CRUISING INTERRUPTED

The follow-up to The Joy Of Cruising,
formerly known as More Joy Of Cruising

PAUL C. THORNTON

Cruising Interrupted

The follow-up to The Joy Of Cruising, formerly known as More Joy Of Cruising

print ISBN: 978-1-09834-465-8
ebook ISBN: 978-1-09834-466-5

Contents

Section Seven: The Passionate Cruisers of The Joy of Cruising...

What Are They Up To Now?

Dedication

Dedicated to the over one million souls and their families who lost their lives to Covid-19. Particularly, the several dozen passengers and crew who succumbed to Covid-19 on a cruise ship, plus the untold numbers who while asymptomatic and/or untested on board, passed away from Covid-19 subsequent to disembarkation.

"*Travel is fatal to prejudice, bigotry, and narrow-mindedness, and many of our people need it sorely on these accounts. Broad, wholesome, charitable views of men and things cannot be acquired by vegetating in one little corner of the earth all one's lifetime.*"

—Mark Twain

Acknowledgements

Writing the prequel to *Cruising Interrupted*, called *The Joy of Cruising* was a blast. Imagining cruising vicariously through the eyes and stories of the passionate cruisers featured in *The Joy of Cruising* made it an easy decision to write a follow-up, *Cruising Interrupted*, which was initially planned to be titled *More Joy of Cruising*. The Covid-19 pandemic tried hard to steal the joy of us passionate cruisers, but the enthusiastic cruise community, including bloggers, influencers, travel writers and ordinary champions of cruising who possess extraordinary passion—some of whom are featured in *Cruising Interrupted*— collectively kept afloat the spirits of the cruise community. Once again it was fun to interview and share the stories of passionate cruisers from all over the world, most of whom will forget more about cruising and travel than I will ever get to experience!

Thank you for enabling me to tell the readers of *Cruising Interrupted* about you: Christine Beehler, Amherst, New Hampshire; Gary Bembridge, *Tips for Travellers*, London, United Kingdom; Doris Vasconcellos-Bernstein and Doug Bernstein, Bonita Springs, Florida; Kandes Bregman, *Sea of Glamour*, Scottsdale, Arizona; Heidi and Donald Bucolo, *EatSleepCruise*, Berkley, Massachusetts; Joe Church, Dover, Pennsylvania; Judi Cohen, *Traveling Judi*, Toronto, Canada; Scott Eddy, *@MrScottEddy* (TV host of *Video Globetrotter*), Fort Lauderdale, Florida; Jenni Fielding, *Cruise Mummy*, Horwich, United Kingdom; Erin Foster, *The Unofficial Guide to the Disney Cruise Line*, Westchester County,

New York; Sarah Gallo, *The Five Foot Traveler*, Redding, Connecticut; Sheri Griffiths, *CruiseTipsTV*, Southern California; Carolyn Howard-Johnson, Los Angeles, California; Steve Kriese, *DCL Podcast*, Lake Oswego, Oregon; Dennis Littley, *Ask Chef Dennis*, Kissimmee, Florida; Carole Morgan-Slater and Paul Morgan, *Paul and Carole Love to Travel*, Gloucester, United Kingdom; Alyson Nachman, *My Virtual Vacations*, Baltimore, Maryland; Laura Pedlar, *Cruise Lifestyle*, Cornwall, United Kingdom; Bill Raffel, Milwaukee, Wisconsin; John Roberts, *In The Loop Travel*, Brighton, Colorado; Heidi Sarna, *QuirkyCruise*, Singapore; Ilana Schattauer, *Life Well Cruised*, Montreal, Canada; Ted Scull, *QuirkyCruise*, New York, New York; Jason Venner, Portland, Oregon; Christine Zimmer, Punta Gorda, Florida.

Thank you to Dr. Toni Shoemaker, Fort Myers, Florida, editor of *Cruising Interrupted*; Cheryl Thornton, my wife who put up with me at the height of the lockdown when it looked like my beloved cruising and the good feeling engendered by writing about it appeared to be in grave danger; and Kalen and LaKi Frazier, my grandkids and the reason I cruise.

Section One:
CRUISING INTERRUPTED

When I started this book late Summer 2019, the second chapter of this section, which is titled *More Joy of Cruising*, was the first chapter. In fact, the title of the book was also *More Joy of Cruising*. I had completed that opening chapter, *More Joy of Cruising,* as well as a number of other chapters when the pandemic happened. Then cruising interrupted.....

Cruising Interrupted

On March 11, 2020, Dr. Tedros Adhanom Ghebreyesus, Director-General, World Health Organization (WHO), strode to the podium at WHO's headquarters in Geneva, Switzerland to address the hundreds of journalists and scientists in the venue along with thousands on the livestream worldwide. Thousands of miles away in Brazil, Doug and Doris enjoyed a private meal featuring aged Parmigiano Reggiano sourced from Italy's Emilia-Romagna region, olive oil from Umbria, buffalo mozzarella from Naples, and ham out of Parma, at La Terrazza aboard Silversea *Silver Shadow*. They were among six couples invited to dine with a ship officer for having booked a future cruise with Silversea. In Willemstad, Curacao, Heidi and Don sipped on drinks in the Vintages wine bar of *Freedom of the Seas* while waiting for the 70's Party. Docked in Colombo, Sri Lanka, Carolyn went to crafts class on *Pacific Princess* to work on her St. Patrick's Day decoration. Chris explored the southern tip of South America, "The End of the World," when *Coral Princess* stopped at Ushuaia, Argentina. On a stop during a Holland America Line *Zuiderdam* cruise, Gary took a stroll around Oranjestad before heading to his Aruba snorkeling excursion. All of their stories follow.

Dr. Ghebreyesus stated, "There are now more than 118,000 cases in 114 countries, and 4,291 people have lost their lives. We are deeply concerned both by the alarming levels of spread and severity, and by the alarming levels of inaction. We have therefore made the assessment that Covid-19 can be characterized as a pandemic."

March 11 was unremarkable for the cruisers above; on that day they each experienced in various ways the joys we all love about cruising. For some, their cruise continued that way. For others, talk of ghost ships, evacuation, armed guards, confinement, even death were part of their story, and in the days subsequent to March 11, their cruises were anything but unremarkable. Fortunately, ultimately all ended up safe at home—a positive Covid-19 diagnosis for one of them notwithstanding.

On March 11 Carolyn returned to crafts class on Pacific Princess and put the final touches on her St. Paddy's Day door decoration.

Chris spent March 11 in Ushuaia, Argentina.
"Oh I adored Ushuaia." The calm before the storm.....

Gary on a port day for HAL Zuiderdam for the world's last cruise ship excursion of 2020
(the cruise lockdown had already been announced.)

A pandemic is an illness that spreads throughout the world. Last declared in 2009 for the H1N1 swine flu outbreak, a global pandemic designation conjures myriad political, public health, economic, and sociocultural considerations. Nevertheless, 4800 miles away, in Fort Myers, Florida, I was oblivious to the ramifications of the Director-General's pronouncement on my two passions: cruising and writing.

I love cruising. So much so that a year prior I published *The Joy of Cruising*, and I was well underway on writing a sequel, *More Joy of Cruising*. I should have paid more heed to the press conference that led all the news programs on the evening of March 11. The signs of the seriousness that the declaration of the pandemic portends were all around me. Just a couple of days earlier, I had returned from a flight to Newark, New Jersey to visit my daughter's just purchased first house. In the airport, perhaps 10% of travelers wore face masks—enough for me to notice something was happening. The university where I work was contemplating a decision to vacate the dormitories—send the students home and teach the remaining couple of months of the spring semester online. That was a monumental decision, one likewise being considered by universities and schools at all levels throughout much of the country. Discussions were underway to send university staff home to work remotely.

Yet, I continued undauntedly to pursue my twin passions of cruising and writing. Just prior to the pandemic declaration, I had paid the remainder of the fees for a July 2020 cruise with our grandkids on Royal Caribbean *Independence of the Seas*, and purchased vouchers for my grandkids to go on the waterslides and hot air balloon during the *Independence* stop at Royal's private island, *Perfect Day at Coco Cay*. We had taken my granddaughter to the water park at *Perfect Day* on our last pre-pandemic cruise on *Harmony of the Seas* in 2019, but my grandson couldn't join us. (We didn't want to pull him out of high school football practice—his dad is the coach!) We were excited that we had scheduled the *Independence* cruise in advance of his football practice beginning so that he could go with us. Around the same time, I scheduled the credit card payment for the balance for the Mediterranean bucket list cruise my wife and I were taking in November 2020 on *NCL Epic*. The Mediterranean cruise included three stops in Italy—I had paid scant attention to the contagion starting to ravage Italy at the very moment I clicked "submit" on the travel agent website.

The writing of *More Joy of Cruising* was progressing nicely. I had completed the first chapter, titled "More Joy" and conducted interviews with about half of the influencers, bloggers, travel icons, and fascinating cruisers I planned to feature in the book. I was in various stages of transcribing the interviews and writing narrative. On the weekend before the pandemic announcement, while in New Jersey to visit my daughter, I conducted an interview with John Roberts of *In the Loop Travel*. John lived only four train stops away from my daughter, so it was an excellent opportunity to interview him for his feature in the section of *More Joy of Cruising* called "The Globetrotters." It would turn out to be the last interview conducted for the book for many months.

On the evening of the pandemic announcement I read a March 10 TheDailyBeast.com article titled "Meet the Insane People Still Planning Cruise Ship Vacations," by Sam Stein. Not sure why he was writing about cruising—Stein is a favorite political pundit of mine, and I always enjoy his articles—about politics. Nevertheless, I cringed at the title. I thought it was sensational; clickbait intended to generate website visits, and at the same time belittling to and impugning the judgment of passionate cruisers—cruiser-shaming at its basest. I defensively thought that the cruisers depicted in the article were not so much planning to cruise in the near future as the title suggested, but were already on cruises they had planned months prior. As late as February and early March, when ready to embark, they were assured by the cruise lines that they were okay to cruise, and reassured by various pronouncements from US government agencies such as the Center for Disease Control (CDC), Health and Human Services, and the President of the United States: "…when you have 15 people, and the 15 within a couple of days is going to be down to close to zero." —President Trump, February 26

Notwithstanding the misleading premise, the article was actually quite balanced and a good read—but that title!

Royal Caribbean *Freedom of the Seas* had arrived in Willemstad, Curacao on the morning of the 11th. After spending the afternoon on a beach hop excursion, Heidi and Don looked forward to the evening's sail away party. While awaiting party time, Don checked in on cruise social media. He had been checking in frequently since shortly after boarding *Freedom* several days earlier, the CDC had issued its first advisory for cruise ships. Heidi sensed some concern in Don's expression. But it wasn't about CDC or WHO. Don leaned over toward Heidi and whispered, "Viking has suspended all cruises for 60 days." It was the first cruise line to cancel cruises.

On March 13, the United States declared a state of emergency. On March 15, Cruise Lines International Association (CLIA), the primary cruise industry group, issued a 30-day voluntary suspension in global cruising operations. Despite all the clues around me, my obliviousness, perhaps denial of the burgeoning threat to my beloved cruising passion continued. I had interviews scheduled for *More Joy of Cruising* throughout March and was busy sending inquiries to prospective subjects seeking their agreement to be featured.

I am not sure exactly when it hit me that my upcoming cruise was not likely to happen; or, when some pandemic milestone such as number of hospitalizations and deaths, grim news feature showing scenes in hospitals, or a White House Coronavirus Task Force press conference jolted me into suspending my writing of *More Joy of Cruising*. The pandemic increasingly raged in March. At the time of the WHO press conference, cumulative worldwide deaths from Covid-19 were less than 5000. Total! By the end of March, Covid-19 deaths were 5000 per day. My native New York City and Long Island area was experiencing the brunt of Covid-19 in the US, and daily images of people suffering, and overstretched nurses, doctors, EMT personnel, medical, and funereal facilities in New York were jarring. New York Governor Andrew Cuomo's daily Covid-19 press conferences became must-see-TV. There were daily poignant stories of the deaths and the impact on survivors of essential workers—first responders, grocery store clerks, bus drivers, and more. More than once my eyes watered watching the moving stories of Americans who passed away, often with loved ones not even able to say goodbye at a funeral.

Like its predecessor, *More Joy of Cruising* was intended to be a fun and upbeat perspective on cruising. Now, as the pandemic raged, there was something incongruous about writing a book that celebrates fun, family and friends, togetherness, luxuriating in food, drinks, and pricey activities and excursions while thousands were sick and dying and often alone and unable to see and touch their loved ones.

On the one hand, quarantining, social distancing and a serious lack of other diversions were the perfect conditions for writing a book. Not one with "Joy" in the title though. As events quickly shifted, beginning with the pandemic declaration, and more and more I read damning articles about cruise travelers stuck on the ocean, cruise ship crews struggling to get home to their families, typically in less-developed countries, and cruise line leadership and US government agencies and leadership offering up imprecise, contradictory and frankly inadequate guidance, my passion for writing *More Joy of Cruising* waned. I was overtaken with concern first for the well-being of my own family and friends, and also for the global community. Jolted from the obliviousness that I suffered from just days prior, within a couple of weeks of the pandemic declaration, I stopped writing or thinking about *More Joy of Cruising* completely.

Just as I don't recall precisely the moment I "canceled" *More Joy of Cruising* the way Royal Caribbean canceled my cruise with my grandkids, I don't recall precisely the moment I decided to start writing again. Even though I had paused writing, and despite the glum cruising news, my passion for cruising continued unabated. So, as usual I made my daily visits to the cruise blogs, social media cruise groups, Cruise Critic forums, etc. A couple of things stood out to me. For one thing, from the perspective of cruise fans I sensed a collective spirit of "I can't wait to cruise again, and we will be doing so shortly." Of course, there was a contrarian view present but it was definitely in the minority, and wishful thinking seemed the overwhelming sentiment. In April and May there were many discussions about cruises booked for the summer—discussions confidently assuming the cruises would happen. I was less sanguine about the early return of cruising, but I hoped I was wrong and those optimistic cruisers were right.

The other thing that stood out was the indomitable spirit and hopefulness of the many cruise community leaders, icons, influencers, bloggers, vloggers and podcasters. They did and continue to perform a wonderful job of keeping the collective spirits of the frustrated cruise community "afloat" throughout the cruise lockdown, and many modified their approaches, including increasing their coverage of news and topical aspects of interest to the cruise community, and creatively incorporating signs of the times like coping advice, live chats, virtual cruise cocktail parties, and the like.

Between visiting cruise websites and social media, and reading optimistic takes, I slowly sensed my spirits lifting. I had eased up on my fear—perhaps overblown by my gorging on media articles (and even worse, their online comments)—that my beloved cruising may not even survive the pandemic. Plus, I had been moping a bit about not being able to take my grandkids on our annual cruise—that was starting to subside. I hadn't yet recovered from my self-imposed "writer's block" but I was beginning to "dig out." I think when I got contacted about being a guest to talk about *The Joy of Cruising* on a cruise podcast, *DCL Duo*—which focuses on Disney Cruise Line—that was the final bit of encouragement I needed… I was back. *Cruising Interrupted!*

More Joy of Cruising

"**A**re we there yet?" My nine-year old granddaughter LaKi was growing impatient. On the morning of August 4, 2019, my wife Cheryl, LaKi and I had left Orlando Florida Hilton Buena Vista hotel—ostensibly headed to the beach—over 30 minutes prior. Cheryl and I live over three hours west, in Fort Myers, Florida, and my granddaughter LaKi was on her annual visit with us from Delaware. On August 3, we attended a banquet in Orlando for the Florida Authors and Publishers Association President's Book Awards, where *The Joy of Cruising* was a Medal Winner.

LaKi's birthday was approaching, August 10, and we promised her that after the banquet we would be staying in Orlando a few days and visiting nearby beaches and waterparks to celebrate. LaKi fancies herself a mermaid—there's never been a pool, beach or waterpark she does not want to conquer. After LaKi fell asleep back in the hotel room following the banquet, I loaded our luggage in the car. In the morning, we told LaKi that we had a short drive to get to the beach so after breakfast she got in the car with her backpack containing sunscreen, Frisbee, and other beach gear and then proceeded to check in every few minutes with an inquiry about our progress in reaching the beach.

After 40 minutes or so, and yet another "how close are we," in the distance the mighty *Harmony of the Seas* cruise ship came into view as we approached Port Canaveral. Up until a little over a year prior, *Harmony of the Seas* was the world's largest cruise ship; it was indeed awe-inspiring and immediately captured LaKi's attention. Perhaps the only thing LaKi likes more than getting in the water is being on the water on a cruise ship. The beach outing was a fun subterfuge; in reality we had decided to celebrate LaKi's birthday with a cruise. She loves cruising; this was going to be the fifth cruise we have done with LaKi in the last four years—most recently the previous Christmas on *Anthem of the Seas*, the culmination of *The Joy of Cruising*. A broad grin took over LaKi's face as the ruse about the beach became clear; the grin did not disappear for the next eight days!

LaKi and me right after boarding Harmony of the Seas.
That smile never left her face for the next eight days.

How has life changed for me since publishing *The Joy of Cruising*? For one thing, I fancy myself as a "travel writer" now; so, whenever I want to book a cruise, I can rationalize it to my wife as conducting research for my next book! I have gone on or booked several cruises since *The Joy of Cruising* came out in the spring of 2019; each cruise's selection was influenced by what I learned in writing *The Joy of Cruising*. The first cruise I took after *The Joy of Cruising's* release was just a few months later. It was on the aforementioned *Harmony of the Seas*, and that quickly became my new favorite cruise ship. That cruise in August of 2019 was exceptional in several ways and was so memorable that I chose my favorite photo from that cruise as the cover for this book.

I had long been intrigued by the Royal Caribbean's Oasis-class, comprised of the four world's largest cruise ships—*Symphony of the Seas, Harmony of the Seas, Allure of the Seas,* and the ship that launched the Oasis-class in 2011, *Oasis of the Seas.* My first cruise ever was on a game-changing ship; then the world's largest ship—by far—Royal Caribbean *Sovereign of the Seas* ushered in the era of mega-ships in 1987. When the *Oasis* concept was announced I knew Royal Caribbean again would "change the game." So enamored was I with the concept of *Oasis of the Seas,* that I incorporated its development and construction as a case study in a course I was teaching about leisure industry marketing as a university professor.

During researching and writing *The Joy of Cruising,* several aspects of Oasis-class ships sparked an interest in cruising on one. Several of the passionate cruisers profiled in *The Joy of Cruising* fondly recalled their experiences with the Oasis-class. In "Cruise Bloggers: The Readers' Choice," Matt Hochberg, creator of the *Royal Caribbean Blog* responded when I asked Matt how the *Royal Caribbean Blog* came about.

"I remember back when *Oasis of the Seas* debuted it was a really big deal, still is, and I was really pumped to go on it. It just redefined what a cruise ship experience could be. My excitement was so great that I needed an outlet for it…I wanted to blog about my experience…" That Oasis blog post was the origin of *Royal Caribbean Blog.*

The Joy of Cruising chapter, "Marathoner of the Seas" featured Joe Church, who famously has run a marathon-length distance on every ship in the Royal Caribbean fleet. The climax of the "Marathoner of the Seas" was Joe's last marathon completed on *Symphony of the Seas,* the newest Oasis-class ship. Joe discussed how the Oasis-class dedicated running tracks enabled him to run during daylight rather than in the middle of the night as he normally does, and Oasis-class' gargantuan size allowed for a running track twice as long as other classes. Joe could cover the 26.3-mile marathon distance in 63 laps on his runs on Oasis-class ships versus as many as 262 laps on, for instance, *Freedom of the Seas*.

I got a vivid, inside perspective of *Symphony of the Seas* from Manny Kellough in *The Joy of Cruising's* "Jazz on the Ocean: The Legendary Manny Kellough." Manny is the Grammy-winning drummer for rock-R&B legend, the late Billy Preston. Manny, who has returned to his jazz music roots, leads the Manny Kellough Experience jazz combo that appears regularly in *Symphony's* Jazz On 4 nightclub.

Between Matt Hochberg, Joe Church, and Manny Kellough piquing my interest in the Oasis-class, as well as several of the other passionate cruisers profiled in *The Joy of Cruising* who shared fond recollections, it was an easy decision to choose an Oasis-class ship for my first cruise after publication. We chose *Harmony of the Seas* because it embarked from Port Canaveral on August 4, 2019. *The Joy of Cruising* had been selected as a medal winner in the Florida Authors and Publishers Association (FAPA) President's Book Awards in the category of Adult Nonfiction. The FAPA banquet was in Orlando, close to Port Canaveral on the preceding night. So, besides the wonderful feelings that always accompany a cruise, the *Harmony* cruise would be celebratory, embarking the morning following the banquet with *The Joy of Cruising* officially a winner. Secondly, during the cruise we would be celebrating LaKi's birthday.

LaKi and her grandmother, my wife Cheryl, celebrating her 10th birthday in the Harmony main dining room.

Harmony of the Seas was all we had hoped for and more. Besides the many highlights of *Harmony*, it was also our first visit to the newly imagined Royal Caribbean private island, Coco Cay. The private island had recently re-opened as *Perfect Day at Coco Cay*, a $250 million transformation of Royal Caribbean's picturesque beach playground into a more kid-friendly space with a water park and hot air balloon rides adjacent to the beach, and theme park style eateries replacing the private island standard picnic-style buffet. Oh, and a newly constructed dock enabling cruise ships to anchor right at Coco Cay instead of requiring ship passengers to be transported to the island from the ship via a tender, a small boat only capable of moving a finite number of the ship's passengers at a time and subject to safety issues related to the weather and getting on and off the tender.

Cheryl, LaKi, and I had a wonderful time at *Perfect Day at Coco Cay* despite a fair amount of trepidation regarding whether we would get to experience it at all. During breakfast before disembarking, a downpour started, and it did not appear our day at Coco Cay was going to be so perfect after all. When the Cruise Director came on the public address system and announced several additional on-ship activities, it brought to mind my dreaded experience on *Anthem of the Seas* just six months prior. (On Christmas morning on *Anthem*, right before we were due to stop at Coco Cay, the Captain announced it was too windy to tender and we had to skip the stop.) This time there was a happy ending: the weather cleared, the sun came out, and *Perfect Day at Coco Cay* was terrific. LaKi loved the water park and the Up, Up & Away balloon ride with me; it offered great views and an incredible vantage point for photos. My wife and I enjoyed a shady spot to sip our Miami Vices while LaKi was on the waterslides, and we sampled the nearby wave pool.

LaKi on the Up, Up, & Away Balloon.

The second cruise I booked post-*The Joy of Cruising* was also chosen directly due to writing the book. Royal Caribbean's *Independence of the Seas*, or *Indy*, as it was affectionately known to the Brits after it was launched and based in UK in 2008, had a significant role in *The Joy of Cruising*. A popular feature in

The Joy of Cruising, was "The Godmother: Elizabeth Hill," which was about the first non-royal, non-celebrity person in UK chosen to serve as a cruise ship Godmother, of then new UK-based, world's largest ship *Independence of the Seas*. Known as *Cruise Like A Godmother* on social media, Elizabeth's story of being plucked from relative obscurity as a leader of a charity working with children on a farm, to be named Godmother (she had never been on a cruise before!) of the at-the-time, world's largest cruise ship, was like a modern-day fairy tale.

In 2020, *Independence of the Seas* was relocated from Southampton to Port Miami, just a couple of hours away from where I live. My grandchildren come down to Florida to see us each summer and we go on a cruise before they return up north. The timing of an *Indy* departure from Miami was per-fect—the week before the grandkids were due to return home, and the itinerary included *Perfect Day at Coco Cay* which my granddaughter loved last year. I knew my 16-year old grandson Kalen—who could not cruise with us last year when we stopped at *Perfect Day*—would be up for the challenge of *Perfect Day's* Daredevil's Peak, the tallest water slide in North America (which LaKi wasn't about to try to conquer last year.)

The timing, departure location, and itinerary was wonderful in terms of helping to choose *Indy*, and a major factor was the the sentimental value I held for *Indy* after the opportunity to tell *Cruise Like A Godmother's* fairy tale! In *The Joy of Cruising*, I included a photo of *The Godmother* standing next to her portrait which is permanently displayed on Indy. My plan was to take a photo of my grandkids next to the *The Godmother's* portrait for inclusion in this book.

Yet another cruise chosen as a result of my involvement with *The Joy of Cruising*, was our first Mediterranean cruise, booked for NCL *Epic* November 2020. I asked each of the passionate cruisers profiled in *The Joy of Cruising* about their most memorable cruises as well as cruises they have on their "bucket list." Several destinations showed up repeatedly: Alaska, Panama Canal, Galapagos, and of course, the Mediterranean, and, several cited Barcelona, Spain as among their favorite ports. Speaking to seasoned cruisers from around the world led us to broaden our horizons instead of always cruising to the Bahamas and the Caribbean. So, the Mediterranean cruise is our first step in that direction and we looked for an itinerary that included Barcelona. For our 28th wedding anniversary we will be spending a few days in Barcelona, and then on November 1 cruising from Barcelona to France, then Italy, and then back to Barcelona. In 2021, Alaska here we come. You know, research!

Alas, our 2020 cruise plans fell victim to the pandemic. In early June, Royal Caribbean made the inevitable official, and canceled our *Indy* cruise. Moping about not being able to cruise and especially not seeing my grandchildren, I then faced a decision about the Mediterranean cruise. It was conceivable cruising would be back by November. However, *Epic*'s itinerary included three stops in Italy. Covid-19 had ravaged parts of Italy. We decided Italy won't be ready for us—nor would we be ready for Italy. Regretfully, we canceled.

It was going to have to be *More Joy of Cruising*…deferred!

Trapped In Paradise

I imagine that for many cruisers, the notion of "living the life" on the ocean—being personally served virtually around the clock filet mignon, lobster, and chocolate-covered strawberries, drinking martinis, fine wine, and champagne, relaxing and luxuriating in the suite accommodations with an unparalleled view of the ocean from your veranda on a six-star cruise line—is an occasional fantasy. A relatively small percentage of cruisers get to experience some aspects of this on their luxury cruises. That was Doris Vasconcellos-Bernstein and Doug Bernstein's experience around the clock for 12 straight days. Sounds glorious, except Doris and Doug had no input to this real-life fantasy except whether to order Lemongrass Beef Nam Tok Nua, or Lobster Thermidor, or Milk Fed Veal Escalope. And, it took place at a time that outside of Doris and Doug's suite on Silversea Cruises *Silver Shadow*—from which they could not leave—the world was grappling with a raging pandemic.

Doris and Doug doing something they did a lot of on Silver Shadow—
sipping champagne in their suite.

Doris and Doug are both esteemed scholars, speakers, authors, and researchers specializing in psychology with courtesy professorships at the University of South Florida. Doug is Professor Emeritus at the University of Illinois at Urbana-Champaign where he was on the psychology faculty for 30 years, and Doris is retired from her psychology professorship at *La Sorbonne*. The Bernsteins reside in Bonita Springs, Florida most of the year, and live the remainder in Paris where Doris teaches at *Ecole de Psychologues Praticiens* of the *Institut Catholique de Paris*.

Doris and Doug have traveled regularly both for leisure and professionally, or a combination of both, to teach, speak, and attend psychology conferences worldwide. "We travel a lot for business, organizing conferences related to teaching psychology; we make the best of it by doing a lot of add-on trips. And every time we go to Paris for Doris to teach, we make side trips to other parts of Europe."

Doris has traveled extensively throughout the world. Doug has traveled mostly in Europe—he lived in the UK for 10 years—and in South America. They enjoy cruising and have done a dozen or so. Although their first cruise together was on the Cunard *Queen Elizabeth 2* in 2008, Doris and Doug mostly enjoy small, luxury cruise ships. The view entering New York Harbor passing by the Statue of Liberty on *Queen Elizabeth 2* is one of their all-time cruise memories. I asked about other cruising memories they recall. One memorable cruise was their 2018 10-day French Polynesia cruise on the 332-passenger *Paul Gauguin*. "We were celebrating a birthday milestone Doris and I both reached that year. We spent a few days in Tahiti and then went on a cruise, and then we spent another few days in Moorea." Doris added, "Oh, and Kotor; I want to go back there, it was fantastic, spellbinding. It's kind of at the end of a long fjord; it's in Montenegro. The ship was arriving maybe 5:30 in the morning or so; it was just starting to get light and there were a few houses with lights on along the fjord on both sides, and absolute quiet. So we were out on our balcony and were able to see that. It was really impressive." Kotor, Montenegro was part of an Athens to Venice cruise on Regent Seven Seas *Voyager*.

The most impressive ship Doris and Doug had sailed prior to *Silver Shadow* was on their cruise just before the *Silver Shadow*. In 2018, Doris and Doug enjoyed a 14-day cruise to Barcelona on Regent Seven Seas *Explorer*. Christened in Monte Carlo by Charlene, Princess of Monaco in July 2016, *Explorer* was Regent's first new ship in over 10 years, the largest in their fleet at 750 passengers, and is considered the world's most luxurious cruise ship. Doris said, "Oh the floors were to die for…marble floors!"

Doris and Doug are not faithful to any one cruise line, although they particularly like Celebrity and consider Silversea their favorite. "We always come back from Paris on whatever is the last boat leaving. Some of our most interesting cruises have been transatlantic because we essentially use them as our bus home."

Doris is from Porto Alegre in Rio Grande do Sul, Brazil. On February 27, 2020 Doris and Doug flew to Rio de Janeiro for a family reunion. They spent a week in Rio, then boarded Silversea Cruises *Silver Shadow* for a 20-day cruise for their return trip to Florida from the family reunion. Silversea Cruises is a six-star cruise line; that is, in addition to being ultra-luxury, virtually everything is included: flights, shore excursions, alcohol, Wi-Fi, gratuities and more. Silversea's fleet is comprised of intimate ships between 100 and 750 passengers. *Silver Shadow* holds 388 passengers; all of its suites offer ocean views and butler service. The cruise was scheduled to make several stops in Brazil and Guyana, and then ports in Barbados, Grenada, Martinique, Antigua, French West Indies, San Juan, and ending in Fort Lauderdale.

Saturday March 7, Doris and Doug arrived at Port of Rio de Janeiro to board *Silver Shadow*. Other than temperature checks for each passenger, embarkation was unremarkable and Doris and Doug were headed to their cabin in minutes. *Silver Shadow* had just undergone a multimillion-dollar refurbishment and reimagination on virtually every part of the ship a few months earlier. Each suite had been redone from floor-to-ceiling, and Doris and Doug inspected what would be their home for the next 20 days. It was the size of a small apartment with a bedroom with beige fabric padded walls; a living room with dining area, refrigerator, espresso machine and bar stocked with their preferences; and, a gray marbled bathroom with double vanity, whirlpool bathtub and separate shower. As he inspected the stunning bathroom, Doug commented to Doris about the plush bathrobe and slippers awaiting them, "Those will get a lot of use!" Floor-to-ceiling glass doors afforded an ocean view and opened up to a sizable teak veranda with a dining table and two chairs as well as two chaise lounges.

Doris and Doug thought the cruise started wonderfully. I asked them to talk about their first impressions. "It was no question one of the best cruise ships and lines we have experienced. The embarkation process was efficient and elegant. The accommodations: it was probably about 400 square feet; separate bedroom, living room, sort of a working area; bathroom with a jacuzzi—it was huge; and then there was a walk-in closet with drawers and cabinets that was impossible to fill up, even for Doris. There was so much storage space it was amazing. And there was a dedicated butler for the suite."

I asked if they engaged in any shipboard activities early on. "The activities we usually engage in on cruise ships are all alcohol-related," Doug and Doris laughed, "we usually find out where all the bars are first. We went to one show shortly after boarding."

I asked them for their early impressions of the ship. "The ship was beautiful. It had been recently refitted, so the ship was in really good condition. Everything was excellent. The dining rooms were very nice; we ate in a couple of the restaurants. They had quite a bit of variety for such a small ship. We checked out all the bars. The service was unsurpassed; all the staff were very attentive. Even though we had been on the ship for only a few days, the staff we met in each one of the restaurants and bars immediately remembered what we like." Doris added, "And the furnishings! One of the cocktail lounges, called simply, The Bar, had these beautiful heavy glass cordless lamps on each table… they were kind of like candles, yellow glass and low light. We like them so much we noted the manufacturer and ordered online and we have them now at the house." Doris laughed, "That's how much we like the ship; probably would have liked to buy some other things. All the furnishings were very nice."

I asked Doris and Doug if they had interacted with other passengers yet.

"For some unknown reason, we were invited to attend an exquisite six-person dinner at La Terrazza, a superb Italian restaurant which specializes in ingredients sourced from various regions in Italy. The ship officer who invited us was in charge of reservations for future cruises. I think it was because we had booked another cruise on Silversea for next year already and I suppose we were invited to the table to help encourage other people to book in advance."

Great looking couple checking themselves out before heading to La Terrazza on night two, March 9, 2020...the calm before the storm.

After a couple of days at sea, *Silver Shadow's* first stop was March 10 in Salvador de Bahia, Brazil. Doris and Doug met for lunch with Doris' brother and his wife, who live in Salvador and weren't able to come to Rio for the family reunion. They were in Salvador just for the afternoon.

Doris and Doug enjoyed a day at sea on the fateful day of March 11—the day the global pandemic was declared. March 12, the day they stopped at Recife, Brazil, on the east coast of Brazil north of Rio, turned out to be a fateful one in its own right. I asked them what was their first indication that all was not right.

"We got off the ship in Recife to buy a fridge magnet as we do at every port. To us Recife was not a particularly exciting place to be. It was not very easy to get from the ship; to walk anywhere where we wanted to go. We thought we'd go in and have lunch. We headed out to do that, but discovered that there were really no interesting restaurants. There was one place we stopped for a beer but that was about it. But the cruise terminal was gorgeous! We came back to the ship to have lunch. Before we left the cabin to go to a restaurant, the Captain made an announcement over the PA system: someone had been taken off the ship sick and they had to follow some international protocols and asked us to stay for the moment in our cabins."

That "for the moment" became 12 days. It became apparent that the "moment" was going to turn into something longer when shortly thereafter *Silver Shadow* Captain Gennaro Arma directed all guests to immediately return to their room and not leave. Doris and Doug never again saw any part of the *Silver Shadow* beyond their cabin until they were led off to be flown home. At that point, little did the guests realize that not only were they confined to their cabins, but that the *Silver Shadow* would not be departing Recife that night en route to their next destination of Fortaleza, Brazil. Pending test results for the passenger who was taken off the ship with a cough, fever, and respiratory symptoms, *Silver Shadow* was held at Recife Port. Port management even prohibited the discharge of *Silver Shadow's* garbage. Furthermore, the pier that the ship was docked on was ordered isolated.

Two days later, Royal Caribbean, Silversea Cruises parent company, released a statement to the media: "Two guests aboard the *Silver Shadow* have been medically disembarked in Recife, Brazil, and one has tested positive for COVID-19." The 79-year-old man who tested positive died a couple of weeks later in a Brazil hospital. The second person removed tested negative.

It was not clear to the *Silver Shadow* guests when Captain Arma made his directive, of the extent to which the Brazilian authorities had exerted control over the situation. At the time, Brazil had reported 37 cases of Covid-19 and zero deaths since the outbreak began. It would become a lot clearer in the ensuing couple of days.

If you have to quarantine, *Silver Shadow* made it reasonably pleasant to do so: rock-solid internet access, hundreds of movies available via the ship audio/visual system, every guest had a suite, virtually all with a private verandah; and, of course, gourmet cuisine and libations brought by room service.

"Some of the guests' accommodations were more modest. For instance, although every guest had an ocean view suite, there were some without a balcony. Also, we were very lucky; some people were on the city side of the boat, looking at this very ugly port, while we looked out on the water and could see all the boats coming and going."

So those passengers on the starboard side of the ship had to stare at an industrial looking, desolate landscape for 12 days—even those in the $15,000 two-bedroom small "houses" known as the *Silver Shadow* Owners Suites.

"There was quite a bit of concern on the ship. But thankfully the crew was fabulous, both in terms of impeccable service as well as exercising extreme caution. The crew and the Captain followed procedures so closely that not one single passenger or crew got sick after that. The Captain would come on the speaker a couple of times a day. We sensed the Captain was very frustrated that he didn't really have control of the situation anymore. All the international protocols were in force; the Brazilian authorities wouldn't let anything happen with the ship that they didn't approve. For example, the Captain wanted to arrange for people to come out of their cabins for an hour each day for some exercise one deck at a time—kind of like in a prison when inmates come out to the yard. He tried that for one day, and then the next day he came on the speaker and said he was told we were not allowed to do that so we had to stay in our cabins."

"We had menus for each day of what we could have for breakfast, lunch, and dinner, and all the meals were brought by room service. And we could drink whatever we wanted. We drank champagne like it was water! We drank plenty of water too…you have to stay hydrated you know," they laughed.

I said sheepishly, "I know this probably sounds frivolous, but talk about your menu choices—I know readers would want to know!"

Doug said, "I think the lunch and dinner menus were fairly similar. There were lighter offerings for lunch. There were various salads, steaks, all kinds of seafood." Doris added, "We tried everything. And there was lobster every night; all different varieties of lobster every night."

I asked, "So how did they deliver your food? Just knocked on the door and left it out there?"

"Yeah, they had us put our luggage rack outside the door, and then they would come with the trays. They were wearing hazmat suits with gloves and masks, and they would drop the food off. We would pick it up and bring it in and then wash our hands."

Filet Mignon and lobster is served!

What about the room steward I asked?

Doris said, "He would change the linen, towels…change everything we wanted but he would not come in to clean." Doug added, "Towards the end he stopped coming at all so we were cleaning ourselves."

So they weren't seeing their cabin steward anymore, and weren't seeing the room service crew who delivered their meals anymore. I asked, "When did you get to see other passengers again after everyone was confined to their cabin?"

Doug said, "Not until we were allowed out of our room on March 22nd, 12 days later."

I asked Doris and Doug if they were in any communication with the states; and then I recalled, "I guess you had communication with the media because I read about you in the *Naples Daily News*." (Doris and Doug's hometown newspaper.)

Doug said, "Yes. The Internet service on this ship was the best I had ever seen. It was utterly reliable, and just as fast as at home. Now of course, we were in a port so that helped as well. We had been in contact with some friends at home in Bonita Springs and I guess they contacted the newspaper as I got a phone call from a reporter."

In the article in *Naples Daily News* where I first learned of Doris and Doug, the interview with the reporter happened just three days into the quarantine. I asked them when they knew it was going to be a fairly long time.

Doug said, "We never really knew. It always was day-to-day. They just said, 'we don't know when we can leave; we'll let you know what we find out tomorrow.' And tomorrow was always, tomorrow. So it was just one day at a time." Doris added, "Europeans went out first; then the Canadians; South Americans; New Zealand and Australia. The Americans were the last ones to leave the ship. It was a question of which state would be willing to accept us." Doug noted, "They wanted us to go to Miami but things were so bad there that it wasn't acceptable to the state of Florida. So we flew to Texas. We weren't angry about it. We felt that our country was being appropriately careful."

I said, "How did you find out you were being—I hate to say it this way— released?"

They both laughed. Doug said, "That was the word, yeah released! The night before we got the announcement that the Governor of Texas agreed to accept us." Doris pointed out, "Yeah but they didn't tell us that we wouldn't see our luggage for three weeks!" Their luggage ended up in Southampton, United Kingdom along with the *Silver Shadow* and then flown back to the States via FedEx.

On March 23, 2020, Doris and Doug, along with the other remaining American citizens onboard *Silver Shadow,* 103 in all, flew to Dallas to be transferred to private jets to take them to their home cities. It was explicitly mentioned in the Coronavirus Task Force in Press Briefing the following day. The passengers arrived late to Dallas and had to be hosted by Silversea for one more day.

"I cannot tell you how good the service was. When we arrived in Dallas we had been wearing masks and gloves for the past five hours, and everyone was hungry and exhausted. They brought us off the plane and there were airport staff lined up in a double row guiding us into a nearby building and saying, "welcome home." We went into the building and they had set up a huge buffet for us with just about anything you can imagine for us to eat, along with wine and beer. We only got to sleep for about two hours. After a quick breakfast they put Doris and me on a 30-passenger private jet—even though there were only 12 of us. We had never been on a private jet before but I tell you, that's quite a way to travel! We flew first to Orlando, and some people got off; then Fort Lauderdale, some more people got off; and then finally to Fort Myers, where there was a limousine waiting for each of the remaining three couples and then they drove us home."

I asked Doris and Doug if this experience would affect their willingness to cruise in the future.

"No. We got so much cruise credit from Silversea, that we're booked for March 2021 to cruise on the brand-new *Silver Moon* from Fort Lauderdale to Barcelona and then onward from there to Athens. We certainly haven't changed our minds about cruising. Anytime you are with other people, you run the risk of being infected with something. This has been true of cruise ships forever and that's not going to change. You can only do so much to prevent infections. The only way to stay healthy for sure is to stay home. We don't want to do that!"

Fascinating tale. It almost all takes place within four walls, the daily routine was virtually identical for the duration, and the scenery never changed—as beautiful as it was. Yet, there are few people in the world who share the experience Doris and Doug had.

Harkening back to the opening paragraph: Imagine a world where the misery, heartbreak, and destruction of Covid-19 was nonexistent. Yes, I can easily fantasize a cruise to nowhere; ultra-luxury accommodations; endless gourmet cuisine, wine and cognac; hundreds of movies; a laptop for writing my books and ability to stay connected to friends, family, and world events via the Internet; and, my non-changing view of the gorgeous ocean vista below. Yeah, sign me up.

Not a screensaver; Doris and Doug's unchanging view for 12 days.

The Love Boat:
Evacuation 2020

Carolyn Howard-Johnson and her husband Lance boarded Princess Cruises luxurious *Pacific Princess* February 19, 2020 in Sydney, Australia. *Pacific Princess* had originally departed January 5 in Fort Lauderdale, Florida for a 111-day World Cruise comprising 42 destinations, 26 countries, five continents highlighted by traversing the Panama Canal, with stops in Tahiti, Seychelles Islands, Phuket, Thailand, and Tanzania, Zanzibar.

Carolyn and Lance were among the scores of cruisers who take advantage of shorter, multi-destination segments of a world cruise. They intended to cruise the leg of the voyage from Sydney, stopping first at Melbourne, and then destinations including Singapore, Sri Lanka, Madagascar, and then disembarking April 3 at Cape Town, South Africa.

The intimate 670-guest *Pacific Princess* is the namesake of *S.S. Pacific Princess* that served as the setting for *The Love Boat,* the iconic ABC television network romantic comedy series set on a cruise ship that ran from 1977 to 1987. *Pacific Princess* was launched in 1999 by Renaissance Cruises, and acquired and renamed in 2002 by Princess Cruises. *Pacific Princess* is easily the smallest ship in Princess Cruises' fleet although numerous experts rate it as Princess' top ship, and it is recognized as one of the best small ships in the world.

Pacific Princess sail away for Carolyn's 45-day leg of the 111-day World Cruise was festive.

Carolyn Howard-Johnson is an award-winning author of fiction, poetry, and nonfiction, and a well-known writing consultant. Carolyn's writing career began when she was hired as the youngest person ever to be a staff writer for the *Salt Lake Tribune,* writing features for the society page. Carolyn went on to become an editorial assistant at *Good Housekeeping,* and then built an esteemed writing career: columnist, reviewer, and staff writer at various publications, poet, novelist, and best-selling author with her award-winning HowToDoItFrugally series including her flagship book, *The Frugal Book Promoter,* who has helped writers and retailers worldwide. Carolyn loves to travel and has visited nearly 100 countries, both leisure travel as well as professional, where she is a popular presenter at tradeshows and conferences, and as an actor that has appeared in TV commercials for the likes of Time-Life CDs, Marlboro, Blue Shield, Apple, Chinet, Lenscrafters, and Disney Cruise Lines (Japan). Carolyn also has traveled extensively to study writing, including at Cambridge University in the United Kingdom; Herzen University in St. Petersburg, Russia; and Charles University, Prague.

Carolyn's first cruise was on the original Love Boat, *S.S. Pacific Princess* in 1978. She didn't immediately take to cruising. "I loved the experience, but

I kept fighting against it because I kept thinking I'd rather stay in a destination longer. I'd like to spend time in museums, I'd like to spend several days in a place. I'm not getting my fill of this place. But then the more we did it the more I realized some of these ports I am going to be back at. After many years we've been back at some ports as many as 10 times."

Carolyn Howard-Johnson at the Pacific Princess chocolate buffet.

After that first cruise Carolyn didn't cruise again for another 10 years. When she returned to cruising, it grew on her rapidly. "The more cruises we took, the more I liked it. As I started to age, being able to unpack once really appealed to me. And I saw the advantage of following my own path, while my husband followed his with the tours and going to different places, yet still being together on a cruise. I also saw that cruising afforded just an ease and a caretaking situation that made traveling alone extremely comfortable. It just makes traveling so much easier."

Carolyn has been on 85 cruises, 34 of them on Princess. Besides Princess, Carolyn has cruised on Holland America Line, Norwegian Cruise Line, Windstar Cruises, and Disney Cruise Line. "I adored Disney; my husband hated it. We didn't do this one with the grandkids; it was just us. They did an admirable job of keeping kids pretty much separate from adults who wanted a regular cruise on their own. The other thing they did extremely well was, because they had to cater to families, the tours were very well set up so the food was available, promptly at noon. I noticed that. The photos with the Disney characters were terrific. It was fun. I just love Disney, so if you are an adult Disney fan, a Disney cruise is highly recommended."

Out of 85 cruises I knew I couldn't expect Carolyn to tell me about her cruise highlights in a way that could give them justice. Carolyn is a prolific writer—I'll leave it to her to tell that story. She did mention a couple of lasting cruise memories. The first, not all that pleasant but undoubtedly memorable was also on a Princess cruise. Carolyn told me about an instance right after 9/11 involving a Princess cruise around South America. Due to the tense political environment and anti-terror sensitivity, the consequently revised, more restrictive documentation procedures, and further complicating matters some miscommunication with Princess Cruises, several couples including Carolyn and Lance, could not board due to revised documentation requirements. At their own expense they rectified the documentation situation in Miami—Princess was of little assistance—and they flew to the Bahamas to meet up with one of the itinerary's first ports. They got to the airport in the Bahamas the day before Christmas. It was packed, and numerous flights were delayed. Carolyn said, "We had to stay overnight in the airport there—it was an open-air airport—and it rained. Not a California rain like I was used to, but a tropical, torrential downpour. Imagine if we were in our 20's taking our first cruise. Think about that as your lasting impression of cruising!"

The *Pacific Princess* cruise is undoubtedly one that Carolyn, Lance, and the approximately 1000 passengers and crew onboard will never forget. I asked Carolyn what other cruise stands out as particularly memorable. Carolyn responded, "I think the most memorable may have been the cruise on the little Windstar ship, the *Star Breeze*. We tried Windstar for the first time a couple of years ago and that was fun. It went places and did things—they are small ships—that Holland America, Norwegian, Princess don't do. Lots of ports we would have never visited otherwise; like the islands off the coast of France. The trip was mostly about the cave art in Southern France and Basque Country in Spain. That's why we chose that itinerary. You could take private tours from the ship; they stayed in one port two nights so you had plenty of time to get inland, to see the original cave art, the neanderthal art. It was fantastic."

And what's on your cruise bucket list?

"I do want to try one of those National Geographic expeditions or clipper-type ships with sails in the Greek Islands. That's on my board of things I want to do. I'm a big Greek mythology and history fan. I've been there several times, but that particular kind of ship has my eye."

On February 19 when Carolyn and Lance boarded the *Pacific Princess*, coronavirus was still relatively insignificant in the United States in terms of media coverage, which had reported 15 cases to that point and one death. There was not a lot of reason for it to be foremost on their minds, or that of the other guests boarding with Carolyn and Lance that morning. At that point coronavirus received scant media attention. And the passengers already onboard *Pacific Princess* had embarked January 5th when coronavirus wasn't discussed at all. However, also on February 19, 4800 miles away there was a major development involving *Pacific Princess* sister ship, the *Diamond Princess*, docked in Port of Yokohama, Japan. *Diamond Princess* passengers were finally allowed to disembark after having been quarantined in their cabins for 14-days due to a coronavirus outbreak which had reached 634 positives out of 3800 passengers and crew. *Diamond Princess* portended things to come for a number of cruise lines, especially Princess Cruises.

I wondered if coronavirus had crossed Carolyn and Lance's minds in the days leading up to the cruise. "Lance and I did think a little about the news reports before we left. We gave some thought to not going even though it was going to cost us a fortune. You know we have had four or five episodes in the United States over the years that could have turned into pandemics but didn't because we had a valid CDC, etc. We did decide to get some masks, only because we were going to be relatively close to China and we knew there was something going on in China. We were operating on the assumption that this would be something like H1N1, Zika, Ebola; none of them reached the US; they didn't go everywhere, and none of them were something where you could not travel. We didn't see any reason to deny ourselves. Furthermore, we were thinking of this cruise as a bucket list cruise—this was the last part of the world that we hadn't visited that was reachable by cruise ship. This was the east coast of Africa, and Seychelles and Réunion Island in the Indian Ocean."

The first two ports on the 45-day leg of the 111-day World Cruise that *Pacific Princess* stopped at went fine: Melbourne, Australia on Friday, February 21, and Adelaide, Australia on Sunday, February 23.

Carolyn said, "By the time we had been to our first three ports, we knew our trip would be quite different than we ever could have imagined. Many Asian ports had closed to us. By the third port they were beginning to substitute cancellations in other parts of the world with more ports in North Western Australia—ports that nobody ever stops at: Brazelton, Geraldton, Exmouth. They were finding ways to get our little ship into the docks. They were unscheduled stops, and obviously not used to having cruisers."

Carolyn and Lance disembarked at those tiny ports and there were some tours and excursions. When they stepped foot on Exmouth March 3, it would be their last time on land until they disembarked *Pacific Princess* for good March 21.

"So these substitute ports were because there was no place else for you to stop?" I asked. Carolyn said, "Yes, one at a time. First it was Shanghai, then it was Bali. Then by the time we knew we couldn't get into Sri Lanka for anything but fuel, we knew there would be a big problem. We had heard rumors about Réunion Island—on a Princess ship, passengers had tomatoes and eggs thrown at them by the locals as they tried to disembark to keep passengers from enjoying their island. Sri Lanka allowed us to dock to pick up supplies—no visits."

I mentioned that it sounds like there was some trepidation on the part of her cruise mates. Carolyn replied, "It's interesting; it was kind of like the nation today. It was sort of half-and-half; there were those of us who felt safe. First of all many had been on the ship for already a quarantine period. So we felt fairly Covid-safe. We kind of felt like a little floating safe haven. And those of us who took that attitude tended to make the best out of it. Some people were like, 'we're fine, we're eating beautifully, we're sleeping well, we're going to the theater.' The other half was mad mainly because they couldn't get more details about what was going on."

So, after the stop in the substitute locales in Australia, the ship began almost three weeks straight of sea days, stopping once to refuel but passengers could not disembark. Until this point, other than the itinerary changes, the cruise felt normal.

Carolyn said, "And they continued to be normal until we got off the ship. The only thing passengers started to worry about as the days, and then weeks started to go by, and no country would allow us to port, was that…we started to worry that we were going to be on the water forever and worried how were we going to refuel again…that this might go on for many more weeks… we just couldn't float around forever."

What, I asked, besides the sudden changes in itinerary were the outward manifestations of the burgeoning crisis. "Did the cruise itself, and the activities and amenities still feel like a high-end cruise?'

"They did their very best. Yes, I'd say it was. We had our meals, and we had beautiful buffets. We were lucky as we had a balcony. We always bring our computers for writing so we did plenty of that. Princess gave everyone free Internet. So the itinerary changes, extra sea days didn't bother us. It didn't bother a lot of people. We were never confined to our cabin—we had the full run of the ship."

So, just a little over a week from the time Carolyn and Lance boarded for their 45-day cruise, the itinerary started changing but the sea days for the cruise were otherwise normal. The *Pacific Princess* casino, pools and hot tubs, restaurants and bars, and high-end shops all remained fully operable. The on-board entertainment was stellar but limited because the ship couldn't dock and pick up new acts.

"Granted, they weren't able to pick up new entertainers at the ports, but the entertainers that were already on the ship were collaborating to come up with new shows, so every night they had different entertainment. The woman who put together craft programs had enough supplies to keep us occupied throughout the cruise. In fact, she doubled up and had two different programs a day instead of only one."

Pacific Princess was refused permission to dock in Maldives, Bali, Singapore, Phuket, Thailand. They tried a couple of ports in the Seychelles—again no luck. In Sri Lanka, the ship was allowed to dock only to refuel and restock—no passengers were allowed to disembark. Under the watch of armed security patrolling with dogs, the ship was refueled and food replenished. With no ports open to the *Pacific Princess* to dock, while at Port of Colombo, Sri Lanka, the Captain announced that he had no choice but to cancel the remainder of the cruise and that it would terminate in Fremantle. *Pacific Princess* reversed course and returned to Australia. "That's when they said we were returning to Australia to evacuate." Carolyn said.

One night during the return leg to Australia, Carolyn and Lance attended dinner with *Pacific Princess* Captain Andrea Spinardi. The ship doctor was at their table and informed them there were no fevers on the ship—clearly a much more positive outcome than what was reported regarding several of *Pacific Princess* sister ships that were on the ocean around the same time.

Carolyn and Lance with Captain Andrea Spinardi at the Captains Cocktail Party.

"Other than uncertainty regarding when we were going to be able to port, I think most of the problems passengers had were because sometimes it felt like Princess was not forthcoming with information; not giving us the full story. But I don't think that was it; I don't think they knew entirely what was going on either. I'm sure that they had access to information we didn't have, but a lot of it was evolving and iffy. A lot of it was still iffy long after we got off the ship."

Carolyn and Lance were among the *Pacific Princess* passengers evacuated on March 21 in Fremantle, Australia. Most but not all guests disembarked in Fremantle for flights home on the ensuing couple of days. 115 passengers unable to fly due principally to medical reasons remained onboard *Pacific Princess* en route to Los Angeles. Princess reported that there had been no confirmed Covid-19 cases on board.

Carolyn and Lance were at the port in Freemantle for about five hours. They took a flight into Sydney where they stayed overnight. In the morning they were scheduled to fly first to New Zealand, but by that time New Zealand was refusing entry to anyone with an American passport. Princess came to the airport and rescheduled everyone, and Carolyn and Lance took the first of two flights to get to Los Angeles.

"Surprisingly, hardly anyone wore masks on the plane even after we offered some of ours to them. Presumptuous, perhaps, but worth a try. We felt 99% sure of being virus-free on the ship. By the time March 21 rolled around, all of us on the ship had been on it the full quarantine time except for the unscheduled Australia tours, so we felt fairly safe. Once home, during self-isolation from the cruise we tried to remain positive. I must say, Princess was there at every step, after several weeks of us floating on the Indian Ocean like a ghost ship with no place to go!"

After disembarking most guests in Fremantle, *Pacific Princess* stopped briefly in Melbourne, Australia, to refuel and restock. On April 13 *Pacific Princess* docked in Honolulu, Hawaii, for service and to disembark four residents of Oahu per arrangement with the Hawaii Department of Transportation. The remaining passengers disembarked in Los Angeles on April 20.

"The guests shared tons of stories about the cooperation of the crew and entertainers throughout the ordeal on *Pacific Princess*: how we were and were not informed of events, the great work of Carnival [parent company of Princess Cruises] and Princess who were continually adjusting to the new conditions of each day. Two weeks with no ports! So, a 45-day cruise turned into a few ports including substitute ports—all in Australia. All in all, Princess was fantastic especially in contrast to our earlier disaster with them on the 9/11 cruise! The *Pacific Princess* cruise adventure could have really been a disaster, but everything Princess could do, they did right. And no passengers sick! They were ultimate hosts through it all, including a really tough evacuation eventually. And they did amazingly well during evacuation."

Got Covid Onboard:
Cruising Interrupted (But Not Stopped!)

I first encountered Christine Beehler when we became kindred spirits, so to speak. We were among a group of cruise enthusiasts interviewed by CNN. com during the pandemic for an article about our interest in cruising as soon as possible, "Cruise Fans Explain Why They Can't Wait To Cruise Again," by Francesca Street (July 24, 2020). All of the cruisers interviewed were "off-the-charts" eager to get back on the ocean again; well, all except yours truly! I came across as the most cautious of the bunch, in stark contrast to Chris. The article began with a depiction of Chris' last cruise which took place in March 2020 on the ill-fated Princess Cruises *Coral Princess,* which was denied docking during the pandemic declaration and then was stricken with a Covid-19 outbreak. That opening to the article immediately caught my attention; then it said, "…Beehler returned home on April 6; she also tested positive for coronavirus. Beehler is 72, with a partial right lung. She also suffers from chronic obstructive pulmonary disease and emphysema....."

Most remarkable of all: Chris can't wait to cruise again!

Chris on a stop in Santorini during the final sailing of Splendour of the Seas in 2016.

Christine Beehler is a 72-year old passionate cruiser. She is married with two children. Chris retired from American Express as a corporate travel agent after a 25-year career. She has lived in New Hampshire with her husband Ron for the past 35 years. Originally from Rhode Island, Chris left the state after high school graduation to live in Switzerland for a year, before returning to Boston for college.

Travel has long been a significant part of Chris' life, beginning with her first trip to Europe when she was 12 years old. "That gave me the bug. We had neighbors from England and their 10-year old son and I were best friends. They were going to England and thought that the boy would benefit by having a friend go over with him and invited me to come. I was delighted to do that and we just had a wonderful trip. Two years later when I was 14 years old, my family and I went on a camping trip across the country. I was just amazed to see all of these sites across the United States that I never knew existed or had just learned a little about in school: the Badlands, Mount Rushmore, Yellowstone, the Grand Teton region. My goal was to see San Francisco and I was not disappointed. From there, we went up to the Seattle World's Fair and then returned. When I was 17, I was offered the opportunity to live in Switzerland after I graduated from high school in the US, as an international high school student. I did a fair amount of travel throughout Europe via train during that year. When I was younger, I would return to my beloved Switzerland every other year, sometimes alone, often with family or friends. "

After years of being a work-at-home mom and raising her children, Chris pursued her love of travel professionally. "I worked at a travel agency and was able to go on seemingly endless fam trips; the travel agency was very good to me. [Familiarization trips offered to travel professionals to resorts and destinations typically in the off-season.] Usually a tour operator would put it together so that we could maybe sell their tours. We would visit several resorts who would entertain us because they wanted us to market their properties. The travel agency was a lovely job but didn't pay very well, and I moved into corporate travel, which paid better but I was not offered the fam trips to the same extent as to when I was in retail travel."

Chris traveled extensively worldwide once her career as a travel professional took off. Through leisure and business travel, Chris took numerous trips throughout the US, Canada, Europe, Caribbean, Alaska, Panama Canal, Canada. In 1988, Chris and Ron's honeymoon was an overland trip to New Zealand, Australia, and Tahiti. "I've also been on a land tour of China with a group travel organization and most recently, in 2019, to Vietnam, Cambodia, and Thailand." In recent years her travel has been mostly cruising; however, she makes frequent overland trips to Germany where her daughter and grandchildren live.

Chris has been on 30 cruises—almost all since 2013–throughout Europe, Australia, New Zealand, the Arabian peninsula, China, Southeast Asia, Caribbean, and South America. Most of her cruises have been on Princess and Royal Caribbean. Chris has also sailed with Carnival and Norwegian, and has been on river cruises with Viking and AmaWaterways. Her first cruise was in 1981 on Royal Caribbean *Song of Norway*. "I was taking advantage of a $5 per day per person discount I got through the travel agency. I took my first husband and two children; my son was celebrating his 12th birthday. It was a lot of fun but I didn't get the 'bug' at that point. I think because I had so many other opportunities." I said, "I guess you could go anywhere in the world just about." Chris replied, "Right, I could go over to London for $30 for the weekend. I just kind of checked it off. Cruising, ok I did it, that was fun."

Chris cruised again three years later on Carnival *Mardi Gras*, again taking advantage of the $5 per day perk. This time she was accompanied by her fiancée and now husband Ron. Again, cruising was just okay for Chris, and Ron did not care for the experience, so cruising was put on-hold for many years. Things changed dramatically when Chris experienced a cruise to Alaska in 2013. She has been cruising non-stop ever since, undaunted by anything until the cruise lockdown of 2020.

Typically, I would ask Chris for her most memorable cruise. For Chris, that's too obvious so I approached it a little differently: "What's your favorite cruise or two?" I asked. Chris said, "My all-time favorite cruise was in 2017, a Princess cruise on *Crown Princess* of the Norwegian Fjords to the Arctic Circle during the Summer Solstice. Three days without night in the beautiful scenery of the Norwegian Fjords. And in 2016, Royal Caribbean's final sailing of *Splendor of the Seas*; a 16-day cruise from Dubai, around the Arabian peninsula through pirate territory, up the Red Sea, passing thru the Suez Canal, then stopping in Israel, Greece, and ending in Venice.

Chris plans to get back on her schedule of several cruises per year in 2021. She has some catching up to do after the lost 2020, when she had four cruises canceled. Chris has five cruises planned for 2021: Bahamas, Norway/ Iceland, Mediterranean, and two Transatlantics. She has some more river cruises on her bucket list. Besides visiting her family in Germany, Chris has no near-term plans for non-cruise travel though she longs to go to Singapore and Bali.

The bucket list discussion with Chris was interesting. I routinely ask passionate cruisers about their bucket list aspirations; that is, where would you like to cruise before you are gone? I was not about to go there with Chris though. With most cruisers it is a lighthearted, frivolous discussion meant to give readers (and me!) ideas for dream cruises, and insight into what seasoned travelers are thinking about doing in the future. However, I knew from preliminary information-gathering from Chris that "bucket list" had a different connotation for her. With most interviews, bucket list is just a figure of speech, and for me it is an interviewing device to prompt discussion. Because of sensitivity I wasn't going to talk about things you do before you die. Without prompting, Chris brought up her bucket list cruise—it was *literally* the cruise she aspired to go on before the very real likelihood of her dying. In 2006, shortly after retiring from American Express, Chris was diagnosed with lung cancer. "I hadn't cruised in years and wasn't even thinking about cruising. When I got cancer, I went through the proverbial thinking of what I wanted to do before I died. I said I'd like to do an Alaskan cruise. And you know, I am not sure where that even came from. I didn't go for years later, however; I was too sick for a while, and then after my recovery from cancer itself, I had to have a series of medical procedures due to complications related to my cancer surgery. I finally was in good enough health to do that Alaskan cruise in 2013, on Princess Cruises *Island Princess*. My husband accompanied me. Even though he had not had a good experience on his first cruise in the 80's, he wanted to honor my bucket list wish." The *Island Princess* cruise hooked Chris on cruising.

Outside of travel, Chris is very involved in animal rescue. She is passionate about rescuing cats from kill shelters, raising funds for their rescue through Facebook, and she also fosters cats at her home when not traveling. There was little surprise that of the many picturesque cruise photos Chris provided me, several featured Chris interacting with animals in faraway lands. Chris also enjoys gardening, design and horticulture, and architecture. She particularly enjoys appreciating architectural design during excursions to city settings.

Chris at a llama farm during Coral Princess first stop in Puerto Montt, Chile (l). With the famous penguins of Falklands Islands (r). The Falklands stop just a week after Coral Princess departure, would be Chris' last day on land during the cruise.

Princess Cruises *Coral Princess* is a 92000 gross ton 2000 passenger cruise ship launched in 2002. It underwent a stunning $1,000,000 refurbishment in 2019 including major enhancements of all cabins. The 32-Night Brazilian and Cape Horn Grand Adventure on *Coral Princess* departed San Antonio, Chile on March 5, 2020, when cruising worldwide was in full operation, Covid-19 did not exist as a term, and the nascent coronavirus was largely limited to China. There had been minor, sporadic outbreaks in other parts of the world, and news coverage on March 5 in the United States was minimal nationally and virtually nonexistent in local media.

This was not Chris' first time on the *Coral Princess*. Once Chris got hooked on cruising on her bucket list cruise to Alaska, she followed that up with what would be another bucket list cruise for many of us: passage through the Panama Canal on *Coral Princess*. Chris chose this South American cruise because of the itinerary. "I have a lot of friends who speak highly of the South American itinerary. I always wanted to go to Machu Picchu; I wanted to round Cape Horn. Some of my doctors advised that I forgo Machu Picchu because of my medical history—I have emphysema, COPD, and only a partial right lung. I just crossed Machu Picchu off of my bucket list but said, 'I can still do the cruise.' So I started planning it perhaps six-months in advance of departure; it was not going to be a straightforward trip to put together and I was torn between a 14-day and a 32-day cruise."

Chris initially planned a 14-day cruise departing San Antonio, Chile, rounding Cape Horn, and then up the east side of South America and ending in Buenos Aires, Argentina, where she would then fly back to the US. Ultimately, Chris decided to extend her time on *Coral Princess,* and booked the 32-day cruise itinerary where the cruise continued on from Buenos Aires to Fort Lauderdale.

I asked Chris if she had any apprehension about returning to *Coral Princess* at that time in the face of the burgeoning coronavirus story abroad. "No, I wasn't concerned. The coronavirus was confined mostly to China and Italy. There was only one reported case in South America at the time I left New Hampshire. A good friend suggested I not go. I downplayed her concern. I said 'It's South America. I'm going to be fine, they'll take care of us.' I did, however, during the days leading up to the cruise have fleeting thoughts about the news out of China—that if I ever did catch the virus I might have a hard time. I probably would need a ventilator. I might not make it. Yet I got on that airplane with complete confidence that nothing was going to happen."

"On the plane over to Chile on March 3rd, word spread regarding a second case reported in South America—this one in Santiago, which was our destination. You could sense a bit of panic on the plane. The thinking back then was that this was a virus that was just connected to China and Italy. Even the one case in South America was supposedly someone who had come back from Italy. And there were a few cases on the west coast in the US that had kind of escaped. The concern level rose—even though it was only two cases on the entire continent—especially when we got to the airport in Santiago and they were taking a lot of precautions: the airport workers were in hazmat suits, we had to complete multiple health forms and have our temperatures taken. It was nothing like that when I left Boston. At the port the personnel very deliberately went through our passports to make sure we hadn't been to China or Italy, and then we boarded the ship."

The cruise was uneventful for the first week; in other words it was glorious. The first day was a delightful day at sea, and then *Coral Princess'* first port was Puerto Montt, Chile. Chris enjoyed an excursion to a llama farm and stopped at a viewpoint at Lake Llanquihue, the second largest lake in Chile, to see the Osorno Volcano. After another couple of glorious sea days including cruising the Amalia Glacier in Bernardo O'Higgins National Park, Chile, *Coral Princess* docked at Ushuaia, Argentina on March 11.

Chris adored Ushuaia. "Such breathtaking scenery everywhere. So much nature, yet also a vibrant city, with even a Hard Rock Cafe. The day was spent largely in the enormous Tierra del Fuego National Park. Most memorable was visiting the End of the World Post Office—I think the southernmost post office in the world. We later visited gorgeous Lake Roca, where we had lunch, then traveled to Lapataia Bay, and saw the end of the Pan-American Highway—with the other end being in Alaska. finished the tour with a stop at a hotel high on a mountain just outside the city, where we had a beautiful panoramic view of Ushuaia Bay and the Beagle Channel before heading back to the ship."

A glorious March 11 in Ushuaia for Chris. Unbeknownst to her, on the same day, 8200 miles away in Geneva, Switzerland, the World Health Organization told gathered worldwide media, health and science personnel and government representatives that Covid-19 was officially a global pandemic.

The following day *Coral Princess* rounded Cape Horn at the southern tip of South America, enroute to the Falkland Islands where they arrived on Friday the 13th. It would be Chris' last time touching land until the *Coral Princess* cruise ended weeks later. Chris told me, "After the first several days, *Coral Princess* was likely the most interesting cruise I had been on, if not the most pleasurable. It was fantastic, and so different. I have this thing going on about fjords; I saw fjords, I saw volcanos, I met amazing people in South America. Everything was going beautifully. Though the pandemic was spreading worldwide, we had been a healthy ship. But then all of a sudden, Friday the 13th, the Falkland Islands was the last port we were allowed into."

I asked Chris what was the first sign that things were going wrong. She told me, "We came back on the ship at the Falkland Islands after a wonderful day with the penguins. We soon learned that we would not be stopping at the next port. Instead, the Captain directed us to turn on our TVs to view an announcement from the President of Princess Cruises, Jan Swartz. Her comments were not specific to *Coral Princess* but pertained to world events and the entirety of Princess Cruises. She said that Princess was voluntarily pausing cruising."

Coral Princess was denied entry into the next two ports, Puerto Madryn, Argentina, on Sunday, March 15; and Montevideo, Uruguay, on Tuesday, March 17. Chris said, "Things got very chaotic. We didn't know where we were going or why we couldn't stop at those ports. It was not relaxing at all. There was all this chatter—a lot of groups organizing in order to talk to their embassies. There were many meetings; the Canadian contingent had meetings happening all the time; the UK contingent met regularly." Despite the tension simmering just below the surface, outwardly passengers and *Coral Princess,* managed to maintain a façade of normalcy. All the ship's venues were open and passengers had the normal run of the ship—sitting by the pool, engaging in classes and activities, and attending *Coral Princess* entertainment productions.

Coral Princess next scheduled stop was Wednesday, March 18 in Buenos Aires, Argentina. The passengers were informed that the cruise was ending in Buenos Aires, and that they should start buying plane tickets home. I asked Chris if at this point there was any discussion of coronavirus cases. She told me, "No, we were still a healthy ship. In fact, other than the confusion and everything being up in the air that came with ending the cruise early and arranging transportation, many of us felt we were right where we wanted to be. We said, 'Just keep us on the ship until this thing blows over in the rest of the world because we are in the safest place possible.' We really thought this was going to blow over in the world in two or three weeks. Just keep us on the ship; we won't have to be buying toilet paper and everyone will be healthy. That was kind of the mindset."

Coral Princess arrived in Buenos Aires on March 18th. Passengers were instructed to purchase plane tickets to depart on 19th because they could not disembark until then—that would give them a 14-day quarantine period from the time of embarkation. Chris said, "At three o'clock in the morning on the 19th the Captain came on the PA and said health officials were on board and they were coming around taking temperatures so we should expect a knock on our door after 3:30. I never did get a knock. I think they came to the realization taking everyone's temperature was not going to be feasible. I went back to sleep as my bus to the airport was not until 10AM. When I got up and went to the meeting place to await my bus, I found many people who had booked their trip with tour operators (mostly in the UK) and those who had originally purchased their air through Princess air had not heard from Princess about alternate air arrangements home. There was massive chaos at guest services although Princess was very good about bringing out officers who were going through the lines offering assistance."

Immigration officers came on board and set up in the wedding chapel for most of the day to clear the passengers for disembarkation. Chris had a flight scheduled for the afternoon of the 19th at 3:00 and was assigned to a 10:00 am bus heading to the airport. However, disembarkation proceeded very slowly. First, the Argentinians were permitted off the ship. At around 1:00 pm a couple of buses headed to the airport. Chris had the impression that immigration officers were giving priority to clearing passengers whose embassies had been involved with their return to their country: the Swiss had a plane waiting for them; an Air Canada plane was held up for a contingent of Canadian passengers who had been in contact with their embassy.

Chris said, "My flight never did get called. About 1000 passengers were able to disembark, but the other half of the passengers, including me, were never cleared by the immigration officers until it was too late—well after our flights had departed. It seemed like the Americans and UK, the Brits, and Australians and New Zealanders were the ones left behind."

Initially, the remaining passengers were advised that the *Coral Princess* was going to remain in Buenos Aires for however many days it took to get everyone on airplanes. However, late on March 19, amid passengers heading to airplanes in buses, the Argentine government announced they were closing borders at midnight. Chris said, "The Captain had to make a fast decision to leave port so as not to be stuck at the port for an indeterminate number of days with very limited supplies. He called back the people at the airport waiting for planes, he didn't want to abandon them: some were waiting in buses, some had entered the terminal. If their flight was not leaving before the borders closed, he didn't want to leave them with no option out of the country. Once they arrived back on board, we took off quickly."

After departing Buenos Aires, *Coral Princess* was no longer a cruise—that had officially ended. It was transportation for citizens of several countries who were stranded at sea with no immediate way to return to their country. When the Argentinian borders closed with only half of *Coral Princess* passengers able to board planes out of the country, the plan was to continue on from Buenos Aires to another country where passengers could disembark and arrange transportation home. Except, there was a pesky problem of fuel, provisions and supplies. Chris told me, "The Captain said we were going to go back to nearby Montevideo because we needed supplies. We were also instructed to again buy airline tickets home, as we would be disembarking there. Montevideo was the port—outside the country of Argentina, in Uruguay—that had refused us docking privileges a few days earlier." March 21, *Coral Princess* made a short stop in Montevideo. Princess had hoped to disembark all the guests there but no passengers were allowed to disembark. Instead, the ship stocked up on provisions and headed 1180 nautical miles up the east coast of South America to the Port of Rio de Janeiro. A Princess Cruises press release stated: "In the continued effort to repatriate guests as quickly as possible, the ship will sail to Rio de Janeiro, Brazil, arriving March 24. Although Brazil has been closed to cruise ship traffic, we are working through diplomatic channels to obtain permission and have received positive responses. Guests with confirmed homeward flight arrangements will be permitted to disembark and go directly to the airport. Regretfully, we do not anticipate that all guests will be able to disembark in Rio due to limited flight availability. From Rio, Coral Princess will sail to Fort Lauderdale as previously announced with a planned arrival on Sunday, April 5."

I wondered, now that the tenor of the cruise had changed dramatically from a pleasure trip to essentially a high seas evacuation, how had the remaining passengers' mindsets changed? Chris told me, "It was a looming question about where we were going and what we were going to do? And because the cruise officially ended in Buenos Aires, a lot of the services disappeared. In terms of entertainment, the crew got together and put on a talent show, which was funny. Normally we would have brought on new entertainers at the stop in Buenos Aires, but of course we weren't able to. The original comedian who was still on the ship put on another show. The passengers pitched in. One couple were Tai Chi experts and they gave Tai Chi lessons. Another were counselors and gave a presentation on stress and how to handle it. And everybody by now was very stressed."

Rio was days away. Many passengers had originally booked the 14-day leg of the cruise which was supposed to end on the 19th and now they were looking at getting home well past that. Chris noted that some people had work to get back to; had to get to animals that were in kennels; doctor's appointments—one man was due to start chemo. The passengers were instructed to buy plane tickets leaving from Rio. Chris said, "At this point, I had $7000 on my credit card of tickets I couldn't use. So I didn't even bother with buying tickets. I said, 'I'll just see what happens,' but secretly looked forward to going on to Florida, ending where and when I was originally scheduled. We still had no worries of the virus being onboard."

Chris was prescient. On March 24, the Brazilian Health Regulatory Agency denied the *Coral Princess* from even entering their waters. Passengers expecting to disembark, including Brazilian nationals and those with confirmed flights out of Brazil would have to continue to Florida. "After sitting outside the waters waiting for the pilot to come on board—because we had been promised that we could get in their port, and that we would be able to use their airport—the Captain announced Rio was not going to let us in and so we were pulling out, heading to Fort Lauderdale. I was alone on the aft deck with a view of Rio disappearing in the distance. A man came through the aft door, pointed to land, pounded his chest, and with tears in his eyes, cried out 'Mi Brasil.' I expressed my regrets, then left him alone. After I went inside the ship, I glanced back through the door's porthole and saw that he had dropped to his knees, watching his country disappear in the distance. He was supposed to go home at Rio, but his country had let him down; now he was headed to an unknown."

The Brazilian man dropped to his knees, pounded his chest and cried out repeatedly "Mi Brasil" as Rio faded into the distance after refusing to allow Coral Princess to enter its waters.

On March 24th the passengers were notified that *Coral Princess* had given up on South America—they were heading to Florida.

"For over a week after we left Rio's waters, we were still believed to be a healthy ship. Then early on March 31st the Captain came on the PA and said, 'a number of people have reported to sickbay, and if you have experienced any of these symptoms—then he went through the symptoms—please come down to the sickbay and there will be no charge for this service.'" I asked if that was the first indication that perhaps *Coral Princess* was no longer a healthy ship. She replied, "That was the first indication for me. But it turns out other passengers knew of people who had been sick days before that. But you know many of the symptoms mimic norovirus, or the flu, or all sorts of things. That's what people thought they were experiencing. But the Captain's announcement specifically said 'experiencing influenza-like respiratory symptoms.' Around lunchtime the Captain came back on the PA and said people were continuing to come to sickbay, and we were ordered into our cabins."

Since half the ship's passengers had disembarked in Buenos Aires, Princess moved all of the remaining passengers into balcony cabins. Chris was already in a balcony room. Also, some crew were moved from cramped crew quarters into rooms normally reserved for passengers so they wouldn't be as crowded. I asked Chris to talk about quarantining in her cabin. "By now I had coronavirus, but I didn't know it. So, I preface by saying I probably was not at my top mental functioning. I often thought it was like being in solitary confinement in jail—with a few amenities. Food was placed outside our doors. Someone would knock on our door, and then run. Princess gave Internet to all the passengers, and opened the bar service so you could order alcohol and soft drinks at no charge whenever you wanted. Breakfast sometimes came at six in the morning, sometimes came at nine in the morning; dinner came at nine in the evening and sometimes didn't come at all. But I don't fault them for this at all. This crew was fabulous. Nobody trains for serving room service three times a day to a thousand passengers. When you missed a meal, calling was futile because the lines were all jammed to get through. To tell you the truth, if I was down in that kitchen I would have taken the phone off the hook. For the most part I imagine you had the same number of people working down there as you would during a normal cruise where you get a fraction of the room service orders. They did put the waiters and some other crew down there to help. The crew was also seeing some of their co-workers get sick. So, if I missed a meal—I just accepted it for what it was. Princess also offered psychological services, counselors and the like."

That evening, the first of quarantine, March 31, *Coral Princess* stopped in Barbados for what Princess referred to as a service call. Chris said, "We had to detour to Barbados for what we were told was to pick up medical supplies. It was so interesting going into Barbados because there were all the empty ships with crew only anchored at the port. It was pretty eerie—distressing. At Barbados we saw an ambulance at the dock and someone was taken off the ship. Supposedly, he was airlifted to Florida. After we returned home I heard he passed away from the virus. So now things moved from stressful to ominous. We were confined to our cabins, and then we see someone taken off the ship." A couple of days later, Princess reported publicly that *Coral Princess* test samples processed in Barbados confirmed 12 positive cases of coronavirus. On April 2, the Captain informed the passengers of the results. That same day, for reasons not entirely clear, the U.S. Coast Guard announced it would not allow *Coral Princess* to dock in Fort Lauderdale on April 4 as scheduled. Chris told me, "Two infected Holland America ships were just ahead of us and were docking the day before us. We heard that Fort Lauderdale didn't want additional Covid-19 cases to take up their medical facilities."

On April 3, *Coral Princess* met up with its sister ship, the *Regal Princess,* in the Bahamas to pick up additional medical personnel and supplies. There were no passengers on *Regal Princess,* just crew. Said Chris, "At this point we had been turned down by several places. There was a collective sense that nobody wanted us. So when our sister ship met us, we received a wonderful welcome from the crew on the decks of *Regal Princess* and in tenders. They started their horns and the *Coral Princess* and the *Regal Princess* were communicating with each other, playing *The Love Boat* theme. When Princess ships leave port, their horns usually play out *The Love Boat* theme. It was…oh my gosh…I think everybody out on their balcony was crying."

Tenders transferring needed medical supplies, doctors and nurses from Coral Princess
in the Bahamas where Coral Princess was en route to Fort Lauderdale. The top tender
contained entertainment crew with signs and playing music.

On April 4, Coral Princess was approaching Florida, and thus far officials there
denied it entry. Chris said, "Even our own country didn't want us. I could
relate to the man from Brazil who couldn't get into Rio. Early that morning
I was awakened by that familiar ding-dong tone signaling the Captain was
about to speak. By this time I had a little PTSD thing going on, and every
time I heard that 'ding-dong' I had a bit of a panic attack. The Captain started
his announcement by informing us that Miami, instead of Fort Lauderdale,
would allow us into their port. Then he broke the sad news that during the
night two *Coral Princess* passengers had passed away."

Coral Princess docked at Port Miami on April 4. Chris said, "Many were
taken away in ambulances, and another person died that night in a Miami

hospital." Florida residents disembarked first and were provided transportation home. The remaining passengers were directed to make arrangements for flights out of Florida on the 5th, but on the morning of April 5 the Captain came on the PA and stated that the CDC ruled overnight that cruise ship passengers were not allowed to go on commercial flights. Chris said, "I thought this was going to take forever to arrange charter flights for everyone. I mean we had a couple on board from Dubai. And that gentleman from Brazil was still on board with family. It was just inconceivable to me how they were going to get everyone on charter planes. I was preparing myself to go back to sea for another 14 days. But they did pull off a miracle. The next morning, on the 6th, I got a wake-up call. 'You're going today' I was told. So I quickly packed, and realized I was short of breath. I figured this was related to my pre-existing condition, plus the stress of the circumstances. In fact, I came home with the virus, unknowingly. As we had been in cabin quarantine for a week, I didn't move around much, so I didn't notice I was short of breath until they told me my charter plane was arranged and to be downstairs in one hour."

A phalanx of law enforcement escorted the bus carrying Chris' group to the Miami International Airport. All highway exits and entrances were closed so the buses could pass undeterred. The passengers boarded the waiting plane directly from the tarmac where protective-suit clad TSA had set up a temporary screening station, as the CDC ruled that the passengers could not enter the terminal.

On the tarmac, headed home; that's TSA in the hazmat suits.

There is a famous image that appeared on worldwide media of Chris standing alone at the top of the steps leading into the plane and waving to the media, TSA, and Princess Cruises personnel gathered on the tarmac. Her glance is slightly skyward as much as it is focused on the crowd below. It was as if Chris was acknowledging a higher power. Perhaps she was—but she was also glancing at the helicopter hovering above from Miami ABC10. Chris had been feeding continuous updates from *Coral Princess*, including cell phone video, to an ABC10 reporter to whom she had become acquainted. The news helicopter was unable to get within a certain distance of *Coral Princess* at the dock. A building blocked the view of the ship, and reporters were not allowed past that building. Her reports and video were picked up worldwide. On the way to the airport Chris told the reporter that she had been in communication with, "Well I guess that's it, I don't have any more reports for you." Chris told me, "I was sad to leave him at that point. He had provided a lot of emotional support to me." After she signed off to the reporter, he cryptically stated, "They're going to be waiting for you at the airport." When Chris climbed the steps to enter the plane, she didn't see anyone from Miami ABC10. "Then I looked up and saw the helicopter and cried." Chris believes their presence hovering above the waiting plane was a thank you for the assistance she had given their reporter.

Before Chris entered the plane, she glanced skyward and mouths the words to the helicopter crew, "Thank you for coming."

Postscript

The day after returning to New Hampshire, Chris got confirmation of what her body had been telling her for a couple of weeks—she tested positive for Covid-19. From networking among *Coral Princess* passengers subsequent to the cruise, Chris surmised the number of positives beyond the 12 officially reported by Princess were many, many times that and she has since learned of the deaths of several other passengers after they returned home. Chris plans to cruise again as soon as the lockdown is lifted.

Section Two:

THE GLOBETROTTERS

The World Is But A Canvas To Our Imagination
—Henry David Thoreau

Each of the three passionate travelers featured in this section, *The Globetrotters*, have racked-up a prodigious number of miles on their journeys—overland as well as at sea. They all have fascinating cruising stories but they transcend travel. I considered introducing *The Globetrotters* with a clever superlative, perhaps approximating the combined cumulative miles traveled by them given their number of countries visited, miles hiked, oceans traversed, etc. On reflection, too much math! Besides, that just quantifies their travel. The richness in their tales is about the places they have been and the stories behind how each one of them became *The Globetrotters* that they are.

Mr. Scott Eddy

There is no one better to lead off this section, *The Globetrotters*, than @MrScottEddy, as he is known on social media where he is the world's most popular travel personality. Scott epitomizes a *Globetrotter*. In fact, he is the star of the new Lifetime television series *VideoGlobetrotter*, which premiered May 2020.

Scott Eddy overlooking the "City Bowl" in Cape Town, South Africa, designated the best place in the world to visit.

Scott Eddy has taken somewhat of a circuitous route to arrive at his current designation as one of the top travel influencers in the world. A Forbes Magazine profile stated that Scott Eddy "is consistently rated as one of the top five luxury travel influencers in the world." Yet, travel wasn't even Scott's first career, although he traveled quite a bit with his family in his youth. I asked Scott to take me back to the route he took that culminated in his current standing in the industry and his own television show.

Scott was born in Michigan. Scott's father's side of the family was American. His mother's parents were from Lebanon, and then moved to Jamaica to be entrepreneurs, and Scott's mom was raised in Jamaica. Scott's father, who was in law enforcement, first raised the family in Michigan where he was a state trooper for 11 years, and then moved them to Florida where he was a Fort Lauderdale police officer for 11 years. So, growing up all of Scott's travels were either to Michigan, or in the Caribbean to see his family on his mother's side. Consequently, the Caribbean travel enabled Scott to do a fair amount of cruising as a child.

"Back in the old days when Carnival *Celebration,* SeaScape, and NCL were all leaving out of Fort Lauderdale, it was super easy to do cruising to the Bahamas, Jamaica, Mexico; those three or four days, sometimes we would do a week—it was very cost-effective travel for a family. It wasn't a big family—my sister, parents and me—we weren't a big family but costs add up and we weren't wealthy; we only had one salary. My dad was a cop and my mom didn't work. So affordable cruising was a good way to go."

While certainly those experiences cruising beginning at about 10 years old perhaps laid the foundation for this globetrotter to see the world, they did not spark a motivation in Scott to pursue a travel career as he entered the workforce. In fact, a travel career was nowhere on the horizon for Scott. The script for Scott's life was that he was supposed to follow in his dad's footsteps.

"My middle school and high school was familiarity with the police station. I went on ride-a-longs, learned to administer a polygraph exam when I was 12. I took my driver's license test in a police car. I was destined to graduate from high school, enter the police academy, become a cop, and retire as one. That was the life plan. Three weeks before my graduation from high school, my father was killed in the line of duty. He was a detective, and was flying to Tallahassee to get a confession from a suspect who was already in jail. On the way back to Fort Lauderdale, there were some fires in the Everglades, a lot of smoke, and as the plane turned towards the commuter airport, it went down in a tailspin. Changed my life forever; went from having a perfect childhood, about to become a cop, to not knowing what I wanted to do but not wanting to be a cop anymore."

So when that happened with Scott's dad, he didn't know what he wanted to do, and for the recent high school graduate, travel did not rise to the forefront as a career path. Instead, Scott's entrée to the professional world was in the field of investment banking. Staid and largely unglamorous—not withstanding depictions in the movies Wall Street, or The Wolf of Wall Street—investment banking was far removed from world travel. Scott worked in investment banking for 10 years.

"I went to an orientation for a stock brokerage firm that was opening up in Fort Lauderdale. They accepted me into the training program. So I became a stockbroker. That was in the 90's when mortgages were going through the roof. So, it was a good time to be a stockbroker."

I asked Scott if he had any kind of business background that influenced his career choice. "Not at all, zero. I knew nothing. I knew nothing about marketing, finance. They were just looking for bodies to put into the training program so they could train people the way they wanted them to be trained. The only reason I got in is because a friend of mine knew someone in that firm."

"What motivated you to go into the field of financial services?" I asked

"Nothing motivated me. I had no idea what I wanted to do with my life, and it was the most promising thing that was right in front of my face. Looking back, it was the best decision I ever made because I learned one skill set, very, very well, and that was sales. I learned how to sell from the best people in the business. And sales, you need that in every industry."

Scott enjoyed 10 years of progressively increasing success in financial services. Then, one Friday the firm leadership came out of their offices and informed the team they had just sold the firm. They told the associates that they could come in on Monday and they would have new investment orders, or they could resign. So, half the firm resigned, Scott included.

On somewhat of a whim Scott moved overseas. He ended up living in Europe and Asia for the ensuing 17 years. Scott made the move with about as much forethought as he did when starting a career as a stockbroker. And, just as he learned sales as a stockbroker, a skill that would serve him well, the move abroad was a fateful one that introduced Scott to a new skill set that would change his life.

"My friend's friend was an ex-pat living in Thailand. My friend said to me. 'Bro you're 29; you've never been to Europe, never been to Asia. What's wrong with you?' So, I bought a two-week ticket to Bangkok, and after four days I just could not imagine leaving there. The people were like the finest people in the world. I couldn't imagine coming back to the US where everybody is so…entitled. I just…it changed my life. I ended up living in Bangkok for 11 years. While living in Bangkok, I started one of the first digital travel and tourism marketing agencies in Southeast Asia, and it remained one of the biggest ones in the region for five years. After selling the agency and spending some time in Europe while building my brand, I now travel full-time, while building digital strategies, speaking at conferences, creating video packages and consulting for the world of luxury travel."

So what is a digital marketing agency, how did you get into that business and how did you succeed, I wondered.

"So you know what an advertising agency does; so a digital marketing agency does everything that an advertising agency does but on the digital side. So anything with marketing strategy for social media, for Google AdWords, things like that; creation of websites, social media ads, developing mobile apps. So, everything marketing-wise, on the digital side. That was when all the islands of Thailand, Viet Nam, Macao, Bali, Singapore, that's when all of these places were blowing up. And that's when all the hotels and resorts were entering this region. And we sort of garnered the name as the go-to digital agency for anything travel. It wasn't me. I am definitely not a genius, and I knew nothing about marketing in the travel world, but I hired some really smart people from other agencies, and I just watched them. And I learned."

I asked, "Similar to entering the stock brokerage career, what motivated you to go into digital advertising? Was it the sales and marketing background you had gained?"

"A friend I worked with in the finance world left to take a big job with one of the Big Five advertising agencies, and was stationed in Hong Kong. He knew that his company was investing millions into this whole digital marketing and social media space. He said to me, 'you need to do this; this is what is going to propel you in life.' I took his advice, and it paid off huge. So, it was a friend who gave me a nudge in that direction."

So that was Scott's foothold into the world in which he would become one of the biggest social media icons in travel. The stage was set for Scott's transition from big digital advertising business to building his own social media brand.

"When social media came around, I was very active. Asia as a whole, the whole continent, was very attuned with being early adopters. So any website, social media platform, anything that comes out, they go all in overnight. When Instagram first came out, three out of the first four years, the most Instagrammed place on the planet was Bangkok. They called Bangkok the center of the social media universe it's so active there and they have so many users. So that's really how I got involved with social; just being around that atmosphere. And I built my audience because it was just natural over there."

Scott sold his agency after five years and worked on his own growth and that of his freelance enterprise. Now, he does the same thing as he did through his agency for clients in the travel space, except he provides all the services under the umbrella of his personal brand, *Mr. Scott Eddy.*

Scott on an Alaska expedition cruise with UnCruise.

An amazing story. Scott's decision to turn a short trip into an 11-year adventure in an unknown land is not a whole lot different than the Scott of today who will visit a new part of the world almost on a whim—although under very different circumstances.

Between Asia and then Europe after that, Scott lived abroad for over 17 years. Today Scott lives—well, everywhere. I ask Scott, "where are you based?" Before he could answer, I said facetiously, "the world, right?" He told me, "That's actually accurate! I technically don't have a home. I rent a room from a friend to keep my clothes, but I literally travel full-time. And I love it this way. Most people want a house. I just want to keep going; I love it. I think it is the greatest thing in the world. It's fuel for me. I got rid of my things a long time ago. I own nothing…I don't have a bed, couch, TV."

I responded incredulously, "No television, and you are about to launch a television show?"

Scott said, "Yeah, and actually I don't watch that much TV and if I do it's Hulu or Netflix on my phone. It's so funny; I probably watched ten episodes of *Anthony Bourdain: Parts Unknown*, and other than that I don't think I have watched a full episode of a travel show, ever."

I told Scott that given what I have read about him, it seems like he would have fit right in on Bourdain's show. "Perhaps. He was definitely the master," Scott said.

That was an excellent segue to *VideoGlobetrotter* which Lifetime describes as:

"Your host and tour guide Scott Eddy is a travel media personality and brand ambassador who visits exotic destinations all over the world to experience vibrant cultures, sample food and drinks from top restaurants and stay at award-winning hotels and resorts."

VideoGlobetrotter collage.

Before the pandemic I chatted with Scott about the show. I asked Scott how *VideoGlobetrotter* came about.

"About two years ago, a lady who had been following me on social for over a year reached out about meeting for lunch. Turns out she owns a huge public relations agency in South Florida. We became good friends and a few months later I signed on with her to be my publicist. She got me an introduction with the television producers of a local studio that had seven shows on Lifetime. They really wanted to do a travel show; it was just perfect timing. We quickly came up with an agreement and I signed on and I am going to be the host."

I said, "I'm not asking for trade secrets but can you clue us in on the format of the show?"

"A lot of sitting down with locals, a lot of eating street foods…my goal in the show is to make you fall in love with destinations that you didn't know you wanted to go to. I can't talk about the destinations at this point but by the time *More Joy of Cruising* [the book's title at the time] goes to print several episodes will have aired."

VideoGlobetrotter started filming February of 2020 and then…travel interrupted—that is, the pandemic hit. The premiere episode aired on Lifetime in May but Scott has no idea when it will resume. I chatted with Scott again after *VideoGlobetrotter* aired the pilot episode.

"We were fortunate enough to get a full episode completely filmed before the shut-down, and the premiere episode went on air during the pandemic, May 22nd. With regard to episode two, I don't have the answer to that question. I wish I knew, but I don't think anyone knows right now."

The premiere episode of *VideoGlobetrotter* featured Scott mingling with and experiencing people, food, picturesque sights, fun local activities, and sharing a little about local customs and history in, respectively, Trinidad and Tobago, Antigua, and Grenada.

The premiere episode was wonderful both in terms of interest-level and of course, the beautiful tropical imagery. In a half-hour I learned a little about the history and culture of each island, and it passed the test Scott alluded to earlier: attract you to destinations that you didn't know you wanted to visit. Airing at the height of the lock-down, *VideoGlobetrotter* was a welcome respite from the stress of the pandemic and boredom of quarantining and the travel worldwide lockdown. It was a welcome escape, visually, to tropical settings and ocean vistas. For me, one word describes my impression of Scott in *VideoGlobetrotter*—authenticity. Scott came across like he was very much at home in the locales he featured. The result is that the first *VideoGlobetrotter* looked like an episode of a long-running series rather than the pilot. When I asked Scott how it felt, what was it like filming that first episode, his response underscores the natural and authentic way I felt he came across.

"Truth be told, filming the episode was not really a great deal different than my normal travels; I usually travel with a video guy. It was just like a typical trip. It felt a little weird because it was going to be on television, and that's never been a goal of mine; it just happened organically. I like that it's going to reach a wider audience than I normally would through my video, and make more people aware that 'you should travel.' I like that aspect, but otherwise it feels just like my normal travels."

I told Scott that jibes with my impression of viewing the show. "I'm not surprised that you say it felt pretty much like you normally do because when I watched it you came across as very natural—like you were in your element. It didn't strike me as the first episode of something; it seemed like it was just part of a long-running series. And that's because, as you just alluded to, it is part of something long-running—not *VideoGlobetrotter*—but your life has been a long-running series of travel, evidenced by great video."

I asked Scott about the *VideoGlobetrotter* airing on May 22nd. How did it feel? Did he host a watch party? Surprisingly Scott responded:

"I actually hate being on video and I never watch myself on video. So yes, prior to airing, when the producer sent over the edits for my input and approvals and things like that, I looked at videos, but on the 22nd I didn't watch the television show. I was staying at a hotel and a bunch of people came over—my publicist, maybe 10 close friends, and we social distanced in a big conference room and I was livestreaming on Instagram while everyone viewed the show but I did not watch it myself."

VideoGlobetrotter would have been fun viewing in normal times; given the time that *VideoGlobetrotter* aired it was just what was needed at a time when traveling was locked down. If only more episodes were "in the can" when the pandemic hit. You can view the premiere episode at *VideoGlobetrotter.com.*

Since Scott's introduction to cruising as a kid on those short cruises to the Caribbean, he has gone on 50 more. Scott liked cruising from the beginning, mainly because it was something done as a family and he always had fun. He notes that back then cruising attracted a much older demographic though. "I always hoped and prayed when I got on a cruise that other kids were going to be on the cruise. But at the end of the day, whether there was or wasn't, I always had a good time."

So, Scott's positive feelings toward cruising were formed at an early age. However, he didn't cruise much after entering adulthood until Scott returned to the States after his extended residence abroad.

"The cruise boom happened when I was gone. For that gap when I was living in Asia and Europe for 17 years, I would come home once, twice, sometimes three times a year; but I didn't come home to travel. I came home to hang out with my family. So, I didn't cruise for that whole gap of 17 years. That was the whole boom of cruising and the introduction of the mega-ships. So, I haven't really done those mega-ships yet. The biggest ship I have been on is *Queen Mary 2*, Cunard; I've done that twice. I think that's around 2600, 2700 passengers."

Scott on Cunard Queen Mary 2 transatlantic ocean liner
just after departing Quebec.

Among all of Scott's luxury travel to virtually every corner of the world, luxury cruising is well represented, including on the unparalleled Hapag-Lloyd Cruises *Europa 2*, the 500-passenger luxury yacht deemed the premier small ship (251-750 passengers) in the world by *Berlitz Cruising & Cruise Ships;* and, Viking Cruises, perennially designated the world's top cruise line. Within his first year after returning to the States, Scott cruised for the first time in over 17 years—a Viking River Cruise down the Danube. Scott has also cruised on Celebration, Costa Riviera, Cunard, Norwegian, Royal Caribbean, SeaEscape, and UnCruise. I asked Scott his favorite ship or cruise line.

"Without a doubt Viking. By far." I said to Scott there's no surprise there. He continued, "Well they just do it right. When I talk about trips, I envision myself as a guest—and I understand that I am not paying for the cruises and I get paid and things like that—but I always think of myself as a guest. The number one thing that drives me crazy when I am on a cruise is when they nickel-and-dime people. When I get on a cruise, I talk to dozens maybe over a 100 of the other passengers and I ask them what their impressions of cruising are, what lines they like, this and that. Everybody says they would like to pay a little more upfront but stop nickel-and-diming them on the back-end. But the cruise lines charge very reasonable prices upfront for what you get, just to get you on because they know all they have to do is get you on—then you have no choice."

Then you are a captive audience, I point out.

"Yep; then you have no alternatives. If you are on a cruise ship, what are you going to do? For instance, they don't allow you to bring your own alcohol on the ship. So if you want a drink, you have to pay for the drink or purchase a drink package. They don't allow you to…just everything, everything. You don't have a choice but to pay for it. Which in essence, that's why I love Viking. They include Wi-Fi; they do have alcohol packages, but it's not necessary if you just want to drink with your meals, because it's provided. The food quality is excellent, the service is on another level, and their ships are phenomenal, the upkeep on the ships is unbelievable. So, I just like everything that they do and I cruise with them at least once, sometimes twice every year."

So when you say that you don't pay for the cruises, the cruise line invites you. What is your role? Why?

"So, inevitably the main thing people know me for is, and I hate this word is, to be an influencer. Where a brand is basically 'renting' my audience to speak to. So I will get hired to go on a cruise; a cruise line will pay me x amount, and they cover my expenses, and my only job while I am there is to talk about the itinerary, the cruise ship, the cruise line, chime in on everything, and I have a certain amount of deliverables on social media."

Scott clarified that his discussion of things like the itinerary, ship, cruise line, etc., are in the digital world. I ask him if there is an expectation he interact with the customers. Does he have any role on the ship?

"No, zero. But all influencers have different roles. For instance, I do not write; I'm not a writer, I don't have a blog. So some influencers' deliverables will include posts on their blog or maybe an article on a website or in a publication after the cruise."

Scott has a similar role with respect to non-cruise travel—he does the same kind of things for airlines, hotels, and destinations as he does for cruise lines.

"So those 'influencer' activities get me the most eyeballs, and gets me the most engagement, and the most exposure. But then what happens, hopefully, is maybe a hotel chain or an airline will come back to me and say, 'Hey, can you build-out a digital strategy for me? Can you consult with me while I'm building up my digital presence? Can you provide me with a hundred drone shots of my property?' So, those are all aspects of my real business. The influencer activities is just stuff on the front-end that everybody sees."

When I first interviewed Scott before the pandemic, as would be expected for someone at the top in the travel digital marketing business, he had a fantastic slate of travel lined up for 2020. Of course, the pandemic derailed all of that. I asked him about his cruise plans once cruising returns. Scott wants to get into much more expedition cruising.

"I've done some expedition cruising but I want to get into much more, stuff like Antarctica, North Pole, South Pole, Greenland, just weird destinations—I want to do all of them."

I asked Scott about non-cruise travel: "For someone who has seemingly done it all, give me one stand-out experience or destination. And what haven't you done that you would like to do?"

"I did my first safari a few years ago in Kenya with Fairmont Hotels. Fairmont has unique safari guides. We went to villages and sat down with Chiefs. We found rhinoceros horns—poaching is a very big deal in Africa—so the rhinos, especially the species that are most endangered and threatened by illegal hunting, they have their own rangers who stay with them in shifts 24 hours per day. So we went out there and talked with the rangers and brought them lunch and sat down and ate with them. It was just an incredible experience."

"And where haven't you been?" I asked. "Antarctica and Greenland, number one and number two. I've got to get there."

The travel lock-down has been emotionally challenging for all of us with a passion for travel. Travel professionals like Scott have also had to deal with the tangible impact on their business, and for someone who is a leading freelance travel entrepreneur, the impact has been quite significant. I asked Scott—besides the awesome line-up of travel he had to forego—how has the pandemic affected him both emotionally and professionally.

"Within a 48-hour period I lost 22 trips, 14 speaking engagements and all my retainer clients—I'm consulting with them, I'm helping them with strategy; I lost probably $160,000 in revenue…in 48 hours. Everything in my life was canceled except for the TV show, but we are not filming anyway. At least it wasn't canceled; it's going to pick back up when this over. Emotionally, I didn't get down because travel will be back. The only way you can be depressed is if you only care about today and you are not thinking about tomorrow and you think this is the end. Travel will be back, so it's going to be fine. Has it been difficult? Absolutely. I was bleeding from my eyeballs like everyone else with no income coming in. I just confirmed my first trip since the pandemic. I am going to Cabo in a couple of weeks. It's with a resort down there that I have worked with in the past. So things are starting to come around."

I asked Scott is there is anything he is doing differently right now with regard to his business during this travel lock-down.

"I am being a little bit more of…turning the camera around and just shooting raw video; telling people why it is important to stay on track, get more digital; telling the hotels about the importance of staying away from the OTA's, online travel agencies, Hotels.com, Expedia, and the like, because they have no control of their database when they do that—focus on direct bookings;

that way they have control if something like this pandemic ever happens again, they'll have the client details to reach out to."

I closed by asking Scott to give us some reassuring words for the future. How will travel change because of this?

"Travel is going to be cleaner! There is never going to be a cleaner time to travel. It's analogous to 9/11. Starting 9/12, there was never a safer time to fly. They were looking for bombs everywhere."

Succinct, insightful words from a globetrotter, travel marketing expert, and social media icon. Just don't call him an influencer!

Scott and The Five Foot Traveler, Sarah Gallo, another top travel influencer, I mean icon, on Windstar Wind Surf off the coast of St. Barths.

The Five Foot Traveler:
Sarah Gallo

Sarah Gallo is professionally known as a Destination Marketer and Travel Expert to the many audiences she stands in front of at international travel and hospitality events and symposia. She is a writer, content creator, keynote speaker, and photographer. Sarah is also known as *The Five Foot Traveler* to the travel blogosphere, her legion of fans on social media, and to the digital marketing world where she reigns among the elite when it comes to travel influencers. Launched in 2013, *The Five Foot Traveler* specializes in luxury accommodations, adventure activities, and cultural immersion worldwide.

The Five Foot Traveler, Sarah Gallo, on Norwegian Encore.
(Courtesy @thestelios)

Home for Sarah is in Connecticut but you are not likely to find her there. She has been traveling full-time for the past seven years. In fact, she has been traveling full-time essentially her entire adult life—Sarah is only 28. Traveling that much she has to have racked up some prodigious statistics, right? During the last six years Sarah has visited a remarkable 114 countries across all seven continents. Sarah visited her seventh continent by the age of 23! Sarah has polar plunged in Antarctica, jumped off the world's highest bungee in Macau, learned to dive in the Maldives, trekked to see gorillas in Uganda, sailed the San Blas Islands, slept in an ice hotel in the Arctic, and road tripped through Mongolia.

Recently Sarah was named by *Porthole Cruise Magazine* to its list of Top 10 Cruise Influencers of 2019. "I was so surprised and incredibly honored. It looks like I chose to focus on cruising at the right time!" Sarah told me. "Has receiving that accolade influenced you in any way?" I asked. "Well, I've definitely incorporated cruising into my life more. I've found that more companies want me to experience their ships and I've fallen in love with a whole new realm of travel. It's been quite exciting!"

Sarah's travel scope transcends cruising and is truly global as the afore-mentioned statistics depict. Sarah is one of the world's foremost travel experts working with leading companies, hospitality brands and national travel and tourism organizations to help them with enhancing their brand awareness, and facilitating promotion of their travel services, products, and destinations. Some of her clients include Olympus Cameras, Air New Zealand, Capital One, Windstar Cruises, MSC Cruises, The Ritz-Carlton, Intercontinental Hotels & Resorts, Raffles Hotels & Resorts, Anantara Hotels and Resorts, Wonderful Indonesia, and Auto Europe, among countless others.

I wondered how Sarah became such a travel enthusiast, at such a young age, traveling the world practically non-stop since graduation from New York University in 2014.

"What really catapulted me into global traveling was getting over my debilitating 10-year fear of flying. My parents used to have to carry me on air-planes, literally. I'd have a panic attack on take-off and then I would pass out."

I said, "Wait what? You are a world-leading traveler, only 28, and you had a 10-year flying phobia? Obviously, in the last several years you made up for lost time, but what's the story behind that?"

Sarah replied, "I used to love flying as a little girl. Then 9/11 happened. I was around 10 years old. I flew on a family trip that following February. There was, to-this-day, the worst turbulence I ever experienced on an airplane. Someone on the plane was very loudly distraught. And for little 10-year old me—that stays with you. Emotions were already running high among the passengers as it was not long after 9/11, and because of the bumpy turbulence that started right after take-off. Then hearing that panicked person, and being an impressionable kid, as illogical as I knew that it was, from that point on I couldn't get rid of this massive fear of flying that would spark panic attacks every time I flew."

I asked Sarah how she continued to travel with her parents.

"From that day forward for the next 10 years, every time I got on a plane, I would have to take prescribed Zanax—quite a bit of it. In theory, it was so I wouldn't have a panic attack, but what would happen is that I would still have a panic attack and then I would pass out. And I would be so tired and out of it afterward. So my vacations and family trips all through my pre-teen and teenage years were characterized by this debilitating fear of flying. When I went off to college at New York University, I wanted to participate in NYU's study abroad program. I told my family, and they raised the issue of flying by myself, and the heavy dosage of medication hindering my ability to get to where I needed to go when I arrived at my destination. After a lot of back and forth, my mom said, 'Alright, you're going to hypnotherapy.'"

After much resistance, Sarah agreed to a session. It didn't start well as Sarah denigrated hypnotherapy in the presence of the therapist, telling her "I didn't believe in what she did and that I was only there because my mom virtually forced me. Long story short, three sessions later my fear of flying is completely eliminated and I have been on an unbelievable number of flights since and I have not had one panic attack," Sarah said laughingly.

I asked Sarah if overcoming the fear of flying lead to her embodiment as *The Five Foot Traveler*. "It propelled me forward because overcoming my fear of flying allowed me to study abroad. A few months after the hypnotherapy— prior to embarking on study abroad—my grandpa took me on my first trip overseas to celebrate my high school graduation. That was incredibly special. We went to London and Paris. He had promised to take me there for my high school graduation when I was in second grade! It was my first exposure to different cultures, different languages, art and architecture, the history, just immersing myself in a new place outside of the Caribbean. I grew up going to the Caribbean, and while I loved the Caribbean, we were always going to all-inclusive resorts where you're not really getting the culture. You are going to spend time with your family. I lived for that one week a year where I got to spend time with my family on the beach. But it wasn't culturally enriching and immersive in the way that traveling overseas is. The trip to London and Paris was May 2011; in August 2011 I left for my first study abroad."

And that was the beginning of Sarah becoming a world traveler.

"I studied abroad in Florence, Italy. I got there—no panic attack; it was my first time on a plane by myself. Within three weeks of living in Italy, my life was forever changed, and I knew that I had to incorporate travel somehow; I had no idea how, but I knew that I had to meet my NYU graduation requirements early so that I could spend the first half of my senior year (which was my last semester) with another study abroad assignment. So I did everything to make that happen, taking an overload of classes each semester. I traveled non-stop that semester, visiting 16 countries in Europe."

Sarah majored in media, culture and communications at NYU. Coupled with her first study abroad semester as a sophomore, and her second study abroad semester as a senior in Buenos Aires, Argentina, Sarah was well prepared to establish herself as *The Five Foot Traveler*.

"Along with my major of media, culture, and communications, I had a minor in the business of entertainment, media, and technology. I use what I learned at NYU every day. I truly believe I live and breathe my degree every day, just in a nontraditional way. And that last study-abroad transitioned directly into the launch of *The Five Foot Traveler*. Prior to heading to Buenos Aires, my first trip to South America, I came across an opportunity that introduced me to blogging. I read about a $3000 study-abroad scholarship offer that required you to blog about your travels. I had never given any thought to writing and blogging but I was certainly interested in being paid to travel and write about it—NYU is notoriously stingy regarding scholarships. I applied and got selected! So when I took off to Buenos Aires, I was required to keep a travel blog. That forced me to document my travels not only through photos, which I was already doing beginning with my first study abroad, but it also compelled me to write about my experiences for people to read and visualize through the images. That was shared throughout the NYU community and my friends and family. And I loved having something that documented my travels...to remind me of my experiences and memories. Just like in Italy, I traveled extensively every weekend; visited almost every country in South America. I walked out of my last ever NYU exam in Buenos Aires and celebrated by visiting, in order: The Bolivian Salt Flats; trekked through Patagonia at the southern tip of South America; continued on to Antarctica where I spent Christmas; celebrated New Year's Eve in Rio de Janeiro; and then flew back home to get what I thought would be some great job in New York City in public relations and publicity. It turns out several job offers were forthcoming, but none of them paid the kind of wages that would enable me to live in New York. I figured I'd supplement my income by bartending on the weekends while I moved up the corporate ladder, but come to find out I needed to be on call on weekends for events. I decided this wasn't going to work out long-term, so I bartended when I could for a while to save up some money. In August 2014, that blog I had created for the scholarship morphed into *The Five Foot Traveler*; I took off for Africa a few months later, and the rest is history."

"So when you took off for Africa, that was the end of the work-a-day-world?" I asked.

"Yes, definitely. I quit my bartending job after turning down the corporate offers. I left for Africa armed with my camera, and my writing. Slept in a tent for almost two months. Ha, I had never slept in a tent! That was the cheapest way for me to immerse myself in the culture. I didn't have much money, but I knew that I wanted to explore and have these amazing experiences. I visited South Africa, Lesotho, Namibia, Botswana, and Zimbabwe. During the same time period, I remember learning what a hashtag was on Instagram while sitting in a tent. My whole brand literally emanated from a tent in Namibia. It was during that trip that I first began to work with companies. So I worked with some safari companies, vineyards, hostels, some attractions like the 'the world's highest bungee bridge,' things like that to try and get my foot in the door. And this was well before the word influencer even existed. Very few people were doing what I was doing, whereas now it's so common and such a saturated market. Back then, it was just me and a handful of others."

Although Sarah only recently shifted her travel focus to cruising, she experienced her first cruise way back in 1999 as a six-year-old, on Carnival *Paradise*. Although Sarah has cruised numerous exotic itineraries since, that first cruise included an experience that still ranks as one of Sarah's most memorable. "My first ever memory of cruising was a no-hands ice cream eating contest onboard Carnival when I was six years old! Also, my parents were 27-year olds on that cruise; they climbed Dunns River Falls as an excursion and I begged them to take me with them, which they wouldn't allow. In 2019, at age 27, I finally climbed Dunns River Falls on my own excursion while cruising on MSC *Seaside*."

The (not quite) Five Foot Traveler at six years old winning a no-hands ice cream eating contest on Carnival Paradise.

Of course, Sarah was too young to get "hooked" on cruising after that first cruise (although she holds on to the ice cream eating contest memory!) Sarah didn't cruise again until adulthood as *The Five Foot Traveler*. "Did you get hooked right away with that first cruise as an adult or did it have to grow on you?"

"It grew on me. I was spoiled by my first two cruises as an adult. They were respectively, to the Galapagos Islands and Antarctica." After I picked myself up off the floor she continued. "Yeah, I guess that's what you call 'setting the bar high.' Those were spectacular cruises but I was this young 20-something that still had this burning desire to see and explore the world, and so at that time cruising was a little too leisurely for me. I didn't like the sitting around, the sea days, having to mingle and chat with people. I want to be up and out and visiting and exploring and doing and seeing as much as humanly possible. That is why there is actually a pretty big gap before my next cruise. I spent multiple years flying to destinations worldwide, then spending months on the road, waking up at sunrise, out sightseeing until sunset, coming back, writing, sleeping and repeating. Cruising didn't really fit in there as much because it is more leisurely, more relaxing; it is for a certain type of traveler and I was on a quicker pace, more adventure-focused pace, and I just wanted to see and do as much as possible. At the time I didn't think that I could accomplish that via cruising."

Sarah went on those first two cruises, to Galapagos on *Yacht La Pinta*, a 24-cabin luxury expedition vessel, and Antarctica on the *Vavilov*, another luxury expedition ship, during her study-abroad semester in South America. Sarah was not working with companies as an influencer yet. *The Five Foot Traveler* had not even been launched, although Sarah did blog about the trips on her blog that was then called *Blonde, Brains, Buenos Aires!* This was 2013; in 2014 *Blonde, Brains, Buenos Aires* morphed into *The Five Foot Traveler* and you can still read about Sarah's trips to Galapagos and Antarctica at *TheFiveFootTraveler.com*.

I asked Sarah what changed. When did she know cruising was for her?

Sarah laughed, "When I realized that it took most of the stress away from travel! In 2014, after I departed New York City for Africa I had an amazing— but exhausting run of travel. After Africa, I came home Christmas, then I left and spent three successive month-long stays in New Zealand, Australia, and Japan, followed by shorter stints in Korea, Hong Kong, Macau, Taiwan and then I flew to China. In China, travel is really difficult to plan but I learned a popular thing to do was to cruise down Yangtze River. It seemed interesting, and I was a little tired because I had been on the road for quite a while. I was like, 'cruising sounds great.' I collaborated with Victoria Cruise Lines to take one of their majestic river cruises down the Yangtze. It was unlike the expedition ships I had been on to Galapagos and Antarctica—it was a luxury 5-star cruise. We were waited on in every way, shape, form or fashion; the staff was phenomenal, the shore excursions were incredible, our rooms were beautiful, the dining was of the highest quality, and they just immerse you in culture. I loved every second of it. 'Yeah, I can see myself doing more of this!' It was only a four-day cruise but was the highlight of my almost a month in China."

Victoria Cruise Lines was scheduled to introduce Victoria *Sabrina*, the largest river cruise ship in the world in April 2020 and Sarah had planned to be a part of the launch but that has been delayed by Covid-19.

Sarah has been on about 15 cruises. Windstar Cruises *Windsurf* has been her favorite ocean cruise thus far. Sarah has had a number of memorable voyages and iconic itineraries, including cruising the Yangtze and Nile Rivers, Galapagos, Antarctica, and most of Eastern and Western Caribbean. Amazing itineraries and vessels. "What are some of your standout memories and experiences," I ask.

Sarah on board Windstar Windsurf.

"So many! Sitting in the jacuzzi on my balcony with a drink in hand watching the sea pass by and listening to music; swimming with stingrays and swimming with pigs in the Bahamas; cruising down the Nile on the *MS Mayflower*; crossing the Drake Passage to Antarctica while cruising on the expedition ship *Vavilov*; watching the sea lions bathe their pups in the Galapagos; seeing the hanging coffins in the cliff faces as we drifted down the Yangtze on the Victoria *Jenna*—there are literally coffins from ancient times, cliffside cemeteries, very unique, very interesting. I've seen nothing like that elsewhere in the world. And the whole experience of filming the commercials for the MSC *Seaside* was incredible too."

Sarah enjoying the swimming with the pigs excursion in the Bahamas.
(Courtesy @thestelios)

Sarah was featured in a series of destination excursions commercials to be shown on the ship's television for a major cruise line. I asked Sarah to elaborate on what made the filming incredible.

"So as part of the process of filming, I got the opportunity to do every excursion available in the Eastern and Western Caribbean: from swimming with the stingrays in Grand Cayman, to bobsledding in Jamaica [4000-foot sled coaster ride down a mountain and through a rainforest], to snorkeling in Cozumel, to the Flying Dutchman in St. Maarten [the world's steepest zip line, from the top of St. Maarten's highest mountain.]"

All sounds wonderful but no thanks on the Flying Dutchman; loved looking at the mountains in St. Maarten but that's where it ends for me! I was fascinated about the Jamaica Bobsled ride; I remember the famous Jamaican Olympic Bobsled team and the fun movie based on their story, "Cool Runnings."

"It's really fun; kind of feels like a wooden roller coaster, but you get to guide yourself and control your own speed. I did it three times and I thought it was so much fun."

Before the pandemic, I interviewed Sarah about her near-term cruising plans. Notably, while still planning to see the world, Sarah emphasized she is focusing more on experiencing it via the seas. "Ideally, I'd love to reach my next seven countries via cruise, bringing me to 120 countries. I'm working on transitioning from overland travel to cruise travel, as I prefer the leisure and luxury of it all."

Of course, the pandemic derailed those plans. It would take several pages to chronicle the travel opportunities—cruise and overland—that Sarah had to forgo due to the pandemic. Her plans to increase her focus on cruising in 2020, following her Top 10 Cruise Influencers of 2019 accolade was thwarted by Covid-19 and the suspension of cruising will have to be deferred. Sarah was able to do a short cruise on Norwegian *Sky* in January 2020. I noted that NCL *Sky*, while small, is more mass-market oriented than some of the specialty and luxury cruising Sarah had done. I asked her how she liked that style of cruising.

"I enjoyed it; I was somewhat spoiled because I did go on the phenomenal NCL *Encore* in November 2019. It was top of the line through and through, and blew me away. Comparing *Encore* to the *Sky*, they're just different ships, different classes, different everything. I like that *Sky* is a much smaller ship. Even though *Encore* is superior in every way, I prefer smaller; the *Sky* is half the size, half the people. I do enjoy the amenities of the large ships. When I was on the MSC *Seaside* for instance—which is something like 5000 people—I had a room with a jacuzzi on the balcony, so I spent all of my time in the jacuzzi on the balcony versus trying to fight for a seat by the pool on a 5000-person ship. Whereas on the *Sky*, a 2000 person ship, every morning I was able to get a seat by the pool with no problem."

NCL *Sky* wasn't the only travel Sarah could get in before the Covid-19 derailed essentially all travel. Her last trip before the pandemic was the kind of grand, sweeping, multi-country excursion that has characterized the growth of *The Five Foot Traveler*. Unfortunately it ran into the realities of a global pandemic and winding down the trip and returning home became an adventure that just adds to *The Five Foot Traveler* lore. Sarah had been invited to tour the Arctic and parts of Sweden and Norway by a couple of tourism boards many months prior. Her flight took off March 2, a week-and-a-half before the global pandemic declaration.

"When I left for the Arctic there was this vague talk about a virus in China—supposedly it was like the flu. I wasn't really stressing about it, but I always take some extra precautions when anything is going around, and I had an N99 mask with me. I'm a germaphobe by nature, so I always travel with a mask, wipe down my airplane seat and tray table and things like that. So the trip itself wasn't anything out of the ordinary for me. For the first part of the trip my photographer and I weren't paying much attention to the news and we were having this unbelievably unreal experience in the Arctic. Then, my photographer, David Rocaberti, received a call from his family in Madrid and was told the virus was getting bad there and that they had shut down schools; he has two girls. We were like 'there's nothing we can do and it will get under wraps soon.' We weren't stressing...yet. The next day we took a train into Norway and as soon as we got there the country was going on lock-down and we were going to be quarantined in a cabin in Norway that we had originally planned to stay in for just one night. So all of a sudden it went from a bad flu to being caught up in a global pandemic and things got really scary. My family is in the states and my brother is high risk and my dad had to go to work every day. My photographer's family is in Madrid which was already an epicenter before New York was. We couldn't figure out how to get home to our families; all the information we were receiving was contradictory."

"So the cabin in Norway, did you have to rough it, or was it decent accommodations for you to spend this difficult time?" I asked.

"Oh my gosh it was stunning. It was like the greatest place I could ever possibly be quarantined," Sarah laughed. "The views were amazing; we were isolated; under normal circumstances it would have been spectacular. Even still we're incredibly grateful for where we ended up. We were in a big, luxurious cabin called Dyrøy Holiday in the middle of nowhere; we saw the Northern Lights dancing overhead. It was spectacular. The only issue was the changing news every day, so we didn't know when we would be allowed out of the country. So, we weren't able to appreciate the luxurious accommodations because we were glued to our phones keeping up with the rapidly evolving news."

Sarah finally was able to head home and after a 48-hour journey involving numerous flight cancellations, deserted airports (but the last connection was a packed flight), Sarah arrived in New York March 20. She could not see her family however, as she had to isolate for another two weeks in an Airbnb; Sarah could not risk bringing the virus home to her high-risk brother. Between Norway and then in New York, Sarah isolated for almost a month.

Travel will return, and Sarah will get right back on her pace of amazing adventures. She was booked solid for 2020 and I'm sure she will pick where she left off in 2021. I asked Sarah about future travels—particularly the few corners of the world she has not yet conquered. "Where haven't you cruised to that you would like to visit," I asked.

"French Polynesia! One of Windstar's *Star Collector* journeys through French Polynesia. I'd love to do a world cruise. Destinations I'd like to visit include French Polynesia, Easter Islands, Madagascar, Seychelles, Amazon, Antarctica again—the first time I went by myself and it was incredibly lonely—Alaska, Greenland, Arctic, Norway, and West Africa ports. I'm on a mission to find the cruises that visit places I haven't already been to!"

While not traveling, which is rare, although that's the new normal right now, Sarah spends her time with fitness and exercise, enjoys live music, and time with her family. And she stays busy with travel, just not on the road. Sarah continues to be engaged with a number of clients doing social media management, and marketing and business consulting for various travel and technology companies. I ask Sarah what she thinks the future holds for travel—how is it going to change post Covid-19?

"I think domestic travel is going to come back before international travel. Road trips are going to be more and more popular. I think, I hope, hotels and venues will make hand sanitizer available everywhere so that after we touch things, we can sanitize our hands; I hope that from a technology standpoint we use the incredible technology that we already have to make more and more things touchless—doors and the like. It's going to be a prolonged build. I don't expect travel to come back to where it was until 2022-2023ish."

I ask Sarah what the future holds for *The Five Foot Traveler*.

"What a big question! My overall aim is to help ignite the passion for travel in others and to encourage them to visit the many amazing destinations the world has to offer. If we're talking big, long-term goals, I'd love to set myself up so that I have a base in the States and a base somewhere else — where, I'm not so sure yet. These days I'm focusing largely on photo and video content, in addition to writing and social media. I'm working hard to capture the world so that people can experience it through me if they're not able to visit themselves; and to inspire those who can travel but are unsure where to visit and how to make it happen."

In The Loop Travel

John Roberts, founder of *In The Loop Travel*, and his wife Colleen got hooked on travel when they took their first trip to Europe in 2005. John and Colleen met in 1997 at Syracuse University, where they were both pursuing graduate degrees. They had married in 2005 and decided to visit Europe for the first time to see John's high school friends, a couple from Rochester, who worked in the Netherlands for the Rochester multinational Xerox Corp. The trip turned out to be an epiphany of sorts for John and Colleen, as it hooked them on travel and exploring the world beyond the United States. They toured locally with their friends, visiting around Amsterdam, Belgium and Luxembourg, and then the four of them experienced a 10-day Mediterranean cruise out of Rome on Carnival *Liberty*. Their cruise director, John Heald, was an up-and-coming star in the industry. Heald is now an iconic figure to the legions of Carnival cruisers as a Carnival Cruise Brand Ambassador.

John Roberts relaxing on a cruise on the new Regent Seven Seas Splendor, the latest "world's most luxurious cruise ship."

"That was sort of the early days for John; he's quite a celebrity in the cruise industry now. We found him to be just delightful; he was part of the whole fun and part of the reason we got hooked on cruising. Plus it was an amazing time on that ship, especially that itinerary, seeing Italy, Croatia, and things like that. So, experiencing Europe really gave us the travel bug, and we were off and running from that point."

John Roberts was born in Rochester, N.Y. and raised there until he was 12, when his mom and stepdad moved John and his younger brother, Bart, to tiny, rural, Bristol, NY, about 30 miles away "to the country and away from the city." He grew accustomed to small-town life, with his high school Bloomfield Central having a graduating class of about 90 students. After earning a management degree from St. John Fisher College in Rochester, John worked for several years in retail and commercial management before deciding, at age 29, to pursue a master's degree in broadcast journalism at Syracuse University. With enrollment of over 20,000, Syracuse was just 80 miles from home yet world's away from how he had grown up in Bristol. John earned his broadcast journalism degree and went on to work in newspapers for 15 years—in Utica, N.Y., Fort Collins, Colorado, and Norfolk, Virginia—as a writer and copy editor covering sports, news, and business before finding his calling and true passion in travel writing.

John lived in Ewing, New Jersey, for seven years, and it's where he started his travel writing via his *In The Loop Travel* website and a freelance travel writing business. He is now back in Colorado, and his freelance business caters to a growing roster of publishing outlets, whether websites or print magazines. John provides stories related to his travels primarily in the cruise segment. He has written for Porthole magazine, AARP The Magazine, Travel Pulse, CruiseCritic.com, TravelAge West and a host of other cruise-specific magazines and websites.

John has operated *In The Loop Travel* since 2013. He creates content for the site and on his YouTube channel and social-media platforms that aims to inform people how to travel in a fun and active way—away from the crowds—to discover interesting and unique experiences. John differentiates *In The Loop Travel* by incorporating a fitness and wellness component "to show that people can enjoy cruises in non-traditional ways."

Despite having been on more than 80 cruises, John and Colleen, who John introduced me to as his "partner-in-cruise," didn't go on their first until 2000—on Carnival *Sensation* out of New Orleans, with stops in Jamaica and Mexico. I'm always intrigued at what motivates someone to cruise for the first time, recalling my own hesitancy to give cruising a try.

"It was our first vacation together. I guess we just thought it would be a cool option to go away for a week and have a sort of self-contained environment that was affordable. We had just started out in the newspaper business and weren't making a lot of money. We were dating and realized we could go and pay one price and have all our entertainment, food all included, multiple locations; we thought we would check it out."

A few years later, John and Colleen went on the second cruise for a friend's 30th birthday celebration aboard Royal Caribbean's *Explorer of The Seas* on a Western Caribbean cruise featuring Belize. For their third cruise, it was back to Carnival; that was the Mediterranean cruise on *Liberty* that was part of the aforementioned Europe trip. By that third cruise, John knew he was hooked.

"We found the value proposition appealing. Being able to unpack once, stay in one room and yet end up in a new location every day; cruising is a hassle-free way to get to see a lot of different destinations in a compact period of time. It's very affordable for the amount of inclusions like meals and entertainment. You have a lot of flexibility and freedom to do what you want, to go on an excursion or not, do things at your own pace or try to join in everything. Each day you can sort of see how you're feeling and then take on that day your way."

Although constrained by full-time jobs in the newspaper business in various locations, and having limited vacation time, John and Colleen began to cruise on a somewhat regular basis—once a year, or every other year, as they could, and often brought friends along.

"We were still attached to a workplace in the newspaper business across multiple locations: New York, Colorado, Virginia from 2005 to 2013. Over the course of that time, we would sprinkle in cruises whenever we could. It became a much bigger deal in 2013. For our cruise planning, Colleen would use the website Cruise Critic to help plan, book, look for the best itinerary, ships, and get an idea what the experiences were going to be like. She found that website to be a great resource. And you know we were in journalism, and one day Colleen says, 'I wonder if Cruise Critic has any job openings.' The newspaper business was consolidating, adapting to the changes presented by the internet, having rounds and rounds of layoffs; we thought we better be a little more proactive about our futures. Colleen checked out the Cruise Critic job board and found an opening to lead their editorial team. Colleen applied and got the job at Cruise Critic and that motivated me to build my own brand, particularly with the access we were going to start to have to more regularly get on cruise ships. Colleen started to go on media trips to see new ships and refurbished ships, started covering the industry quite intently, and often she was able to bring a 'plus one guest.' Lucky me! So I get on more and more ships."

Seven months later, John left his job in Norfolk, Virginia, and relocated to New Jersey to join Colleen who had moved to assume her position with

Cruise Critic. Partners-in-cruise indeed; Colleen had successfully converted her avocation for cruising into a vocation. And John was able to enhance the growth and reach of *In The Loop Travel* by gaining exposure to even more cruises.

"I spent those seven months kind of processing everything, and making sure Colleen loved her job, and that she was definitely going to want to stay in Jersey. I said to Colleen 'I should make my schedule more freed up to be able to go on some of these trips and ships and experiences with you as often as possible.' I don't have enough vacation time to be able to go cruising all the time. So, I decided to leave the newspaper business and start my website and freelance business from scratch. So it's been a long process of over seven years of sort of riding Colleen's coattails in the industry for a little bit, and then eventually making my brand stand out and finding my own niche with things like fitness and wellness and things like that, and raising my profile enough that opportunities like *Cruising Interrupted* find me."

So John started *In The Loop Travel*. I asked if it was exclusively focused on cruising at first.

"Actually the name kind of predates the establishment of the brand. It was based on cruises and other travel we would enjoy when we were still in the newspaper business. It was more of a diary or blog just built for my family and friends to read about what we were up to and sort of keep them 'in the loop.' So I took the name that I had generated a little bit of an audience for and then tacked *Travel* on the end so people would know it's about travel. Cruises, yes, take up probably 75 percent of the subject matter, because that's where my connections are, that's my preferred method of travel, but initially it was established as a travel site."

John has been on more than 30 cruise lines. After starting mostly with the mass-market lines and sailing and enjoying them all as chronicled extensively on *InTheLoopTravel.com,* John now prefers smaller ships, loves river cruises and especially enjoys expedition cruises with UnCruise Adventures.

John on an expedition cruise with UnCruise Adventures in Hawaii.

"Colleen and I loved big ship mass-market cruising in our early years of travel. The ships had so much going on from entertainment to food to amenities like pools, hot tubs, lively bars and fun people to meet. We loved it. The 'one price gets you almost everything' aspect was appealing as an affordable, hassle-free vacation. We have evolved, though, into travelers who cruise, instead of people taking a cruise vacation. Our best experiences now, by far, come on small ships, expedition voyages to exotic places, traveling among like-minded people. I really enjoy AmaWaterways on the rivers in Europe, and Avalon Waterways on the exotic rivers in Southeast Asia in Myanmar, and the Mekong River in Vietnam and Cambodia. For ocean ships, Viking Ocean Cruises, 930 passengers, amazing experiences…those are fantastic. We have sailed on Viking *Sea*, Viking *Sky* and Viking *Orion*, visiting places like Norway and Tunisia.

"I do like the expedition ships; I like the rustic old ships. Not the ships per se but the experience that an expedition line like UnCruise Adventures gives. They have an amazing program in many exotic places, and they offer great expeditions. And the thing about them is the program is focused through the energy and enthusiasm of their guides and the daily activities and fascinating places you go."

John has enjoyed dozens of cruises on ships ranging from the world's largest with every conceivable amenity to very small vessels with their own levels of luxury. John has experienced Alaska and Hawaii several times, the river cruises with Avalon Waterways and AmaWaterways, Tahiti with Paul Gauguin Cruises, a luxury Antarctica expedition cruise with Abercrombie & Kent and Ponant, and more voyages that many of us would consider "once in a lifetime" cruising adventures.

I asked John if he could highlight one particularly memorable cruising experience for himself:

"Going to Alaska with UnCruise; it was my first experience with them," he said, "and it was my first time seeing Alaska not from a big ship, and going to unique, remote places where only 40 of us are there; whether you are in a bay or an island, or way deep in a fjord; or going off the ship to go kayaking, going on 20-mile hikes during the day through the backcountry, and things like that."

"Certainly in keeping with your fitness niche," I said.

"Yeah, it really played up to what I enjoy doing; being active and fit and finding those kinds of thrilling, adventure activities. It was just an incredible experience. And Alaska on its own is one of my favorite destinations anyway. That's one memory."

"What about the expedition ship itself? A lot of creature comforts, a lot of luxury, or not really?" I asked.

"It's pretty bare-bones. Their ships are functional. You might say the staterooms are cozy. They don't have any TV reception or anything. There are DVDs you can get to watch in your cabin, but the idea is you're not there to watch TV. By the end of the night you are going to pass out from being so active. You just want to drop off your gear and get a good night's sleep. You can easily wander around the four decks of the ship. There is a top sun deck that's open-air, and maybe you get in some yoga, get in a workout in the morning and a stretch and get ready for your daily of excursions. They have a main lounge, dining room and open bar, and just friendly, well-traveled people onboard who are out for the same type of adventure as you are. So, everyone hits it off really well. It's just a great environment and a lot of camaraderie. But the ship itself is not really that flashy. They've got nice refurbished ships that are built to get into small intimate places around the coastline. And they are great home bases—that's pretty much all they are. Get you where you are going safely and fairly comfortably, but they are not like these big shiny, new luxury ships."

I mentioned to John that I am hearing in the expedition cruise space there are some more luxury vessels coming on.

"Absolutely. Scenic Cruises just had one launched; it's called Scenic *Eclipse*. They have a range of fine restaurants onboard; a submarine on it, two helicopters, really shiny finishes, luxury everywhere onboard."

"Have you been on it? Did you ride the helicopter and submarine?" I ask like a fascinated kid.

"Yes. We got helicopter rides! Where we happened to be cruising off the coast of New England, the submarine wasn't allowed to go in the waters. Expedition cruising is an evolving space, and there are something like 40 expedition ships planned to launch over the next few years. It's a huge new segment for people who are maybe getting older and have built up some retirement savings and want to start splurging and going to some exotic places around the world. Maybe they've done all the Carnival and Royal Caribbean cruising with large crowds and they want something more intimate and want to go to some bucket-list destinations. We just got back from Antarctica; that was a great luxury cruising experience."

"What ship was that?"

"We went with an outfitter called Abercrombie & Kent. What they're really well known for, their legacy, started with African safaris; they do luxury boutique travel. And they partner with Ponant for their cruises; Ponant has expedition ships that they use in Antarctica and places like New Zealand and other parts of the world. So, Abercrombie & Kent charters a Ponant ship and puts their clients on so it's a luxury experience on a Ponant ship."

Prior to Covid-19, John had an amazing slate of cruises scheduled for 2020—sounds like it would be a series of bucket-list cruises all in one year for most of us: Thailand and Malaysia on *Star Clipper* in April; Galapagos in May on Silversea *Silver Galapagos*; Japan in September with Windstar; Portugal on Uniworld River Cruises; and with AmaWaterways on the Danube.

"Early on, we knew we weren't going to Thailand and Malaysia; that has now been shifted to November and been redirected to Morocco. Galapagos was a bucket-list cruise. The positive aspect of that trip not happening is that *Silver Galapagos* is being retired and that was going to be its last voyage. They're replacing it with a brand-new ship, the ultra-luxury *Silver Origin*, so hopefully that trip gets rescheduled for the new ship. The Japan trip has been rebooked for 2021."

I wondered with having experienced such an eclectic variety of cruise ships and unique itineraries, what could possibly be John's ideal cruise he still wishes to take. Without hesitation, he told me, "A world cruise with Viking Ocean Cruises. And I still haven't been to the Galapagos. I would love to do that. Need to get to Australia; that would be my seventh continent, and I know cruising around the entirety of Australia is a great way to see that vast country. I want to do a river cruise in Russia. And I would love to do a combination safari, and Chobe River cruise in Africa."

I asked John if he has time for much land-based travel.

"We like to plan a series of U.S. land-based shorter trips around our busy cruise travel schedule. We get to places like Scottsdale for hiking and relaxing and Portland, Maine, Austin, Texas, weekends in New York City, trips to North Carolina, Wisconsin and up to Rochester or Cape Cod to see friends. A very memorable trip we did was to drive across the country on a big baseball stadium trip. We are big sports fans."

What were your favorites?

"The ones that really stood out for us were Wrigley Field in Chicago and Busch Stadium in St. Louis."

"In terms of land-based travel bucket list, I would love to hike the Camino de Santiago in Spain, it's sort of like a religious pilgrimage trail; I saw a movie based on it: *The Way* starring Martin Sheen, and ever since seeing it, I have wanted to walk at least a portion of it. I want to do an extensive Ireland biking trip; we still want to go to Machu Picchu, and an African safari."

Other than travel, John enjoys television and movies, sports, a broad array of exercise activities—running, biking, hiking, kayaking, snorkeling, and lifting weights—and craft beers. He said he often seeks out craft breweries in the destinations he visits.

His interests clearly favor sports and fitness...and beer. John mentioned biking in Ireland, 20-mile hikes during his UnCruise expeditions; fitness and wellness owns significant space on the *In The Loop Travel* website and in John's life.

"We've always enjoyed working out and staying fit," he said. "It's an easy, seamless, and I think sensible part of travel. Key to prepping for travel, and better enjoying travel is to stay active, and stay fit, and be ready. There are some simple things I always preach about, how travel and fitness go hand-in-hand ...you can handle your luggage better on airplanes; you can have more energy when you go out and do excursions. That's just in general for anybody. But for Colleen and me, we like to more actively seek out fun things to do while at a destination. So we're more likely to go to places where you can snorkel or kayak or go for hikes. In Europe, you pull up on a river cruise, get off, grab the bikes they have on the ship and go for a ride around the city or along the river. Go for a run and get lost in the city. I try to lean my stories toward finding active ways to see a new place. You know the larger ships have the traditional reputation of a lot of people lining up at a buffet and eating all day and drinking. I instead try to find a unique niche to write about ways people can enjoy their trip in a more active or fitness-focused way, on the mega ships as well as the expedition ships where it is incorporated into the programming. I try to write about and do reviews of the gyms on the big ships. Talk about what the fitness program might be on a Carnival ship, or try to tell people about a cool excursion you can do at certain destinations. My idea is to try to break the mold as to how you can have a better cruising experience in an active way."

I read "9 Ways to Get Physical On *Anthem of the Seas*" on *In The Loop Travel.* (I only did one of them, "skydiving" when I was on *Anthem* a couple of years ago. I am disappointed John didn't include my riding of the bumper cars in his list!) Fitness is clearly an integral part of John's life. I asked John how the lock-down has influenced his relationship with fitness. He lamented that with the gyms closed he cannot work out much with weights, so he has shifted his workouts to include more biking and hiking. And, a major response John has made to this unscheduled downtime is to enter his first marathon—at age 53.

"I decided to take this downtime, this window of opportunity where I have many hours of the day; and that was the biggest barrier to training for a 26-mile run—I was never going to have the time to do training runs for two-to-three hours at a time. But now I have nothing but time, and I figure I'd give myself a challenge. I figured if I am ever going to do it, I better get going at it now."

I mentioned Joe Church, and his amazing feat of running a marathon length distance on every ship in the Royal Caribbean fleet. It turns out that John has featured Joe on *In The Loop Travel.* Other than the impact on fitness, and obviously the postponed cruises, John said the cruise lockdown has offered time for reflection.

"Everything was such an unknown early on when we had to shut down. I know a lot of people were thinking, 'we'll lock-down, flatten the curve, and then we'll all get back out there cruising. It won't be so bad.' We were all very positive and optimistic. But you know as things dragged on, it kind of got depressing; I missed travel and more and more trips got postponed or canceled. We had to adjust to living in close quarters … and figure out a way to occupy our time each day. When I don't have travel, there are no stories to write for *In The Loop Travel.* It's been a hectic past several years traveling the globe, doing a lot of cruising, being out there in the world interacting with people, learning new cultures and customs. That was really what my life was like, and it has just taken a 180. But now that we are months into it, you sort of get reflective and you appreciate the smaller things, and what you've been missing out on, and time with your spouse and family and friends—if you are able to be in small bubbles and do things like that safely. We have two friends with a lake home and we visit them—they're our bubble partners."

I asked John for his thoughts on the future of cruising given the post-pandemic new normal.

"I do imagine that in the short-term that maybe they are going to redesign some things. One of the short-term changes we know about—suspension of buffets—I believe that may be adapted for the long-term. I think maybe they are going to redesign ships and re-envision those spaces and not have buffet-style dining. Otherwise, in the short term there are going to be some modifications; it's kind of disheartening that we may not have the level of engagement and interactions that we are used to. To get back cruising, we are going to have to incorporate social distancing, maybe temperature checks, testing, the queues for venues...not being able to eat with new friends at your dining table; multiple dining venues—more so than you already have—spread out all over the ship; it's just not going to be that engaging experience that we are used to. Initially, people are going to be wary of each other, a little distant...people wearing masks—you can't see a smile; can't give a hug, can't give a handshake. Longer-term, I'm just very hopeful that when we get a vaccine or the virus goes away, essentially cruising goes back to be the carefree sort of getaway that we all enjoyed. Hopefully, we can forget all this ever happened because that's what everyone likes about cruising: the interaction you can have with people. The main thing I try to get across to people who really love cruising as much as I do. I would go in with realistic expectations; it's not going to be exactly like what you remember, but you can still have a good time. Cruising traditionally has been special because you get to go to these amazing places and do fun things, try new foods, dance in the clubs, or just have a casual drink and meet new friends; have intense, intimate experiences. But, for now, at least in the short-run, it is going to be different."

When cruising does return, one quote from John sums up what could be the *In The Loop Travel* credo:

"There really is a cruise out there for everyone. You know, I don't think I've ever had what I would call a bad cruise. They all were fun and special in their own ways."

Section Three:

SPECIALTY CRUISING:
FUN AND QUIRKY

I have had conversations with many cruisers who have gone on dozens, even over one hundred cruises but have never experienced a cruise on a non-traditional cruise ship; that is, a small ship designed to hold as few as 300 or less passengers, low double digits, even single digits! These small ships can range from spartan to ultra-luxury, and because of their size and design can access destinations that mainstream cruise ships cannot. Likewise, the vast majority of cruisers have not experienced the fun, excitement and sense of community among like-minded fans on a music-themed charter cruise. After reading *Specialty Cruising: Fun and Quirky,* you may add a small ship cruise, or music-themed charter cruise, or both, to your bucket list.

Cruise Entertainment Producer, Director, Creator, MC Extraordinaire! Jason Venner

I almost titled this feature, *Cruise Director to the Private Sector*, as Jason Venner calls himself. It is an apt description for Jason, but probably wouldn't be meaningful to you until after reading his story. On the other hand, the title *Cruise Entertainment Producer, Director, Creator, MC Extraordinaire!* leaves little doubt about Jason's impact on a cruise, even if you are not sure exactly what he does.

Jason Venner has spent essentially his entire adult life in the cruise world, mostly in a variety of cruise music and entertainment capacities. In other words, bringing the fun! Jason got his start in cruising June 2002 as a DJ with Holland America Line (HAL), a high-end cruise line owned by Carnival Corporation. At HAL, Jason progressed through the ranks from a DJ to over 10 years as a Cruise Director, to Corporate Trainer, to three years as Producer and Host of the joint ABC/BBC HAL production, *Dancing with the Stars: At Sea*. Since 2015, Jason has been self-employed as a Producer, Director, and Host of full ship music charter cruises, primarily in partnership with StarVista LIVE.

For StarVista LIVE, Jason hosts the following annual cruises, each of which features scores of legendary performers as well as comedians, activities, and ship décor in keeping with the musical genre: *Malt Shop Memories Cruise; Soul Train Cruise; The Country Music Cruise; Flower Power Cruise; '70s Rock & Romance Cruise; Southern Rock Cruise;* and, *Ultimate Disco Cruise.* The hundreds of entertainers Jason has introduced, interviewed, escorted and accompanied include Smokey Robinson, Frankie Avalon, Kenny Rogers, Charley Pride, Chubby Checker, Lynyrd Skynyrd, The Beach Boys, Earth, Wind & Fire, and The Temptations. "It's crazy to be on a first name basis with the legends of the music industry."

Jason Venner, on stage introduction, 70s Rock & Romance Cruise.

There was little in Jason's upbringing that would suggest a future of world traveling in a highly visible, public role so deeply enmeshed with popular music and musical celebrities. Born in Seattle, Washington and raised in the Columbia River Gorge area of the Pacific Northwest, Jason grew up off grid, literally—no running water, electricity, middle of the woods, no cars, dirt roads, until at 14 Jason moved with his parents to Portland, Oregon.

I was curious if Jason's austere background had any influence on the route he followed as an adult.

"Mostly on my personal life, not on my professional life. What I do for a living, cruising and entertainment, that all came out of left field; that all really came out of nowhere. Living like that and growing up like that though, no people, nearest neighbors miles away, I think that plays a big role in my being an introvert. When I'm on my downtime, there's nothing I want more, mentally, than to be in that situation. It pushed me to being...I'm really good at being alone; really good at quiet; just enjoying a book or being outdoors."

I expressed surprise that Jason describes himself as an introvert. He told me, "For someone that has been on stage with big crowds as well as intimate gatherings, yes, I am an introvert." I asked how that can be for someone whose very existence in the world of cruising is defined as being the public face of a cruise; not just any cruise but ones whose business model is live, big name entertainment and fun.

"When I'm down—I don't mean emotionally but I need downtime. When I'm off, so to speak, I'm very much off; I'm hidden, not the center of attention at parties and events. Unless of course I'm working; then I absolutely am the face or voice of any event I'm in. I do my best to try to be the biggest personality there or at least one of them; my desire is to make it a fun time and a good experience for all. If that means I need to get the dance floor started, I grab a mic and get a crowd fired up and ready to go, let's do that; if that means I need to buy a round of adult beverages at a bar I lean into that." In other words, Jason compartmentalizes the personal and the professional.

Neither travel nor music played a significant role in Jason's youth. His life centered around football. Jason was a high school football star. He was selected as a High School Football All-American and garnered over 20 full-ride scholarship offers. Then at 18, six months from high school graduation, while driving home from an event, Jason was rear-ended by a drunk driver and fractured his back. He lost all of his scholarship opportunities. After recovering, Jason went on to attend Linfield College where he was a student player/coach for their football program and graduated with a degree in business and marketing.

I asked Jason, "Did that traumatic end to your athletic career influence you in your professional life?"

"It humbled me a lot. When you have success in sports in high school it is very easy to think you are 'it.' It's very easy to fall under the misconception that you are a big deal in the world. All of a sudden, I get hurt and I lose my sports career and the world kept on moving. It brought me back down to earth from where I was a big deal…or thought I was a big deal. It reinforced to me that everyone is going through something; there's no one who doesn't have a drama or trauma that is affecting them. It did affect my professional life in that it gave me the capacity to exhibit compassion. It gave me the ability to hear people out. If someone was complaining, I didn't tag them as a whiner—I listened to them. Tell me your problem. How can we make it right? If you're on vacation, and you have a problem, I want you to have a great vacation. That's my only goal. If it means you need help with something, or you are angry about something and you need someone to listen to you, whatever it is, let's figure it out. So it gave me compassion, empathy."

Jason with Smokey Robinson and wife Brittany Venner.

After graduating from college, on a whim, 21 year old Jason applied online for a job with HAL. He had been on a cruise ship once as a kid with his grandmother but doesn't recall much about it. "I didn't apply to HAL knowing much about what I would be doing. I certainly hadn't heard of the concept of a cruise director. Honestly, I applied for the travel. I figured I would travel the world before getting a real job. I quickly fell in love with the travel, the experience."

I asked, "Other than the cruise as a kid, had you traveled?"

"A little bit," Jason told me. "I went to school in Ireland, I studied abroad my senior year in college at the University of Limerick. At the end I took an extra month and backpacked around, visited several countries. In high school, they took the All-American football team for some exhibitions in Australia, Hawaii, and a couple of other places. So I traveled a little."

Talk about your first cruise after getting hired.

"My first cruise as an employee was out of Vancouver, Canada. I joined the ship in Vancouver; we were headed to Alaska. We sailed out passing under the Lions Gate Bridge, and I remember standing on deck and I was absolutely terrified. I didn't know what was doing; I started to question why I took the job. I had a girlfriend I was leaving back home. I was petrified. I'll never forget standing on deck, in the middle of a huge sail away party; 1000, 1500 people on deck, dancing, drinking their champagne, and I was almost in tears."

Obviously, Jason didn't develop a passion for cruising on that first cruise for HAL. I asked, "When did it occur to you that, hey, I really enjoy this?"

"For lack of a better phrase, HAL played me really well. I was going to do the DJ job for one six-months contract, and then I was going to go and get a real job. About four months into the contract I got a call from the head office. They said my reviews have been great, my cruise director speaks highly of me, and they're going to do something they don't normally do for new staff, which was offer me a really big cruise. They said they needed someone to do their world cruise which was a 90-day Asia Pacific cruise from Vancouver including stops in Japan, China, South Korea, Cambodia, Singapore, all the way down to Australia and New Zealand, up through the South Pacific and ending in Los Angeles. Having taken the job to travel, I made a deal with myself. I thought ok, I'll do one more. How can you pass up that many countries and that much travel? So, I take that cruise, it was a blast, and as that cruise is ending, I get a call. They told me the cruise director on my first cruise—he was a huge mentor and influence of mine—he just took a a big contract for HAL and he requested me. Would I be willing to do 5-months doing 17-day roundtrips back and forth in South America—Antarctica, three days in Rio every cruise, three days in Buenos Aires every cruise, and so on? Again, I'm a kid; this is more travel, more countries, how do I turn that down? So I make another deal with myself. I take those five months, and then I'm going to get a real job! They kept doing that to me. For my first six contracts. During that time I got to live in Venice helping to build out a new ship, *Oosterdam*, and then doing an inaugural cruise on it. HAL just kept offering me unbelievable experiences. And I couldn't turn them down. They were life experiences. Looking back on it, like I said, they played me beautifully. After that first contract if they had offered me another contract for Alaska, or for the Caribbean, I'd have turn them down. But they basically kept me moving all over the world and offering me great experiences. Now I was hooked. And then I got promoted to Cruise Director."

Clearly from the progressively more enticing contracts, HAL was pleased with Jason. I asked Jason to talk about getting elevated to Cruise Director at HAL after a couple of years as a DJ.

"I can only speculate about being selected as I can't answer directly for the Director of Entertainment at that time. HAL had just introduced their new Vista Class of ships. Vista Class is comprised of: *Zuiderdam*, which inaugurated the Vista Class when it was christened December 2002, followed by *Oosterdam*, *Westerdam*, and then *Noordam*. Vista Class was the first time HAL went bigger and different in the design of its ships. On the existing HAL classes, Rotterdam Class (R-Class) and Statendam Class (S-Class), everything was in the same place—cookie cutter casino, ocean bar, show lounge, shops—until they got to the Vista Class. The Vista Class was bigger, brighter, the décor was different; it was just a different animal. If nothing else, HAL was traditional, and so were their cruisers. Their Mariner Society, HAL's repeat cruisers, rely on and expect that consistency; they want to know where to go on ship a, b, or c to find everything, and this was the first time HAL, in their minds, was 'pulling the rug out from under them.' The *Zuiderdam* in particular was big, bright gaudy; it was vibrant bright greens and golds and blues and oranges; there was cow print seating in the Northern Lights Disco! *Zuiderdam* was challenging to run because it was way bigger, and the clientele was very challenging in the beginning because they came onboard and they were already upset because it was not like the other ships they had grown accustomed to. I believe the main reason I got promoted is because I was young enough, and brash enough to tackle that in a time when other Cruise Directors—and I don't mean to lump them into one basket because we had some wonderful CD's—but they were traditional and had been running in the HAL circle for years. That big brand new ship was challenging and they didn't have enough bodies that they could put on it, that could handle it. I was just young and dumb enough. I think I was promoted somewhat out of necessity, and somewhat out of curiosity. Let the kid on it and see if he has the energy and the brashness to make it work."

Jason interviewing Mike Love and Bruce Johnston of The Beach Boys on the Malt Shop Memories Cruise.

That sounds like quite an adjustment moving from largely behind the scenes to be the face of a cruise ship as Cruise Director. "I had wonderful mentors that taught me how to speak on stage, deal heads-up with guests good and bad, to produce and direct, and so on. It was an adjustment, but mainly because of the nature of HAL. I became a Cruise Director at 23—HAL's youngest ever at the time. HAL is not a young man's game; they have mature captains, mature hotel directors, and mature cruise directors. Plus, they have a mainly foreign staff—Dutch, British, not a lot of Americans; I was kind of a shot across the bow in that company."

I asked Jason to talk about serving as Cruise Director. What's life like day-to-day?

"The Cruise Director is the face and voice of the cruise ship. So they are often the person a guest will vent to, applaud, compliment, blame. I come from a background where you take that head on and let's see if we can't make things better if it is a negative sentiment being expressed by the guest; or pass it on to my co-crew members if it's praise. At the end of every cruise we got a card with a rating scale of 1-9 for the cruise staff collectively; the only person that got an individual rating was the Cruise Director. Everyone else was a general group rating: food, service, cabin steward. So you knew exactly where you stood; in the beginning I got beat up; I got a lot of plusses, lot of minuses, a lot of constructive comments, lot of aggressive comments."

"I was the highest ranked CD for HAL for the better part of my career, and certain perks and accolades came my way as a result. I was the inaugural CD for the launch of multiple ships; was chosen as the face of HAL for big launches, new programs, etc., and ultimately that led to *Dancing with the Stars*."

In 2012, HAL partnered with the hit ABC TV show *Dancing with the Stars* to offer its cruise passengers *Dancing with the Stars: at Sea*. After 10 years at HAL, eight as Cruise Director, Jason became Producer and Host of HAL's *Dancing with the Stars: at Sea*. Just as with the television show, the program was a runaway success and in 2013 won a Travel Weekly Magellan Award for Entertainment. *Dancing with the Stars: at Sea* was a major part of HAL entertainment and the pinnacle of Jason's career at HAL. I asked him to talk about how that came about.

"I learned to ballroom dance… you know as I was a very young cruise director, and it's one thing to be a brash, funny guy; but you also want to appear intelligent, refined, debonair as much as possible. As a young man I was trying to learn different things that would enable me to do that. Being able to walk into one of the bars and lounges, particularly the Crows Nest lounge at the top of each HAL ship, every single night it was all the ballroom dancers. They would waltz and they would jive, and cha cha; let me tell you, walking in as a 23 year old—I'm not a small guy, 6'3, 215 pounds, I'm a big kid—walking in wearing a tux and being able to ask a lady to waltz, or cha cha, or to teach someone to dance. I learned that was a great asset, a wonderful ability to have. I just kept learning, and honestly, I taught myself. Watched a ton of YouTube. I paid very close attention when I was dancing with really good dancers onboard. Am I an expert, am I classically trained? No. If I was going into a room and tried to teach a seasoned ballroom dancer, I'd get my butt handed to me. But, compared to the average person, I know a lot more. I can ballroom dance. No, I'm not world class but I know what I am doing. So I started teaching ballroom dancing and for my entire career as Cruise Director, it became one of my go-to's. Every class I taught would have 60-150 cruisers in it. So I would teach maybe five times a week; classes were complimentary. Come learn to cha cha, waltz, with the Cruise Director. So anyway I knew how to dance."

"So 2012, I had inaugurated ships, I had done a lot of their bigger events; I had done it all and I was planning to step away. I got a call from the HAL Director of Entertainment and he informed me that HAL had just signed a partnership with *Dancing With the Stars*. 'Will you help us launch it, help us create what this looks like onboard?' So we had a producer and director from *Dancing With the Stars* come out and they created the show. We would do two shows on one night of the cruise. In conjunction with that was a dance class, dance competition aspect to it, where we judged and hosted and used HAL's pros to dance with the guests, and I created all of that on the HAL side."

So this was a partnership with the TV show, not a *Dancing With the Stars*-themed HAL takeoff?

"No, this was a 100% partnership alongside *Dancing With the Stars*. We had the stars that you've seen on TV come out and sail with us: Carson Kressley, Joey Fatone, Sabrina Bryan, Florence Henderson. We had a bunch of people from the show, and then we had a bunch of pros as well: Derek Hough, Kym Johnson, Sharna Burgess, right down the line. We were an actual branded partnership. I ran the branded partnership; they brought their own producers and the show, and I was the liaison between the cruise ship and *Dancing With the Stars*. We did six cruises a year—with the pros and the celebrities—plus the rest of the HAL fleet ran a competition all year long. The partnership was a three year run, from 2012-2015. That was a wonderful experience, both for HAL and for me personally."

Jason retired from HAL and day-to-day cruising in 2015. "I actually planned to retire in 2012. The only reason I stayed on for an additional three years was because of *Dancing with the Stars: at Sea*. I had a phenomenal run at HAL and a wonderful time as Cruise Director. When I retired it had nothing to do with HAL. I want to grow and want to learn and I want to experience. Honestly, I wanted more. I had done hundreds of cruises at that point. I wasn't challenged anymore. I don't mean to say I had it mastered; it wasn't that at all. I very humbly say and any good Cruise Director will tell you—it doesn't matter how talented you are—you'll come up against a cruise or group of guests that will still kick your butt. So I don't mean to imply I had it mastered, but I wasn't growing at the rate I wanted to anymore. HAL had 14 ships at the time. You know just like McDonalds—if you go to McDonalds in any country, you still should be able to get your basic McDonalds meal. HAL doesn't care which ship you're on, you still should experience Holland American Lines as it is meant to be, anywhere in the world, on any date, on any cruise. By that I mean I was not able to exercise a ton of creativity. They were standardizing their brand somewhat, and because of that I felt stagnated a little bit. I wanted to create. I wanted to do more."

I told Jason he sound like he has a bit of an entrepreneurial bent.

"Yeah. My dad has been very successful and he always said, 'There's two ways to make money in this world: You either own it or you know how to sell it.' That's kind of my mindset. Own the business yourself or you are on some kind of commission and know how to sell it, and that makes you incredibly valuable to the business. And that always motivated me. So when I retired from cruising, I had already started my own business."

Jason had started his own production/consulting business, JBV Innovations, and was contacted that same year by StarVista LIVE as they were looking for a new producer/host. So the transition from HAL to be a theme cruise Producer/Host was seamless and immediate. "When I walked off the HAL ship after the final *Dancing with the Stars: at Sea* championship cruise, my wife and I flew from Fort Lauderdale to Key West and walked straight on to another ship to host the *Country Music Cruise*. So I literally walked from one career to the next!" Jason has worked with StarVista LIVE as a client ever since. In addition, he consults for cruise lines and cruise charter companies on several levels ranging from "how to be a cruise director" to "how to turn an idea into a charter (theme) cruise."

I said, "So, you worked with StarVista LIVE as a host and producer; what exactly does a host and producer do?"

"For StarVista LIVE, I work with their senior vice presidents, both executive producers for the charter cruises. They'll come up with a concept because they have longstanding relationships and experience in the music business. They'll come to us with an idea—for instance, the *Flower Power Cruise*—we want to do a Woodstock 60s themed cruise; let's talk about it. They'll propose a line-up of the kind of stars that fits that kind of cruise. And then I work with my counterpart at StarVista LIVE and together we turn that concept into a cruise: lay out the poolside show, the big theme night, early performance/late performance. Create an ebb and flow; fill around the major stars with your non-headliners, tribute bands; and then finally your Q&A's, trivia, games, smaller events. So that's primarily what the producer aspect is. Once we've created it, built it, scheduled it out, and reworked it a dozen times, and finally onboard, I assume a number of different roles on the cruise. I play a combination of Hotel Director/Cruise Director, so I liaise with the cruise line's hotel staff. Then at showtime and daily events, I am the Host."

Jason maintains a similar role for each of the various StarVista LIVE theme cruises. What varies from cruise-to-cruise is that for each cruise, as host Jason is partnered with a "celebrity" host specific to the theme of each cruise. The celebrity host is someone who is known and knowledgeable within the industry; not necessarily a musician, could be an actor, someone who represents that era or theme. For instance, for the *Soul Train Cruise*, the celebrity co-host is Tony Cornelius, son of the late Don Cornelius, creator and host of the nationally syndicated long-running dance and music television show *Soul Train*.

Jason interviewing the Jacksons: Marlon, Tito, Jackie (middle) and Tony Cornelius (left) on Soul Train Cruise.

"I'm a 40-year old kid! I say that to underscore a point. When I am standing there as the host on the *Malt Shop Memories* cruise, which celebrates the music of the fifties and sixties, the audience looks at me and they know I wasn't there. They know for a fact that I didn't grow up on Frankie Avalon, Frankie Valli, Chubby Checker, the way they did. So we like to have a celebrity host as well. I am the tie that binds, meaning I host maybe 80% of the events—many of the big interviews, etc., but we also like to have a cohost to lend authenticity; to have a face and a voice who was there, so to speak; can infuse knowledge and experience that I just don't have: Jerry Blavat ("The Geator with the Heater") for *Malt Shop Memories;* Micky Dolenz of the Monkees and Grammy Award-winning record producer Peter Asher on *Flower Power* cruise, Deney Terrio of *Dance Fever* on the *Ultimate Disco Cruise,* and so on."

Jason interviewing Cheech & Chong on Flower Power Cruise.

In the course of interviewing fascinating cruisers in the writing of *The Joy of Cruising* and *Cruising Interrupted,* I have learned of and chronicled several cruising superlatives: Mark and Leanne Weston of Australia with 21 cruises in 2018; Joe Church, the marathon runner who has run over 1300 miles—on cruise ships! And others. Well, add Jason to the list of fascinating cruiser with prodigious accomplishments on the ocean. Jason has sailed on over 500 cruises! Among those are a world cruise, a dozen inaugural cruises, and 50 major ship live music charters. Cruising has allowed Jason to visit all seven continents and well over 100 countries. I asked Jason, "What haven't you done yet? Where else would you like to visit?"

"I'm a skier, snowboarder; there's not a lot of that in the cruising world. I'd love to snowboard the Alps. I'd love to get in the Matterhorn area. I'd love to get into Austria, some of the little Bavarian-style towns you get a little ski in, ski out villa and spend some time just hitting some mountains that not everyone gets to hit. That's A1 for me; A2, my wife hasn't been as fortunate as me with respect to travel—I have been very fortunate—way more than most. So anywhere she wants to go. She has the travel bug way more than me. I've been so many places. I'd love to experience with her places that she wants to see. First two on her bucket list are Hawaii and Thailand. Happy wife, happy life."

As with all passionate cruisers, Jason and StarVista LIVE are in a state of uncertain anticipation as to when cruising will start up again. The timing of the return to cruising for charters lags behind the start-up of conventional cruising—and that restart continues to be a moving target given the lingering pandemic and uneven recovery in different parts of the world. Consequently, the cruising lockdown has been very challenging.

"In a word, it has been devastating. You know earlier I referred to myself as Cruise Director to the Private Sector. Charters are a very big business on the private side of cruising; that is, cruises open to the public but private in that for full-ship charters, that cruise is essentially a private party of people. On the *Country Music Cruise* no one is on that ship unless that have chosen to partake in the *Country Music Cruise*. And for the people who put it on, it's a lot of people taking a very big shot once a year—and we don't know when we will be able to take that shot. Each one week charter is hyper-focused; it's not as if we have 52 cruises a year like with traditional cruise lines. *Soul Train* has one cruise a year; *Malt Shop Memories* has one cruise a year. Obviously, every cruise from early 2020 was postponed, and that's a lot of planning that goes down the drain; the early 2021 charters have been deferred to late 2021 and some even to early 2022. I'm hosting some virtual interviews and events, and staying engaged with the executive producers who lead StarVista LIVE, and with some of the performers, but by and large the pandemic has definitely put a giant stop sign on the industry. Until we know how the cruise lines are going to respond, charter companies and theme cruising is sort of on the back burner."

I asked Jason what he foresees in terms of changes to cruising.

"It's all speculative at the moment of course; so it's hard. Having worked on cruises for as long as I have: cruise lines are incredibly resilient; they are heavily regulated; and, they don't have a lot of room for error. They are under a microscope. When gastrointestinal illness, norovirus became a thing, people called it the cruise ship virus. A complete misnomer—it comes from hospitals, nursing homes, day cares, but that was labeled as the cruise ship disease. Reason I bring that up is because cruise ships have done a masterful job considering all the illnesses that are out there and considering how fast they can spread on board—recirculated air, close proximity, buffets. The level of care that's taken on board is pretty epic. I am completely confident that once cruising begins again things are going to be safe. I think the biggest change you're going to see is going to be the terminal; it's going to be before you even see the ship, because really that's where the prevention starts. I think cruise lines are going to ramp up how they allow, and who they allow onboard. As far as the onboard experience: I think we will see a slow roll; cruises lines are going to come out slowly. Cruise lines will likely release a couple of ships at a time; maybe for the big players they'll have perhaps five ships or so, at a reduced capacity over the first 12 months. And that's going to be very challenging for the cruise lines. They're like the airlines; you don't make money on the first 85% of the seats or cabins sold; you make money on the last 15% or so. You are going to see a strong push from brands to re-establish themselves with their clientele, create trust. I don't think buffets are gone. I don't think a lot of traditional cruising activities are gone. Where you served yourself—you're now going to be served. Where you got to put your hands in the bowl of peanuts, you'll now get cups of peanuts."

Jason's insights on cruising post-pandemic are good (and I am especially reassured about buffets continuing to have a place on cruises—never met a buffet where I didn't try to get my money's worth!) I wondered if there were any particular considerations for charter cruises.

"In the short-run chartering will be on the back-burner as long as there is not the full complement of a cruise line's fleet operating. The catch for charter cruises is that most of them, if they are music-themed, need the main theater to hold 50% of the passengers. So, charters can't be done on just any ship. There is an ideal size of ship where that 50% passenger capacity holds up—generally about 2000-2500 passenger ships. For bigger, or smaller cruise ships the required venue sizes don't match up. So with a reduced fleet operating at first it will be hard for charters to get in there. All this is short-term; in the long-run theme cruise passengers will come back. Chartering will come back. As long as the artists are there, then the guests will come. If Smokey is there, if The Beach Boys are there, then the guests will show up."

I recall during the writing of *The Joy of Cruising*, I asked one of the features—who was exclusive to one cruise line, what was his favorite cruise. He snapped facetiously (I think), "that's like asking me which one of my kids is my favorite." Mindful of that, I said to Jason, "Let me close by asking—and you may not want to respond—of the hundreds of music stars you have introduced and interviewed on StarVista LIVE cruises, who is the most memorable?"

"When Paul Anka gets on stage, talk about a Las Vegas quality epic production, Paul Anka is probably one of the single greatest performers that we have had of any age on any cruise ever. Phenomenal show; he was on our *Malt Shop Cruise* and he blew me away. Most awe-inspiring for me, probably was Chubby Checker. You know, the man is in his 80's; still gets up and does two full 90 minute shows in a night—active, moving, singing, dancing the entire time—kills them. Kenny Rogers—so endearing, so charming, just unbelievably good rapport with an audience. Out of all the artists I've seen, if I could be an artist, I would be Eddie Levert of The O'Jays. I want to grow up to be Eddie Levert. He is just the smoothest, coolest…I love him. Then there's the comedians. Watching real pros work a stage, work a crowd—that's my craft— Jeff Foxworthy, Larry the Cable Guy, Bill Bellamy, that's a real inspiration."

Why go on a music charter cruise?

"There's nothing like seeing the person 'that sang the song, sing the song!' You watch Smokey do all the Miracles hits and then his solo stuff. You watch the Beach Boys…that's the Beach Boys! Why take a charter? You can't do this anywhere else in the world."

Quirky Cruise

QuirkyCruise was cofounded in 2015 by Heidi Marie Sarna and Theodore W. Scull. The two friends met in the '90s when both were working in New York City—Heidi was an editor for a travel and cruise magazine and Ted was a freelance writer, travel guide author, and lecturer on cruise ships. Among several things they share in common—long-time travel writers, extensive and diverse travel background, deep appreciation and knowledge of history—Heidi and Ted have a mutual affection for small-ship cruising. Heidi said, "We have each done many small-ship cruises all over the world and so we created *QuirkyCruise* so there would be a place for quality small-ship articles to live and be shared with the world."

The business partners work together from a great distance apart year-around, so operating *QuirkyCruise* during this pandemic feels relatively normal—if only there were cruises to write about! Heidi has lived in Singapore since 2006 with her husband Arun and their twin sons. The family plans to move back to the United States in the next few years when the boys have started college. Ted lives in Manhattan with his wife, Suellyn.

QuirkyCruise is an ideal outlet for the two itinerant adventurers. It is the culmination of essentially lifetimes of living and traveling abroad, exploration, learning, and cultural discovery for both Heidi and Ted.

Heidi in Hanoi on a small-ship Windstar Cruise.

Ted on the luxurious Hebridean Princess, a 50-passenger five star Scottish cruise ship.

Heidi was born and raised in Pennsylvania near Hershey, until leaving for college at Drew University in Madison, New Jersey, where she studied political science and English, and then graduate school at New York University for an M.A. in English and American literature. Besides writing about and experiencing travel, Heidi is a history buff, and enjoys bicycling around Singapore and wherever she is traveling. "Cycling is the best way to really see a place," Heidi says. She's about to have a book published called *Secret Singapore* about hidden and forgotten things and places in Singapore.

Heidi has traveled to 80 countries across six continents—Antarctica remains a bucket list aspiration. For most of the 14 years Heidi has lived in Singapore, she has traveled at least once a year with her husband to India where he is from. Heidi started her travel career with one of her first "dates" with Arun: a six-month trip around the world, hitting 20 countries on six continents in 1992. "At the time we had been dating for just over a year, but were ready to take the travel plunge together. Arun took a six-month leave of absence from work, and I had just finished grad school, so it was a good time for me to go. We did it on the fly and on the cheap. That made it all the more adventurous. From spending several memorable days cruising down the Amazon aboard a rickety fishing boat (a precursor to quirky cruises to come!) to taking a 24-hour bus ride from Buenos Aires, Argentina all the way across the High Andes to Chile and a train ride across New Zealand's North Island. Traveling the slow way, by water or rail (as opposed to only flying), really lets you soak up your surroundings."

I interjected, "That was a good way to find out if you and Arun were compatible."

"Totally; by the end of six months you're sort of sick of each other," Heidi laughed. "This was before cell phones and iPads so you couldn't take a break and stare at your screen—you had to interact... for six months nearly non-stop! We purposely didn't see each other for a few weeks afterwards to reboot! But yes, our bond was cemented during that trip and we married a few years later. The amazing trip also gave me an excellent background to pursue travel writing. As I had been to so many places during the six months, including Asia and South America for the first time, my world view had grown exponentially. When I got back from this whirlwind adventure, I landed my first publishing job at a small cruise magazine in New York City. The rest is history as they say."

Ted was born and grew up in suburban Philadelphia, and has lived in New York City since the '60s. He studied history at Trinity College in Hartford, Connecticut, and earned a master's degrees in history at University of London, and in counseling at Bank Street College in Manhattan. After returning to the States from earning his degree at University of London, Ted got a job as a teacher at an independent elementary and middle school in New York City and has lived there ever since. Ted has traveled to all seven continents, approximately 180 countries, cruised along three dozen rivers, and visited all 50 of the United States. At 18, Ted drove round-trip from Philadelphia to Anchorage, Alaska; at 21 he worked for an Anglican missionary doctor in what is now Tanzania in East Africa; and, a couple of years later Ted spent six weeks in the Soviet Union.

After teaching roles at a couple of schools Ted decided to become a travel writer. "I didn't want to be a teacher for the rest of my life, although I loved it. I had done all this traveling so I thought that maybe I could become a travel writer. I had so much experience traveling by that time—not only in the United States but abroad—that I felt I had a feel for other parts of the world. Eventually I started to get stuff published, at first mainly in newspapers."

Ted had attained that travel experience first through family travel. "Mother wanted her two sons to see some of the world. We started off visiting various parts of the United States. My mother and father visited Europe without us once and when they came back, they told us that as soon as we were old enough they wanted to take us to Europe—which they did. So it was in me from an early age. I loved traveling by road; I loved the whole process of getting to where we were going; I was fascinated by the huge variety of trains and about the different ways roads were designed and built; I poured over maps."

Ted sold his first story in 1980, to the *Christian Science Monitor*. He was officially a travel writer. During the course of his personal travels abroad and around the country, he would pen related human interest stories that would capture the attention of editors. "One time after I visited my brother living in San Francisco, I decided to go on the Alaska Marine Highway which ran from Seattle up to the Inside Passage of Alaska and British Columbia, Canada. It was a vehicle and passenger service that served all these little towns along the way. I made a seven-day round-trip on this ferry, and talked to all these people who lived in Alaska and had spent time in the Lower 48, and they were going back home. Plus people who were going up to Alaska to look for a job. And I landed a wonderful story. I sold that article to 13 different newspapers all over the country. It was my biggest hit. The *Washington Post* had this veteran old-time travel editor. He said, 'this is too long for me, but it is such a good story. I'm going to run it over two weeks and I have never done that before'"

Ted's articles began to get published often, supplemented by frequent appearances as a lecturer, mostly on travel-related subjects. Ted also wrote a dozen books, about his travels by ship and one called *100 Best Cruise Vacations*. One of the books he proposed to his publisher would be a forerunner to the idea behind *QuirkyCruise*. "I wanted to do a cruising book just on small ships. There was a burgeoning number of companies starting to create these small ships from 150 on down to 75 passengers or so. However, no contract was forthcoming as the publisher didn't foresee a market for a book on small ships."

When he is not traveling or engaged with *QuirkyCruise*, Ted enjoys studying and lecturing about New York, leading walks and hikes, learning more about railroads and ship history, collecting ship posters, and reading.

Add to those well-rounded backgrounds an amazingly diverse and extensive cruising history for both Heidi and Ted. Heidi has cruised 110 times and Ted 180. They each have sailed all over the world, with an emphasis on Europe and Asia, particularly in the latter half of their cruising careers given their fondness for small ships. Heidi said, "Earlier on, I did a lot of cruising to the Caribbean and Alaska, but now, generally worldwide. I like to explore as much as possible."

I asked both to take me back to their beginning in cruising. Heidi's first cruise was in 1993, on the 959-passenger *Cunard Princess*, from Málaga, Spain. "This was my first ever travel writing assignment, for the magazine job I landed after I returned from my trip around the world. The magazine, now defunct, was a trade magazine called *Cruise & Vacation Views*. Although I had never been on a cruise, I was hired as an editor. Lucky me!"

I had to interrupt Heidi: "You landed a job writing for a cruise magazine and you had never been on a cruise?" She responded, "Right, exactly. I guess it was more important to the publisher that I was well-traveled and had writing experience from an internship I had done with the United Nations Association. It didn't matter to him that I hadn't been on a cruise—we'd figure it out. In fact, I may never had taken a cruise if I hadn't gotten this job! A couple months in, the publisher sent me to Miami to tour some cruise ships to start learning the ropes—that was fun. This was my first experience aboard several Carnival and Royal Caribbean ships; I certainly couldn't complain about this "business trip!" Then about six months after getting the job, my publisher called me into his office: 'So, you want to go to the Mediterranean?' I'm like, excuse me...."

I laughed—and cried a little at the same time—as Heidi shared that story. Laughing about her exclamation of surprise, 'excuse me,' but also being reminded of my own Mediterranean cruise scheduled for this November, but in jeopardy due to the pandemic. Wow, first cruise is a Mediterranean cruise, on a press trip as a VIP! What was her impression of cruising?

"We flew to Málaga, and called on Sicily, Taormina and Naples, Italy. An amazing itinerary and honestly, being part of a small press group made it all the more exciting for a 20-something young writer. It was incredible that cruising was now part of my job. Free cruises were my "business trips!" Though a newbie, I took to being on the water and enjoyed the intimacy and sense of community that develops during a cruise. I loved the sound of the waves shushing against the hull, the foamy wake behind us, and the breeze in my hair on deck. I appreciated that the Cunard *Princess* was an older ship, from the 1970s, with classic features like beautiful tiered aft decks—best place for sail-away cocktail parties—and a pointy bow."

Heidi left the cruise magazine after three years and has enjoyed an exciting and satisfying freelance writing career ever since, having penned articles for magazines and websites from *Conde Nast Traveler* to *CNN.com, Frommers. com, CNBC.com* and many others.

Heidi on the 112-passenger SeaDream Yacht Club SeaDream II
on a cruise from Singapore to Bali

Ted's introduction to cruising was under very different circumstances. It likewise was an older ship—much older. Ted's first cruise was a July 1958 transatlantic crossing on the *SS Liberté* owned by the French Line, Compagnie Générale Transatlantique. "My mother took my brother and me to Europe by ship. I was 17 and my brother was 14. Back then it was called a transatlantic crossing as opposed to a cruise, and it was a common way to get to Europe. In those days half the people who went to Europe went by ship, and mother wanted me to have the experience because she had it."

I asked Ted what his impression of his first cruise was. He said, "I didn't want to go at first because I had a part-time job at the Nantucket Cottage Hospital. The liner was the *Liberté*. What do I remember about it? The ship wasn't completely air conditioned because it was built in 1925. It had been German but after the war the Germans lost all their ships and the French took this one over. They modernized it, but you know air conditioning wasn't a thing in Europe yet. The dining rooms were air conditioned, but the rest of the ship was not. We sailed in July from New York and it was like 95 degrees outside and we had an inside cabin and it was 95 in there too." Ted told me that once they got out into the Atlantic air flowed through the ship and the temperature was fine. So, I wondered, besides the climate issue at the beginning of the voyage, what did Ted think about cruising. He told me, "Early on, I liked ships because they took me someplace. As a more experienced cruiser, I particularly like sailing to Europe, because you meet a lot of people from the countries you are going to visit. A cruise to the Caribbean is comprised of mainly Americans. I just have not been particularly interested in that. On a voyage to Europe I like the fact that you meet a lot of people you have never met before—different kinds of people that you don't have an easy opportunity to do so otherwise." Of course, Ted went on to do cruises all over the world—deep sea, coastal, river, lake, expedition. Ted has done dozens of "quirky cruises," but he proudly cites among his greatest cruise memories transatlantic travel on each of the major national flag ships: French Line, Italian Line, Cunard Line, Swedish American Line, North German Lloyd, Hamburg Atlantic Line.

QuirkyCruise was founded in 2015. Ted said, "After my publisher declined to move forward on the proposal for a book on small ship cruising, it lay fallow for a couple years. One day Heidi called me up; I'd known her maybe 20 years. She said she had this great idea, and of course the market for small ships had continued to grow. And she explained the concept of what would become *QuirkyCruise* to me and asked if I would be interested. And I responded, let me think about this for about five seconds!"

And so *QuirkyCruise* was established as a worldwide guide to small passenger ships—river, expedition, coastal, sailing and oceangoing boats and ships of many styles—carrying less than 300 passengers. Its audience is international, with the biggest portion being from North America, followed by United Kingdom, Australia, Germany, Singapore, India and other countries. In addition to the thousands who go directly to *QuirkyCruise.com* each month, *QuirkyCruise* has more than 10,000 subscribers to its newsletter, as well as over 10,000 social media followers. *QuirkyCruise* covers 93 cruise lines, and counting, that meet its small-ship criteria. "We look at *QuirkyCruise.com* as an online guidebook. Ted and I used to do guidebook work for Frommers, for instance. In fact, I was the author of the *Frommer's Cruises & Ports of Call* guide for years and contributed to several other guidebooks as well. In addition to *QuirkyCruise.com* offering profiles of more than 90 small-ship cruise lines, we feature news stories and have a reader review section for small-ship cruisers to share their trips with us." Heidi adds, "We are continuously building on our pool of high quality long-form first-person articles about small-ship cruising by top writers, and it's becoming a very deep pool indeed." (A couple of whom are featured in *Cruising Interrupted*, like John Roberts, *In The Loop Travel*, and Judi Cohen, *Traveling Judi*.)

I asked about the name *QuirkyCruise*—it certainly rolls off the tongue. Heidi told me that the best way to think about it is that quirky means unusual, and many of the cruises they cover meet that criterion, especially relative to more traditional cruises. Unusual works for me; my conception of cruising is principally mainstream big ships. It was absolutely fascinating to listen to Heidi and Ted talk about voyages on 1916-built steamboats and six-passenger barges.

I asked Heidi to talk about the small ship market—the cruise lines, types of vessels, and destinations that are covered by *QuirkyCruise*. "Well there are the river lines—I'm sure you have heard of some of those. The ones in Europe are like mini (long and skinny!) cruise ships, such as Uniworld and AmaWaterways, and offer similar, albeit scaled down versions of what big cruise ships offer, such as multiple dining options and lovely lounges and bars. They sail on well-known rivers like the Rhine, Danube and Garonne, to ports rich in history and beauty. Then there's quirkier stuff we truly relish; for instance, there's a company called Pandaw, with a fleet of vessels that each carry just 20 to 60 passengers. They were designed and built to look like traditional, old steamboats that the British used in Asia to transport passengers, spices, and sugarcane a century and more ago. Pandaw sails the rivers of Southeast Asia, from the Irrawaddy River in Myanmar to the Red River in Vietnam and the Mekong in Laos, Vietnam, Cambodia and China. We also cover canal barges in France and Sweden, and expedition vessels that explore the Arctic region, the Galapagos island, and Antarctica. Our reach also includes yachts in the Greek Isles and off the coast of Croatia, and very small wonderfully quirky vessels that cruise in Scotland's breathtaking western isles. There's not enough time for me to mention everything *QuirkyCruise* covers."

I asked Heidi and Ted to explain how *QuirkyCruise* works. "Do you send a writer to chronical the various cruises?"

"For *Quirky,* Ted and I travel and write as much as we can, and we also work with a stable of freelance travel writers, many of whom we have met and traveled with over the years. We ask them to go on a certain small-ship cruise or they tell us what they have planned coming up, and we assign them stories. We pay writers for their articles, though it's not a lot. Our writers seem to appreciate supporting a start-up like us and they like what *QuirkyCruise* is all about—high-quality travel articles about small-ship cruising. I mean we have a freelance writer who was with *USA Today*; once I asked him 'why do you write for *QuirkyCruise* when you are not getting paid very much?' He told me he appreciated being able to write about off-beat places, places he really wanted to go even if they weren't mainstream—in his case to the Ukraine on a river cruise, which he wrote about for us. It was a great trip and a great article for us. Furthermore, freelancers love that they can write in first person, and that they can write a longer article. There are not many outlets for first-person writing anymore, where a writer can tell a story, and not just regurgitate bullet points and sound bites. So, for writers, *QuirkyCruise* is a creative outlet, which is nice."

Heidi and Ted are very proud that *QuirkyCruise* was selected as a winner of the 2018-2019 Society of American Travel Writers Foundation (SATW) Lowell Thomas Travel Journalism Competition, in the category of Travel Journalism Sites. *QuirkyCruise.com* was accorded honorable mention in a category won by *NationalGeographic.com*. The SATW competition judges said the following: "*QuirkyCruise.com* has distinguished itself as a destination for people interested in alternatives to the corporate cruise experience. The site offers a deep dive into more than 80 cruise experiences on rivers and lakes, as well as the high seas. Warm and friendly writing invites readers into the experience."

Ted on an expedition cruise around Svalbard in search of polar bears.

With the unique and diverse nature of the small ship cruising market they cover, their respective lists of their most memorable cruises is comprised largely of, well, "quirky cruises." How about Heidi's Gota Canal cruise in Sweden aboard an historic 19th-century canal boat, *M/S Juno*? Launched in 1874, Juno is the world's oldest passenger vessel offering overnight accommodation, offering canal cruises through the lovely pastoral landscape of Sweden. High on Heidi's list of memorable cruises are several Star Clippers cruises: French Polynesia, the Greek Islands, and the islands off western Thailand, in the Andaman Sea. Star Clippers is a Swedish-owned cruise line comprised of a trio of super atmospheric full-rigged tall ships meant to re-create the classic sailing clipper ships of the 1800s. Or perhaps one of Heidi's last cruises before the pandemic makes her top 10—a Kerala India backwaters cruise in October 2019 on the 18-passenger *Vaikundam*, (of Adventure Resorts & Cruises). In true *QuirkyCruise* fashion Heidi called that cruise "very quirky, loved it!"

Heidi at Gota Canal, Sweden.

Ted quirkiest cruise might be a cruise around Lake Victoria—one of the African Great Lakes and Africa's largest lake—on a 1916-built coal-fired colonial steamer. He also cited the Swan Hellenic educational/cultural cruises. Swan Hellenic is a British cruise line specializing in high-end small ship tours, expedition tours of historical interest featuring renowned lecturers. Ted has done several Swan Hellenic cruises. Ted said, "One trip I went on was from Greece to Turkey to Syria to Egypt to Lebanon. The first morning we went down to breakfast and we sat at a table for four. Moments later another couple joined us. They were much older, and they introduced themselves. And it was the former Archbishop of Canterbury, the head of the Anglican Church in England. He was a medieval scholar, and he gave this extraordinary lecture from the setting of stadium ruins. He had the ship passengers sit at the top—maybe 20 levels up, and he would stand at the bottom and show how the acoustics worked in the ancient world. He would talk in a normal voice and we would hear everything he was saying. It was remarkable." Another memorable small ship cruise for Ted was the Islands of Japan cruise featuring Intrav's *Clipper Odyssey* to small ports, receiving a formal welcome at each one, with tours to wonderfully varied gardens. Or, aboard Orion Cruses *Orion* sailing along the remote coast of the Northern Territory and Western Australia where he never saw another human being apart from his shipmates for 10 days. "We were alone amongst the most amazing landscapes inhabited by some of the world's weirdest creatures," Ted told me.

Ted in bow netting on Star Clipper.

I am always particularly interested in the bucket list of someone who has seemingly done it all in terms of destinations, as well as the breadth of ships Heidi and Ted have cruised on and written about. Nonetheless, they both have ambitious bucket lists.

Heidi stresses, "As far as cruising is concerned, all small ships for me." Besides attaining that seventh continent, Antarctica, Heidi looks forward to future quirky cruises to the Arctic, Scottish Isles, back to the Amazon—she last went in 1992—the Kimberley region in Western Australia, the Fiji area of the South Pacific, and a Mississippi River cruise. "Any land-based dream trips?" I asked Heidi. "Some cool train rides across Canada, and do some more of them in India; the national parks and states in the US I haven't seen yet, especially in the mid-West; we would like to hike in the Alps; I want to explore Japan on a walking trek ideally; and, of course, do more touring by bicycle, for example, in Laos, Vietnam, the US, countries in Europe."

Ted wants to revisit the Upper Amazon and its tributaries, return to the Scottish Isles, explore the Senegal River in West Africa, and to sail across the South Atlantic with calls at South Georgia and the South Sandwich Islands, and truly remote Tristan da Cunha, in the southern Atlantic Ocean. In addition, Ted aspires to add to his exotic train travel: London to Shanghai by train (not by fancy cruise trains), and from England across Europe, Russia, Mongolia, and China.

I wondered how the pandemic and cruise lockdown particularly impacted the small ship cruising market. "These are strange times and companies are not going to make it, in both the small end and the big end. With respect specifically to small-ship cruising, you know it's been said that they can rebound faster because they are small and there are fewer cabins to fill; but there are many variables that go into the financial well-being of a company." Heidi adds, " I think the potential for private charters is a bright spot for small-ship lines, and I definitely think private travel will be all the more appealing in the COVID-19 era—with small groups of friends and family, say 10 or 20 people, going in on a yacht charter. Luxury barges in France carrying just 6 to 12 passengers are also great for private charters and so are the small coastal cruisers off western Scotland; I know I would feel safer traveling with a small group of friends and family versus strangers, and I think other people feel that way. Let's see, we're living in extraordinary times; we're doing our part to continue supporting small-ship lines."

What about *QuirkyCruise*? How has the pandemic impacted *QuirkyCruise* and are you doing anything differently other than of course not being able to cruise? "It affects us from an advertising standpoint, as companies have had to dial down their marketing budgets, understandably. But this is temporary. In the meantime, we are focusing on news and developments with small-ship cruising. Writer Anne Kalosh is a long-time contributor to *QuirkyCruise,* covering news for us. She writes a thorough and very useful news update for us every week or two—reporting on which small ship lines are starting back up or further cancellations. I do have a backlog fortunately—articles writers have filed in the last six-12 months. Plus we love interviewing and writing about figures in the small-ship sphere, like Steve Wellmeier and Captain George Coughlin. We also do a lot of round-ups; in addition to the in-depth articles from travel writers, we do things like 'An Overview of Small-Ship Scottish Cruising.' Ted just did one recently contrasting The Arctic versus Antarctica. You know, do you see polar bears at the North Pole or at the South Pole?" I actually read that article before Heidi mentioned it. (And it underscored for me the fact that I stopped attending high school geography class way too soon!)

What does the future hold for *QuirkyCruise*?

"Our goal is to keeping building on our reservoir of high-quality articles and to improve our site design and functionality — in fact, by year-end 2020, we will launch a redesigned *QuirkyCruise.com*, with a fresh new look and improved navigation. We're also working on curating exclusive special offers for our readers, especially for full-boat charters. We also enjoy engaging with our audience by running "free cruise" contests, which we'll offer more of in 2021, and we continue to build our Reader Reviews—think *Trip Advisor* for small ship cruising. At the end of the day, we want to inspire and entertain our audience with high-quality travel articles and so we always endeavor to grow our fan base to become the #1 source for small-ship cruisers and travel lovers!"

Section Four:
CRUISERS LIKE YOU
AND ME...SORT OF

The Joy of Cruising featured several public personalities who are passionate about cruising and act on that passion in creative and fascinating ways. These individuals could be readily searched online: a Grammy award winner, Poker Hall of Famer, winner of the TV series Last Comic Standing, a cruise ship Godmother. *The Joy of Cruising* also introduced a number of "ordinary" cruisers doing extraordinary things, and featured them in a separate section; I thought the readers of *Cruising Interrupted* would find a similar section interesting as well. While it was a lot of fun sharing the stories of people that many have heard of, many of us cruisers would appreciate reading about passionate cruisers who are just like us...sort of.

Ask Chef Dennis

Dennis Littley, known as *Ask Chef Dennis* to his prodigious fan base—830,000 followers on Facebook, 76,000 on Twitter and 65,000 on his Instagram accounts *Ask Chef Dennis / Chef Dennis* Travels—is a Food and Travel Blogger. Chef Dennis resides in Kissimmee, Florida with his wife, production assistant, editor, and travel companion, Lisa. Although among the leading food bloggers in the world, Food and Travel Blogger hardly seems a sufficient title for the multifaceted Chef Dennis, so add to that: Retired Professional Chef and Culinary Instructor; Live Stream Show Host and Producer; Social Media Consultant; Brand Ambassador; Keynote Speaker; and oh yes, World Traveler.

Chef Dennis has long been involved in the culinary arts. He started traveling much later, and only experienced his first cruise in 2017. It was just seven years ago, shortly after moving to Florida from New Jersey that Dennis began traveling professionally—that is, in the public persona of *Ask Chef Dennis*. Initially, Chef Dennis travelled as a food blogger throughout Florida, which led to travel opportunities around the US and in Europe as a food blogger/travel blogger.

Ask Chef Dennis

Chef Dennis got his start as a blogger as an offshoot of his culinary career. In 2005 Chef Dennis started working as the Chef/Director of Dining Services for a suburban Philadelphia school district.

"I found my way into blogging via this culinary class I was teaching at Mount Saint Joseph's Academy in Flourtown, Pennsylvania, an all-girls, Catholic high school. As food service director—it was the only school I ever worked at—I didn't know what to feed them, coming from being an executive chef. So I was feeding them like I did adults. Things worked out really well— they loved me. It was like a TV movie; they painted murals of me on the wall. I was loved and hated at the same time: they were really eating well, but they were putting on weight because they were eating so well! I started a blog as a resource for my culinary students so they would have somewhere to go to for recipes, and to interact with each other. They could leave questions, and I could answer them. It turns out the culinary students didn't read it much, but I started getting readers from around the world, and then I officially became a blogger!"

How did that develop, the readership beyond the culinary class, I asked.

"First some of the other students and teachers at the school started to read it. As it got more popular, I joined an organization called Food Buzz, and I started to get an international presence, bloggers and readers all over the world because of this organization. That revitalized my interest in food because I started to see food from all over the world, different types of food. It gave me ideas, got the creative juices flowing again."

I asked Chef Dennis how an executive chef ended up working at a school.

"When I came to The Mount, as it was called, to interview, I didn't want to go there. The kitchen was old and dirty; it just wasn't...the kitchen was obviously the last area they spent any money—that just wasn't where their priorities were. I said no, this not what I thought it would be. Then the principal said, 'well you only work 161 days of the year.' I said, 'when would you like me to start?'"

She said the right thing, I laughed.

"Yea, she had lost me up to that point. Then when she mentioned 161 days, I said to myself, 'Oh, I could do that.' It was a lot less money than I was making; I had been working in corporate dining services, and was a chef in a fine restaurant. But my wife was making a pretty good living as a teacher, and this would give us a better quality of life. I would have my summers off; snow days off; all the catholic school holidays; this would put me on the same schedule as Lisa. In the school system we even got a day off after the Phillies won the World Series!"

After working in the school system from 2005-2013, the physical challenges of being a chef caught up to Chef Dennis. He had already dealt with carpal tunnel surgeries on both hands prior to joining Mount Saint Joseph's Academy.

"I was a chef in a restaurant, and my hands started to go. I had carpal tunnel on both hands so bad the pain would radiate up through my arms, and into my neck, causing severe discomfort. I eventually had surgeries on both hands. I really shouldn't have cooked anymore at that point; my hands were shot." Subsequently, Chef Dennis developed rotator cuff and back problems, and a recurrence of the hand problems because he persevered in the kitchen. Chef Dennis loved what he was doing and he had a strong connection with his students. "I stayed an extra year because students who had started cooking with me as freshmen were entering their senior year and I wanted to see them graduate." He would have continued to work but was informed in no uncertain terms: "Do you want to be a cripple? You're done."

Chef Dennis and his wife retired to Florida. Lisa retired from teaching, and Chef Dennis couldn't work anymore. So, going to Florida, "Everything turned wonderful," Chef Dennis said. It definitely wasn't wonderful up to that point. Prior to leaving the Philadelphia area, Chef Dennis struggled emotionally when he learned he needed to stop working. He endured a bit of rough time after having to give up his culinary career. "My career, my livelihood, the thing that defined me…" Dennis sought some professional help in dealing with the transition from what he loved to an as yet undefined future.

Then, a progression of positive events happened, starting with an omen: Dennis and Lisa selling their Philadelphia home on the first day it was listed, to the first person who looked at it. They were soon driving to Florida.

"We packed up the dog and whatever we could load into the car and headed to Florida…and everything was perfect. I started blogging more. I had been blogging quite a bit up north, but just didn't have the time to put into it. I had started doing things for Google. For Google+, I was an early adopter and a power user in Philadelphia, and they rewarded me by putting me on a follow list with Emeril Lagasse, Martha Stewart, Anthony Bourdain, Rachael Ray; so here were all these huge chefs, and me!"

What does a food blogger write about when you are no longer cooking, I asked. "Oh, I would still create and cook at home; I just couldn't cook for 600 people a day. I was still pursuing my passion. I had lost a little bit of the edge and got depressed after I stopped working. Fortunately, about that same time my relationship with Google flourished. I was livestreaming before livestreaming became popular. I was using Google Hangouts—which were the best thing going, the hardest thing to work, but they were amazing. I would run hangouts and I would have a couple thousand live viewers. I had a variety show called *Good Day Google+*. I would bring in people from different walks of life and we would have a discussion—writers, people playing live music. I'd be around the kitchen table with an *Ask Chef Dennis* segment. I had a cohost, Susan Serra, an award winning kitchen designer from New York, and I would make something and we would talk about kitchens and things."

You said concurrent with relocating to Florida everything turned perfect. You started blogging more; what else changed, I asked.

"I took my blogging on the road. I started *On the Road With Chef Dennis*. So I would take my complete set-up out and set it up on a table with Wi-Fi, and I would have my Yeti microphone and my cameras and do a show and interview people at restaurants. I did a show at Sea World and different places where I would do live broadcasts. At one point I had three different live shows. I did a fourth with a friend from Denver called *The Food and Booze Show*; we would go to restaurants and eat and drink whatever they put in front of us. One of us would be there and the other would be at home running the cameras and everything. Of all the shows and platforms, I've done over 800 live broadcasts."

At this point, Chef Dennis was not a travel blogger but rather a food blogger who travelled with a live show. That was about to change in a big way. I asked, "How did you become a travel blogger?"

"I've been called the accidental travel blogger. My career as a travel blogger began in 2017 when I was asked to apply for a stay at an oceanfront motel that was looking for bloggers. I was a food blogger not a travel blogger;

nevertheless I applied, and they asked me to visit. I was picked, and was given a not-so-great room on the third floor; it was a little old, twin beds. However, they had just installed these nine foot floor-to-ceiling sliding glass balcony doors facing the ocean. So I just stood there overlooking the beach, looking out at the ocean. At that point I decided, I could be a travel blogger!"

Chef Dennis began working with the Florida boutique hotel group that this oceanfront motel was a part of as a blogger and guest speaker, and was well-received at each of the group's properties he stayed at over the next three years.

"I've also spoken at local conferences and food blogger conferences on how to become a travel blogger. These kinds of speaking opportunities led to me attending a Travel Bloggers Exchange (TBEX) conference in Minneapolis; I made many connections and met an agent who helped me transform my media kit and way of thinking about blogging and interacting. My upgraded media kit opened so many doors and made me more appealing to travel and food brands and I began getting even more work and opportunities. I was invited to speak at my first TBEX in 2017 at Huntsville, Alabama and again at TBEX in 2018 at The Finger Lakes in New York."

On social media, Chef Dennis has two "personas," *Ask Chef Dennis*, and *Chef Dennis Travels*. I assumed that *Chef Dennis Travels* was created in conjunction with his new status of being a travel blogger.

"*Ask Chef Dennis* is my blog name. *Chef Dennis Travels* came about because on Instagram every time I would post a travel photo on my food account, it would tank. It would not do well. And I had all of these beautiful travel pics that I wanted to post, but every time I would post them, they would do terrible. Followers just wanted food on *Ask Chef Dennis*. So I decided I would start another Instagram board, *Chef Dennis Travels*. So it's a secondary page. Now I post my food on *Ask Chef Dennis* and when I travel, I post photos on *Chef Dennis Travels*. So, that's the difference. Relative to *Ask Chef Dennis*, *Chef Dennis Travels* is not that big. *Chef Dennis Travels* has 15,000 Instagram followers and another couple thousand on Facebook. *Ask Chef Dennis* on the other hand, has over 52,000 Instagram followers and 720,000 on Facebook."

Chef Dennis had been a travel blogger for a couple of years and was beginning to make a name for himself—asked to keynote at conferences, be on expert panels, and had top-tier professional travel writer association memberships like National Association of Travel Journalists and Society of American Travel Writers among others. Then in 2017, Viking asked Chef Dennis to go on one of their cruises, signaling to Chef Dennis that he had officially hit the big time.

Chef Dennis had only cruised once when Viking reached out to him. His first cruise was on Disney Cruise Line to the Bahamas on Disney *Dream* in January 2017. Trying cruising for the first time by going on a Disney ship is quite a way to start.

Chef Dennis and Lisa at Castaway Cay, Disney Cruise Line's private island in the Bahamas.

"It was a Christmas present to Lisa. We had talked about cruising but neither of us had cruised, and we were in Florida, the home of cruising. The ship was beautiful, it was Disney of course. You could eat all you want, the shows were very nice, they had some great entertainment on board, nice clubs. I said to myself 'This is really nice, but we live in Florida; we've got miles and miles of beautiful beaches. We can go out and eat anywhere.' We came off of it unsure if we were cruise people. Shortly after the cruise on Disney *Dream*, I got an email from Viking—totally unsought and unexpected. We went with some trepidation. I didn't know what to expect, if we were going to like it. So, we did our first Viking cruise and it was magical."

"So the Disney cruise was nice but you didn't immediately get hooked on cruising?"

"No, I don't think I am a big ship cruiser. And it's got to be about the destination; the Disney cruise was only a few days to the Bahamas. The Viking cruise on the *Forsetti* was along the Danube. And when I say the Viking cruise was magical—the wonderful aspects of my first brand ambassadorship started even before the cruise. First off, I asked them what they wanted me to do. They said, have a good time! There was no expectation of social media posts— although I did posts anyway. We boarded and they told us we upgraded you to a suite, we hope you don't mind! And we couldn't pay for anything either; even all of our excursions were taken care of. The trip was amazing; we made some really good friends. The hotel manager would sit and chat with us, the cruise director was wonderful. We made a number of lasting friendships."

So began Chef Dennis' brand ambassadorship with Viking, as well as similar relationships with several other luxury cruises lines. He told me, "With that initial relationship where nothing was expected of me, that started a series of opportunities that have enabled me to cruise all over the world. After getting started with Viking, I went to work learning how to be a better travel blogger and how to become an asset to the brands I worked with."

As a brand ambassador, *Ask Chef Dennis* has been fortunate to sail some exotic itineraries on incredible cruise ships. For Viking, Chef Dennis cruised Viking *Danube Waltz* river cruise June 2017; Viking *Bordeaux Chateaux & Wines* river cruise July 2018; Viking *Portugal River of Gold* river cruise July 2019. On European Waterways, Chef Dennis went on a Northern Burgundy Barge Cruise on *La Belle Époque* in 2018.

Chef Dennis, Northern Burgundy Barge Cruise, La Belle Époque

In 2019 Chef Dennis continued his impressive foray into small ship luxury cruising with CrosiEurope, sailing a Barge Cruise on the Seine in August on the *MS Deborah*. In December Chef Dennis and Lisa brought in the New Year on a UnCruise Sea of Cortez cruise on the *Endeavour*. All of these luxury cruises have been as a brand ambassador. Often, like that first Viking cruise, there is little expected from Chef Dennis, but he has shrewdly done things on behalf of brands in the social media realm that endear him to his clients and have certainly contributed to his success and growing roster of brand ambassadorships.

"For instance, I had sailed on a CroisiEurope ship, but I had been engaged by France Cruises, a travel company specializing in cruises in France—barge cruises, river cruises, luxury small ships. I promoted France Cruises and Croisi on social even though I only was working with France. That got Croisi's attention, so I asked if it would it be possible to work together. They said, 'Absolutely, we'd love to have you. We followed you last time you were on board.' So I sent him all my social media pictures from that last Croisi cruise. They were ecstatic; they said, 'We can use these?' I said, 'absolutely, what am I going to do with them?' They're on my blog, they're on my hard drive, and when I die someone is going to throw that hard drive away and no one will get to see them. So I always give my pictures away to whoever I am working with. I just gave photos to UnCruise; they were so pleased and said, 'Do you need credit?' I said credit would be nice, but no, just have fun with them. I love seeing my photos on social."

Besides cruise lines, *Ask Chef Dennis* has collaborated with numerous major brands, destinations and resorts including Spain (Visit Spain), Madrid Tourism, and Barcelona Tourism; Discover Atlanta, Visit Greensboro, and Visit Florida; Waldorf Astoria Orlando; Margaritaville Resorts, Omni Resorts, Disneyworld, SeaWorld, and numerous others.

Chef Dennis' cruise bucket includes visiting the destinations of New Zealand, Tahiti, and Alaska. With respect to cruise ships, Chef Dennis would like to sail on Windstar, Paul Gaugin Cruise Line to French Polynesia, and a Viking Ocean Cruise.

Ask Chef Dennis and pretzel in Munich, Germany.

Though Chef Dennis is relatively new to cruising, he and Lisa have travelled internationally since the nineties. Their first time out of the country was a trip to Paris, followed by bringing in the New Year, December 31, 1999 on the Grand Canal in Venice. Chef Dennis continues to enjoy land-based travel abroad as a brand ambassador, as well as when traveling professionally. For instance, until the pandemic locked down travel, Chef Dennis was slated to go to Sicily in March 2020 for a travel conference and then travel through Southern Italy as well. The trip included staying in Verona for a month, cooking with local ingredients and inviting food and travel bloggers visiting the area to stop by for dinner. Chef Dennis laments that he and Lisa will miss out on that trip and an amazing line-up of other travel, overland as well as cruises for 2020.

You talk about your travel screeching to a halt. What about the other aspects of what you do, food blogging and the like. What is *Ask Chef Dennis* doing in the pandemic? I asked. "You don't seem to be hurting from what I can see on social media."

"Oh God, no. With everyone staying at home, traffic tripled, shot through the roof. But brands were so weary at the time that what we were getting paid dropped by 40%. So, I made more, but had the brands not cut back it would have been unbelievable. I had three quarters of a million page views in April. I'm actually getting paid more now than I did last year at this time. The brands have cut back on advertising and social media, but you know they're reaching more people through bloggers because people are reading food blogs more than anything now looking for recipes. So people are still hiring me to do work. I'll post recipes sponsored by a brand."

I asked Chef Dennis how have things changed for him since becoming so popular...other than cruising around the world in luxury.

"That's pretty much it. You don't know how visible you are. I was at a conference of bloggers, it was so cool—they had fashion bloggers, food bloggers, motorcycle bloggers, a guitar blogger. I'm like 'this is amazing,' and I'm Tweeting stuff out and then I hear, 'Is Chef Dennis here?' I look up and there I am on the big screen. Or, I was out to dinner with a client during a conference in Boston and she checks Twitter and sees all these different shares of my posts on her feed, and she says, 'You're everywhere.' Being popular on social media makes you more attractive to brands. They know it's more eyes that are going to see your social. And then again there's sharing. Collette Tours loves me because the first trip I did with them I got them almost 1,000,000 impressions on social media; but of course it was 150 social media shares. That's kind of what I do for a brand, that kind of publicity and promotion."

The more I spoke to him, and learned about Chef Dennis, the more I realized how much of a "rock star" he is in the world of blogging, social media and brand influencing. And he gets to do it all in the pursuit of his passions—food and travel.

"I've enjoyed a lot of success as a blogger and feel fortunate to have met people along the way that inspired and helped me, which is why I always try to pay it forward. I love traveling and meeting new people around the world and cruising is my favorite way to travel. They take all the work out of travel and I love it!"

Sea of Glamour:
Kandes Bregman

When you go to the Holland America Line (HAL) homepage, there should be a photo of Kandes Bregman. I am not implying Kandes is HAL's most prolific cruiser, or biggest fan, but she would be a good personification of the joy of cruising on Holland America Line. First, from a sheer quantitative perspective: Kandes has cruised virtually all of her 90 cruises on HAL, visiting 76 countries in six continents and spending the equivalent of three years of her life at sea with HAL. (All the more remarkable given that Kandes has been cruising with HAL for less than 20 years.) And, while perhaps there are those out there who exist, it is hard to imagine someone who is more of an ambassador for HAL. Over 100 referrals of cruisers booked and sailed on HAL, several of whom are now four and five star Mariners—HAL's customer loyalty program. And, Kandes has created and cultivated a website and blog, *Sea of Glamour*, dedicated to all things HAL.

After researching Kandes and reviewing *Sea of Glamour*, I opened up my interview with Kandes by stating facetiously, "You should be in a Holland America Line advertisement!" Kandes responded, "Well, I was...."

Kandes was born in Seattle, Washington, lived in Saratoga, California, and spent a portion of her life in Cary, North Carolina before settling in Scottsdale, Arizona where she lives with her husband of 40 years, Cor, who is originally from the Netherlands. Kandes and Cor have three children, one of whom recently got married on, surprise, a HAL cruise.

Kandes at one of her favorite destinations, Venice, on Ponte dell'Accademia wooden bridge originally built in 1933 spanning the Grand Canal.

As a marketing communications executive for technology companies for over 25 years, Kandes traveled for business throughout the United States, visiting most of the states, as well as parts of Europe. "During that time I traveled extensively for work and traveling monthly became part of who I am." Cor was a corporate executive when Kandes met him and later a real estate brokerage and investment entrepreneur, and also traveled quite a bit professionally.

Cor was born in the Netherlands; thus Kandes and Cor's affinity for HAL. However, HAL wasn't their introduction to cruising. Kandes' introduction to cruising was in December 1998 on Royal Caribbean *Grandeur of the Seas*. "It was our first cruise; it was a President's Club event for the company

I worked for. I was Vice President-Marketing, and I hosted the trip. The President's Club was a sales incentive for the company's sales force where the top sales people were awarded a weeklong cruise with senior management for reaching certain objectives for the year. For me, because I did corporate events and meetings, it was a work week."

So unlike many first time cruisers, Kandes didn't take to cruising right away. "It was fun, but I didn't think I would ever go on a cruise again." If only she knew....

Kandes second cruise, in January 2002, was her introduction to Holland American Line, and she never looked back. Their Dutch travel agents invited Kandes and Cor to join them along with their children and grandchildren for their 40th anniversary celebration cruise to the Caribbean aboard HAL *Veendam*. Cor had first come to the United States as a foreign exchange student, and the travel agents operated the agency that Cor used to arrange travel between the States and home. "Because my husband is from the Netherlands, they wanted us to experience the ship heritage, culture, artwork, food and customs."

Unlike her first cruise, The *Veendam* resonated with Kandes. "Our friends who invited us owned a chain of travel agencies, and when they took us on a cruise it was more fun because they are travel agents, it was vacation as opposed to work, and I had my family with me. So it was different. And it was a Dutch cruise line which was my husband's heritage. So, they made a special arrangement where they had a big table every night for the group, they arranged excursions, we went to the shows; our hosts made sure that we got the full value out of that cruise."

Now Kandes was hooked! I said, "It sounds like that second cruise left an impression on you." Kandes responded, "Yes! We said we are going to do this again. Soon!" And they did, later in that same year. That began a series of cruises—some just Kandes and Cor, and many with their children—all on HAL. After that first Royal Caribbean cruise, Kandes never cruised on a cruise line other than HAL.

In December 2002 Kandes went on the first of many family holiday cruises. They sailed the new HAL *Zuiderdam*, the first ship introducing HAL's new Vista-class. *Zuiderdam* was larger, glitzier, and laid out differently than HAL cruise ships to that point, and made a lasting first impression on the family. The *Zuiderdam* cruise to the Caribbean started a holiday HAL cruise tradition that would take Kandes and family to Hawaii, Panama Canal, Mexico, and the Mediterranean over the 2-week Christmas through New Year's period. "I would bring a trunk with a three-foot tree, stockings and small gifts like snorkel gear, watches and cameras. These were great family vacations. As adults our children now tell us, 'we don't remember holiday gifts as much as we remember every cruise!'"

Over the course of the next several years, between her role as a corporate executive, as well as Cor's responsibilities operating his real estate investment firm, the Bregman's saw the world via HAL. They sailed every ship in the fleet, to every corner of the globe that HAL covers. Then came the cruise that forever changed Kandes' life.

"The turning-point of my life was when we had the opportunity to take a 50-day cruise in November/December 2005 on HAL *Statendam* from San Diego to Sydney, Australia. It was a dream cruise, a once in a life-time event. We met other professional couples that shared our same interest. There were a lot of sea days and we had dinners, parties and lived the life."

I asked Kandes what the circumstances were surrounding the 50-day *Statendam* cruise; I was curious about her referring to it as "an opportunity."

"We were working; both had careers and were working all the time, and we had kids in school. So, the only time we could cruise was Christmas, New Years, and Spring Break. The corporation I was working for…we were selling the company. We had done all the work and now were in what the corporate world refers to as the quiet period. [Technically, the period as regulated by securities laws that prohibits corporations from divulging certain information to the public.] There's nothing I could do—can't do an advertising campaign, no marketing, no press releases, nothing. I'm a Vice President of Marketing and I couldn't carry out marketing. So, there was nothing for me to do. I'm the person that works all the time. I love my work; I am always working; I never took time off. So I asked if I could take my unused vacation. I had all this vacation accrued because I never took off, I took it to go on this 50-day cruise."

Kandes and Cor on their 68th cruise, The Far East Passage, from Singapore to Rotterdam, on the Rotterdam VI in 2016.

Ok, so the opportunity to go on such a long cruise presented itself given what was going on at Kandes' job. Why, I wondered had Kandes referred to the cruise as a turning point? What is it about the 50-day cruise that was such a life-changing event?

"First of all the cruise itself: we left from San Diego, we went to Mexico, to South America, to Easter Island, Bora Bora, Tahiti, New Zealand, Pitcairn Islands. Those are places you read about; you see them in movies. I never thought I would be going to Easter Island. I was the first person standing at the gangway to get off *Statendam* at Easter Island. The sun is coming up, there is no one there—just a couple of cabs—and we get someone who is going to take us all around the island and we will be the first people to see the Moai statues early that morning; it was serene. Those are the kind of experiences that don't happen every day. And then we went to Bora Bora, and Tahiti. We just saw so much and I realized 'well, you can do this if you want to; but I've been so busy working that I never thought about that.'"

So by saying it was a turning point in your life, you were kind of moved by the experience.

"Absolutely I was moved by the experience. The cruise was a turning point not just emotionally, but also with regard to my career. I had a choice to make; I was at a crossroads. The company we were merging with was in New York, and my family lived on the West Coast. And did I want to be traveling for the company half of each month; living out of hotels?"

A few weeks after the cruise, Kandes left the corporate world.

With all of her days at sea with HAL, Kandes has a myriad of unique experiences and memories to choose from: visiting the Great Wall of China; seeing Petra in Jordan and having tea with the Bedouins, the Nomadic people of deserts in Jordan; off-roading in the Falkland Islands; 16 Transatlantic and Mediterranean cruises; 11 cruises to Alaska; numerous cruises to Asia, Africa, South America, Hawaii, South Pacific, Polynesia; and over 50 Caribbean and Mexico cruises.

Not surprisingly, some of Kandes greatest cruise memories revolve around her children. One was part of that 50-day *Statendam* cruise.

"Our three school-age children flew from Los Angeles to Auckland, New Zealand and joined us for two weeks of the cruise over the holidays. They had done the Panama Canal, Hawaii, Mexico, Caribbean with us for the holidays, but this was a big new adventure. My 14-year old son was in boarding school in Los Angeles and my daughters were in school in Arizona. They were nine and ten. When holiday break came, a friend took them to the airport and the girls flew to Los Angeles International Airport. My son got himself to the airport and these three kids met up and flew all the way to New Zealand. They got on the HAL shuttle transportation and got to the HAL hotel. At that time, you did not have cell phones; you just hoped they would be there somehow.

So we were sitting there at the terminal watching buses discharge passengers, and they never got off any of the buses. So I'm wondering 'what happened, and how am I going to find them?' I'm almost in tears as we walked back up to our suite and opened the door to the three of them enjoying the room service they had ordered."

I noted that's pretty amazing; Kandes has some very responsible kids. She said, "Well they were very savvy cruisers as they had cruised every holiday season.

Kandes' children are adults now. They are committed HAL cruisers— they are all HAL Mariners, each having attained 100 sea days before they were out of high school. For one, Kara, Kandes' middle child, HAL will forever be a part of her life and not just because of the indelible memories of spring break cruises and Christmas and New Years cruises and "growing up HAL."

In October 2018, Kara was married on a Mexican Riviera cruise on the bow of HAL *Eurodam*. That wasn't quite the original plan though. Kandes had planned for over a year a storybook destination wedding for Kara with the ceremony for 40 guests at a stop at Puerto Vallarta. However, Hurricane Willa, which peaked as a Category 5 hurricane with winds of 160 mph caused *Eurodam* to be diverted and bypass Puerto Vallarta.

"We were on the *Eurodam* with our whole family; we had this big group with us. We had a near tragedy of the whole itinerary being changed and the wedding ceremony in Puerto Vallarta being cancelled, and Holland America was unbelievable in what they did to correct the problem or handle the situation. I had a binder with every detail of what we had planned to do on land, and HAL reproduced the whole ceremony down to the programs on each seat, flowers and music, on the ship. And it was beautiful."

As a result of an amazing effort by the *Eurodam* officers and crew, Kandes, Cor and the newlyweds, Mr. and Mrs. Guerry, and guests experienced a fairytale wedding. A post about the wedding is on the HAL blog at Hollandamerica.com.

*Kara and Adam Guerry, Kandes, Cor and the wedding party on the bow of the Eurodam,
with Catalina Island off the coast of Southern California in the background.*

Just a couple of months later, Kandes boarded yet another very memorable cruise. *Nieuw Statendam* is *HAL's* newest ship. Christened by ship "Godmother" Oprah Winfrey, *Nieuw Statendam's* inaugural voyage was on December 5, 2018, and Kandes and Cor sailed the transatlantic crossing from Rome to Fort Lauderdale. Kandes had been invited by HAL's Head of Guest Relations, Sissel Bergersen, to go on the cruise loaded with HAL top leadership—Holland America Line President Orlando Ashford, Sr. Vice President Michael Smith and Vice President Fritz Van Der Werff and their executive team, and the European press.

"My love right now is the *Nieuw Statendam* because it is the "New Holland America" and I was on it when it first sailed from Rome. We joined the *Nieuw Statendam* with long time Mariners, world-wide media and HAL executives, who immediately knew who we were. We were at one of the many media events and Orlando Ashford walked up and said: 'Oh, I know who you are, you're the Bregmans. Your daughter just got married on the *Eurodam*.' And they asked us if they could do a full-page advertisement in travel publications about the fairy tale wedding."

HAL quickly turned around an advertisement, a photo of Cor walking Kara down the aisle. The ad promoted HAL's customer service orientation and excellence, and highlighted the proactive efforts of crew in the face of the last minute re-routing of the *Eurodam* and having to miss the stop in Puerto Vallarta due to Hurricane Willa.

The HAL advertisement about Kandes and Cor's daughter Kara and Adam's wedding on board Eurodam.

After leaving corporate, Kandes joined Cor with his real estate investments. "We now have created a virtual vacation rental business. We handle marketing, reservations, bookings, arrivals and departures from wherever we are. We bring our mobile office on cruises and we book a balcony room with a desk." Kandes' other interests are family, fitness, fashion, photography, and of course, travel.

In 2017 Kandes created *Sea of Glamour*. The name of her blog combines Kandes' love of the sea with hints of her past life as a beauty pageant winner. She is the former Mrs. Southwest for the Mrs. Globe organization. Kandes likes glamour and feels it fits in well with cruising and traveling—thus the name, *Sea of Glamour*. She notes that more importantly through her past life in pageants she worked with some important causes and is the spokesperson for a charitable organization called *Women In Need*. I asked Kandes about her motivation for starting *Sea of Glamour*. She told me, "People who were first-time cruisers were asking me: 'Where do you like to go? What were your best trips?' They know that I cruise all the time so it was natural they would ask me those kinds of questions. Then they booked their cruise and they want to know what each of the ports is like: 'What do you wear? What do you do? How does it all work?' So, I started a blog. And then I added Instagram because I wanted to post fabulous pictures from great places."

Kandes is happy with the blog and Instagram and is pleasantly surprised at how many followers she has garnered already. She laments that with the cruise lockdown she has little to post right now.

Nowadays, Kandes and Cor primarily travel via cruise ship unless visiting family or traveling to a destination event. They take about five to six cruises a year. Cor speaks five languages which comes in handy when traveling to foreign ports. Kandes says she has been everywhere she wants to go and loves going back to her favorite places.

Assuming the world health situation allows, Kandes is planning to cruise again in October 2020 on the HAL *Koningsdam* for a family reunion Mexican cruise. She is booked in January 2021 for the Caribbean and is booked for the maiden voyage of the HAL *Rotterdam*, HAL's new flagship scheduled for August 2021. Kandes has no trepidation about returning to cruising. "Cruise lines understand the norovirus and have been dealing with it for years. All the things we are doing right now in our daily life in response to Covid-19, I know how to do because HAL has been conscious of hand washing and sanitizing for years. I have no fear of going back on board, because ships will be the safest and cleanest places to be."

I asked Kandes to reflect on her amazing 20-year run of cruising with HAL. "There are some ships that I fall in love with and are in my heart because of what I have experienced on them. And it's the experiences and people that make a memorable trip. You meet a lot of different people from different backgrounds and cultures and it opens your mind and makes you a more well-rounded person. I truly believe that travel fuels your soul. My belief is you can create the life you want. I did this by working virtually and intentionally building a business around my travel."

Kandes, the personification of the joy of cruising Holland America Line, on HAL Oosterdam transatlantic July 2017.

Traveling Judi

Judi Cohen is a retired engineering and transportation executive who lives in Toronto, Canada with her husband Lawrence. Judi and Lawrence are junior high school sweethearts and have been together for over 50 years. They have two children, daughter Alison, and son, Dustin. Judi was born and raised in Toronto, graduated from the University of Toronto and spent the majority of her adult life in Toronto. And, Judi is a passionate cruiser just like most of us...well, sort of!

Judi is the creator of *Traveling Judi* which was launched officially in 2018. These words from *TravelingJudi.com* encapsulate Judi's approach to travel and the content on her blog:

> *Judi Cohen has traveled the world in search of unique experiences and off-the-beaten-path destinations. She is also a connoisseur of small-ship cruises that pack big adventure, and local cultural and dining experiences.*

After her 35-year professional career, Judi decided to capitalize on her long-time passion for travel, especially cruising, mainly on small-ship vessels to unique and far-reaching locales. In 2015 Judi became a full-time traveler, travel writer, and travel advisor. All along the way, Judi has enjoyed sharing her travel stories through *Traveling Judi*, and nurturing and growing the *Traveling Judi* brand.

Judi aboard Viking Jupiter for the Viking Homelands Baltic Cruise departing from Stochholm.

Traveling Judi was in the making before its official launch. Well before, considering that Judi and her husband had been traveling together since the 70's. They celebrated their honeymoon on a cruise! In addition, Judi traveled extensively as a corporate executive. What Judi did not know at the time she left the corporate world was that *Traveling Judi* was about to be borne. While the brand was not a thought at the time, it originated in the wake of a conversation Judi had with Alison. Judi told me, "My daughter Alison said, 'Mom, you're not a lunch mom; I don't want you to just play golf and hang out at cafes.' I responded, 'Honey, the only things I want to do at this stage are to travel and eat—the two things that I love.' She said, 'Then do it!' And, so I did."

"What did that look like?" I asked Judi. She said, "I went to work. I learned the travel business; actually, I served as a luxury travel concierge with a couple of top tier companies specializing in luxury and experiential travel. I learned to put together very, very high-end trips."

I wondered what kind of things one does when working for luxury travel companies—what was that like? What does arranging very high-end trips entail? Judi said, "At Zebrano Travel, I was focused on understanding what trips people wanted, putting together itineraries, and suggesting experiences for them while they are away. It really was about learning the travel business—of being a luxury travel agent. So I attended many travel conferences and went on familiarization trips to learn and network, and trained via numerous webinars. I did webinar after webinar on the DMC's, (Destination Management Companies) all around the world just to gain an understanding as to what is possible. So if someone called, for instance, and said they wanted to go to Morocco, I was able to make recommendations and rely on a company in that destination, the DMC, to deliver the services."

"Then when I started working with the next luxury travel company, Tully Luxury Travel, my title there was Director of Experiences. I oversaw a small group in there that did what was called Private Travel Design, for people who were primarily cruisers, who also did some land trips. What they were focusing on initially were just the cruises, and came to the realization that those cruisers also did all the shore excursions and pre- and post-cruise stays, and so that's what I worked on. Another big area that they focused on was Africa. One of the divisions at Tully was called African Dreams, and I had the opportunity to learn about Africa and experience Africa so that I could make recommendations as well, and know the suppliers there to put together safaris and other trips for passengers who arrive there either on a cruise or just doing an independent trip."

"I then moved on to another company in Toronto; I thought I wanted to do group travel. So I moved on to a company in Toronto. I was there for a relatively short time but I escorted a trip to Morocco with 16 people. So the small group trips, that required a different skill set. You have to try to understand what a small group would like, and then go out there and market it—within an existing database to repeat clients."

And these were also high-end clients? I asked Judi. "No, they were not. And that's why I didn't continue there. I was much more attracted to the high-end clients, and my personal preference is very experiential and very off-the-beaten-path travel. So I left there and by that time I was doing a lot of posting on Instagram, and I was getting a name and gaining a following. I was posting all my photos from my travel, and I came to realize people were interested in off-the-beaten-path journeys and some of the small-ship cruising and different things I had done, and that's how Traveling Judi was born."

Given that travel was a significant part of Judi's life right from the beginning of her relationship with Lawrence, I wondered what led her to gain an appreciation of travel. I asked, " Did you travel a lot with your family growing up? Did you study abroad? Where did you get the travel bug?" Judi said, " No, my parents were poor. We hardly ever traveled together as a family. The first trip we ever did with our family, we would drive to the Catskills in New York. My parents would go there because my uncle owned a resort. My father would work as a waiter and my mother as a hotel maid. We would spend the summer—while they worked, my brother and I played. We did that for many summers. Eventually, when I was 14 we took one trip where my parents drove us down to Miami Beach, Florida. Actually, I started going to Florida fairly regularly after I met Lawrence. I met my husband in junior high, and his family always had places in Florida, and by the age of 16 I was flying with his family to Florida. We went back each year, and I loved Florida. And, oh we drove to Montreal for Expo 67 as a family. That's the extent of my traveling growing up."

I asked, " Did those kinds of experiences, as sparse as they were, influence you to travel?" Judi said, "They did. As my friends all talked about summer camps—we never went to summer camp because we were always taken to the Catskills—that kind of left a mark on me. And those road trips back and forth to the Catskills were the highlight of my year. Driving from Toronto to the

Catskill Mountains was a major adventure. So they were no less valuable—I don't know how to say it—for me, at that stage of my life, that was like traveling the world."

Judi has been to over 90 countries on six continents traveling with her family, leading organized trips, or on assignment as a freelance travel writer. In addition, Judi's corporate career enabled her to see much of the world. "Through my work I had a lot of conferences and projects throughout the world. I lived in China for instance, working on a big project for the World Bank, and Lawrence came over and met me. So by virtue of handling that project we got to spend time exploring China. Many times a year there would be conferences and I would put my hand up to go on as many of them as I could. So I did fall in love with travel and all these different places, and really immersed myself. Everywhere I went it was not just the business, but what else can I do and see while I am here."

Judi and Lawrence on an Antarctic expedition aboard the Akademik Sergey Vavilov, a Russian scientific research vessel, in December 2017.

As Judi's corporate career progressed, her family grew, and Judi and Lawrence quickly got the kids into travel. Judi said, "My husband is a huge travel enthusiast; he loves travel and adventure. So it was that combination of my husband and me—whenever we had the ability to go we did, and we took the kids from the time they were very young. My son's first trip with us was to Miami when he was eight weeks old. And he accompanied us regularly. He's older than my daughter and that's how she started traveling as well. We spent a lot of time with the kids in Florida—Disney World in Orlando, the beaches on the gulf coast, and Miami Beach—and then we started going to all kinds of places. At first land journeys, but then we started doing cruises as the kids were growing up—we did Mediterranean cruises, we did Caribbean cruises. We started off doing big mainstream ships because they had a lot of activities for kids. As they got older the kids became really curious travelers, and very comfortable travelers as well. So they wanted to do more adventurous and exotic things with us, and so they traveled with us to China, Japan, and throughout Europe. And as they became adults...my daughter, for example, when Lawrence and I did our Antarctica cruise my daughter saw the photos and said, 'I want to do that,' and booked the exact same cruise a few months later. So, my kids are passionate travelers, and they can feel our passion. They have learned from us how important it is to work hard and play hard!"

Many of those over 90 countries that Judi traveled to were reached, or explored, by ship. Judi has been on over 25 cruises since her first cruise way back in 1979. That first cruise, on Chandris Cruises, was quite memorable. Judi and her husband slept in bunk beds—on their honeymoon! "It was a Mediterranean itinerary starting in Italy, with stops in Greece, Spain, Turkey, Egypt and ending in Israel where we spent an additional 10 days. We could only afford a cabin with bunk beds, which has always been a bit of joke, but we saw great places."

The bunk beds on the honeymoon is now part of the *Traveling Judi* lore. Seriously, Judi has incredible memories of that first experience cruising, which was coupled with a land-based trip to Israel. "The cruise ended in Israel and then we got off and spent another 10 days there and did a land journey.

Seeing Egypt at that particular time also was a pretty incredible experience. They took us into Alexandria and then on to Luxor and then to Cairo. So that was a great trip—a pretty extravagant honeymoon even if we could only afford bunk beds. When I reflect back now I say, wow, to take all that time and to do all of that was pretty amazing."

Most of those cruises were on small ships, that is, vessels generally carrying less than 500 passengers, and in Judi's case a lot smaller than that. "While we have been on a number of larger cruise ships, my love is small-ships with less than 200 passengers. I've done small ship cruises in Antarctica, Alaska, France, Germany, Switzerland, Russia, Myanmar, Vietnam, Cambodia, Canada, India and the United States. Some of the cruises were with just my husband, others with family and friends. The more immersive the trip, the better. Remote, untouristed areas attract me the most. Fresh local food is important to me while I travel."

I asked Judi to talk about how she gravitated away from big mainstream cruise ships to her predilection for smaller vessels. "Somewhere along the line we discovered Pandaw Cruises. We went on a Pandaw Cruise in Myanmar. It was our first small-ship cruise—it had 16 people on it. And that's when we absolutely fell in love with small vessels. We loved it. It sailed a short stretch of the Irrawaddy River between Mandalay and Bagan in Myanmar. We landed in Yangon, Myanmar, and then flew to where we were going to board the vessel. Our first sight of that boat, the Pandaw *Kalaw*—it was so simple, a two-deck river boat. And the crew, and an onboard guide who accompanied us on our adventures off the ship at each stop was so welcoming, so genuine, we knew that we were going to be looked after well. It was just wonderful how they ran everything. Two excursions a day; if you wanted to stay on the ship to relax and read you could, but if you wanted to leave you could get off the ship twice a day. The adventures that we shared were into the smallest remote villages along the Irrawaddy. It was such a memorable experience."

So small ship cruising seemed to appeal to Judi right away. I asked her how soon after the *Kalaw* did she do another small vessel. "Immediately;

we got off that and then we took our kids, as well as two of our friends on the exact same itinerary with Pandaw the following year. And then we went back with the kids only and we did Vietnam and Cambodia with Pandaw." Judi's first three small ship cruises, done in succession, were with Pandaw. A new passion was born. Judi has essentially done almost exclusively small ship cruising since, ranging from very small ships barely holding double digits of passengers, to the 100 passenger *Akademik Sergey Vavilov,* a former Russian scientific vessel converted to an expedition ship to Antarctica, and up to luxury ships like Crystal *Serenity* which holds about 1000 passengers. By the way, of Judi's many small-ship cruising lasting memories is a less than wonderful one on an otherwise wonderful cruise on the *Vavilov,* operated by One Ocean Expeditions. "I really enjoyed the *Vavilov;* the cruise was fabulous, everything was first-class; seeing Antarctica, spending time with the penguins, learning as much as we did was a tremendous opportunity. I will add probably one of the most memorable—maybe not in a good way—was crossing the Drake Passage. It was rough, it was crazy, and my husband gets seasick in a bathtub," Judi laughs.

Yet Lawrence loves to cruise. "He loves to cruise. He knows there is a price to be paid, but he is prepared to do it. I asked him if he would be willing to go back to Antarctica and he said, 'I'd go in a heartbeat.' He considers crossing the Drake a rite of passage." That actually wasn't Judi's first experience crossing Drake's Passage. She had done so prior to becoming a small-ship cruising aficionado on a cruise on Celebrity *Infinity.* That cruise on the *Infinity*—wonderful as it was—as compared to Judi's small ship experience starkly depicts the contrast between big ship versus small ship cruising. "It is very different whether you go on a small or big ship—no less beautiful, but different. Our first cruise to Antarctica was in 2013. It was a wonderful experience. Celebrity *Infinity* departed from Buenos Aires and took us down through Argentina, Venezuela, a stop in Ushuai, and then into Antarctica. But we were sitting on the deck on a big cruise ship. Because the *Infinity* was larger, we could not get off the ship and explore. We crossed the passage, we went into the Antarctic Circle, and we saw all of these other people on Zodiacs and small vessels, and then going to land and hiking. Lawrence and I looked at each other and both said, 'We have to do that. We need to come back here and do that.' We knew we wanted to come back and do it in a more adventurous and immersive style. So in four long years, we did."

Judi even took advantage of an opportunity for small shipping cruising close to home. "Lawrence and I did cruises in Canada; we went out to the east coast. They weren't big ships because they went up through the fjords but they were ocean-going because they went out to Newfoundland and came back into New York City. Anytime we had an opportunity we would take advantage of these short cruises."

So many cruises and so much diversity—large and small vessels in virtually every region of the world. I asked Judi to pick some favorite memories. "One of them is definitely One Ocean, the *Vavilov* and crossing the Drake. Celebrating New Year's Eve a couple of years ago on the Pandaw *Kalaw* in Myanmar with all of the crew and the Captain and the other guests was unbelievable. Another memorable family cruise and land journey was in 2015, over Christmas, with Pandaw to Cambodia and Vietnam. A 2019 cruise we did to the Baltics on Viking Ocean's *Jupiter,* which was tremendous; going to St. Petersburg, and enjoying the small group excursions like visiting the Hermitage Museum, and going into the subway system there—my background is in transportation—I loved doing that. Loved Berlin, Stockholm, Gdansk, Helsinki and Tallinn as well. Although the ship had 930 passengers, it nonetheless had a small-ship feel. I also did another Viking cruise along the Rhine River traveling solo. I would get back on a Viking River Cruise down another river in a second and would not hesitate recommending it to solo travelers. I was there in Basel, Switzerland; I was asked to go there by *Quirky Cruise* to write about the naming, christening, of seven new river ships. Then we did a short cruise down the Rhine. For me, it was a real eye opener to the opportunities that river cruising in Europe brings. I always thought of those river boats as being full of people a lot older than I, doing nothing, just floating along. It was a good mix of people, many younger. It was active, and when you pulled up in the cities, you could walk to your destination in some places. They dock in ideal locations; they are not ports. With these river cruises, there is no time wasted. You are right where you need to be. The food was great, the drinks were great. There is no entertainment; it's not like you are on the ship for entertainment; it's really relaxation, and being immersed in the destinations along the river. The other one I have to mention is the Brahmaputra River Cruise in India. I'm a big India traveler. We've been several times. In 2018 we did the Brahmaputra River Cruise in Assam, North East India, which is totally untouristed. We went with a couple of friends and my children. The *MV Mahaabahu* was a wonderful, tiny little ship which carried 46 passengers, but there were only 23 guests aboard."

In 2020, Judi got in a land trip to India following a visit to Nepal before New Years. I asked her how the cruise lockdown has impacted her cruising plans. "When the pandemic started, we had to cancel a scheduled cruise, Panama and Costa Rica with UnCruise on the *Safari Voyager* in March, right as the pandemic was about to be declared. In August, we missed out on a Pandaw cruise out of Burma, to Nagaland, India. During the lockdown, I have been hoping to experience *LeBoat*, which are small self-drivable river vessels along the Rideau Canal in eastern Ontario Canada in September 2020. We are able to drive there from Toronto and it would be completely private for my family only. We would even captain the boat ourselves. Unfortunately we were not able to get a reservation, but we are still hoping. Our next booked cruise is a 10-day Thailand, Cambodia and Laos with Pandaw on the *Champa Pandaw* in October 2021. And, we're combining that with a side trip to Australia. So, another adventurous trip. Fingers crossed!"

I wondered about *Traveling Judi* during the lockdown. "What do you do about the lack of content for *Traveling Judi*?" I asked. Judy said, "I don't worry about it right now. I talk about things that I loved from the past. I talk about what I am doing in the moment…growing and using my herbs that are in the backyard, cooking a lot more than I ever did…it's a focus on my life during lockdown."

Judi on UnCruise SS Legacy preparing to go kayaking at John Hopkins Glacier, Alaska.

I asked Judi about her long-term travel plans, beyond 2021. "I don't like the term bucket list; but I'd really like to take a small ship in the Amazon, the Galapagos, the Canadian Arctic and Svalbard. I also want to get back to Antarctica at least one more time! I would also like to do more Uncruise Adventures, like the one in Alaska, in places like Costa Rica, Panama and Hawaii. Lastly, visiting Australia and New Zealand on a ship is a dream I'd like to turn into a memory soon. Oh my, that's a lot of planning to do!"

I sheepishly asked Judi what it is about the term bucket list? (I 've interviewed dozens of passionate cruisers for *The Joy of Cruising/Cruising Interrupted*, and have asked each in some form or another about their bucket list. I was afraid I had committed some kind of travel *faux pas*.)

Judi smiled, "I liken bucket list to 'before I die.' For me, I am much more forward thinking than that. I want to do these things while I am healthy, while I can, and while I am still interested. I don't know, talking about what I am going to do before I die just has a negative connotation….."

I'm more about turning my dreams into memories every day."

A Voyager of Distinction

Christine Zimmer is a voyager of distinction. No, she is not a celebrity, or a Cruise Ship Godmother or anything like that. She hasn't cruised hundreds of times—she hasn't even cruised dozens of times. She is a cruiser just like you and me…well, sort of.

Christine Zimmer is originally from Rochester, New York and has lived in Punta Gorda, Florida since 1985. Chris has two daughters and four grandchildren. After retiring from a distinguished career as a middle school and high school educator and administrator, Chris has settled into a part-time career working with adult learners at a university. Emphasis on part-time: when not helping lifelong learners keep their minds engaged, Chris travels the world helping seasoned cruisers keep their minds, bodies, and spirits engaged on luxury cruise ships.

Chris welcoming a group of Distinctive Voyages passengers.

Chris is a Host for *Distinctive Voyages*. What that means is Chris leads and coordinates cruise activities for passengers that have availed themselves of the services of *Distinctive Voyages*, a selection of hosted cruises whereby a *Distinctive Voyages* Host serves as a private expert to answer questions, provide advice, and coordinate the services and amenities available to each traveler in the group: a private Welcome Reception frequently attended by the ship's officers; an Exclusive Shore Event, a private excursion lead by the *Distinctive Voyages* Host; and select luxury amenities for special cruises such as the Culinary Collection sailings, or cruises of 14-plus days, etc. *Distinctive Voyages* is a program of the Travel Leaders Network, a community of travel professionals comprised of thousands of travel agencies selling luxury travel, cruises and tours.

I asked Chris to help me understand how *Distinctive Voyages* works. She told me, "Travel Leaders Network is a network of travel agencies. The member travel agencies pay dues to Travel Leaders Network, who in turn helps them with marketing and helps agents get better deals for their customers like discounts, onboard credit, and upgraded staterooms. It's kind of analogous to professional associations, like the American Association of University Women, or the Downtown Merchants Association here in Punta Gorda. They provide support, information sharing, training, and generally help member agencies to be successful."

"So, *Distinctive Voyages* is a program, an incentive that member agencies can offer to their travel customers at no additional cost. So, let's say a customer wants to book a Panama Canal cruise. A member agency can offer the customer a *Distinctive Voyages* cruise with a Panama Canal itinerary that is going to get them a Host, a unique shore excursion, a welcome reception with included drinks and hors d'oeuvres with ship officers, and they get to meet the other *Distinctive Voyages* passengers, people who are going to be on the tour with them and perhaps strike up friendships that will last throughout the cruise and maybe beyond."

Distinctive Voyages is a way for members of Travel Leaders Network to offer a "value-add" benefit to the travel that they are trying to market to their customers, at no extra cost to the customer, thus enabling these agencies to be more competitive.

Chris told me that Hosts who are accepted are required to take online training. There are a couple of mandatory Travel Leaders Network training modules: the first covers all the aspects of being a *Distinctive Voyages* Host; the second covers the different cruise lines with which Travel Leaders Network partners. Furthermore, the cruise lines offer additional online training hosted on their platform focusing exclusively on their cruises.

I asked Chris, "When you are a *Distinctive Voyages Host*, are you always "on duty?"

Chris smiles, "I'm on duty for the Welcome Reception; I have a folder for each of the members that I deliver to their cabins on the first day with an invitation to the Reception and information about the included shore excursion and some other things; and then I am available for what we call 'Office

Hours' for an hour each day on sea days in case anybody wants to stop by and ask any questions. I always provide my stateroom number to my guests in case they have questions or need assistance with something. Once I helped a guest get a tuxedo shirt as he had forgotten to pack his. Otherwise, I am on a cruise! Really I am much more of a passenger just enjoying the cruise than being on duty. Sometimes though, being 'on duty' comes with some really nice perks. Like being invited to a private dinner with senior members of the crew and special guests, who might be people who have sailed on that ship quite a few times or who are in one of the very high-end suites. Or, I get invited to a special, intimate cocktail party."

Sign me up...

Chris did not travel much as a child and young adult. She grew up in a large, middle-class family. "I am the oldest of six children. We did not have a lot of opportunities to do much traveling other than going to visit relatives and do day trips to places like the zoo." Chris was, however, curious about the world around her. Growing up, she was a history buff and was always intrigued by other places and other cultures. That lead her to study Spanish language and culture and history in high school, which became her springboard to an education career. "Because I thought I could do a better job as a Spanish teacher than anyone I had been exposed to in high school, when I went to college I majored in Spanish and minored in Latin American studies."

Chris married during college, and was holding down a job during her late teens and early twenties. Traveling was not foremost in her mind. Chris did not get on an airplane for the first time until she was 21 years old and flew from Rochester to Philadelphia for a weekend. Chris said, "Fast forward from that point to 10 years, two kids later. My husband had a good job, I was teaching, and we wanted to go someplace warm for the February break from school. When we talked to the travel agent we learned we could go to Spain for about the same cost as we could go to Florida. So we flew to the South of

Spain. Here I am escaping the winter of Rochester, and guess what—it snowed in that part of Spain for the first time in 25 years!"

Chris' route to be a *Distinctive Voyages* Host was somewhat atypical given her professional background in education versus travel. However, Chris has traveled internationally for over 40 years, beginning with that trip to Spain in 1980, a destination Chris has come to love and has been back to several times. "Spain is probably my favorite place—so far—due to being a Spanish major in college and all that I learned about the country and its people. The ability to communicate in Spanish while in the country helps significantly. The Spanish influence on many other parts of the world also draws me to those places. I love all of Europe because of the history and architecture, as well as the great variety of geography." Besides Spain, Chris has also experienced international land-based travel to France, Portugal, Italy, and across Canada via train. Unsurprisingly, Spain finds a place on Chris' over-land travel bucket list, specifically, to live in Spain for a couple of months. Chris also aspires to re-visit Italy and travel in Central and South America, as Latin American Studies was her college minor. Concerning cruises, she would like to visit Greece, South America, the Iberian Peninsula, Australia and New Zealand via cruise. In addition, Chris wants to do a Transatlantic cruise.

Several years after her first travel abroad, in 1987 Chris experienced her first cruise, a short jaunt to the Western Caribbean on Holland America Lines. "My father-in-law owned a travel agency at the time and he decided to take his eight children and their spouses on a Caribbean cruise. We visited Cancun, Jamaica, and Grand Cayman. I thoroughly enjoyed my first cruise—being out on the water, the restaurants, being with family and going to the shows, and I loved going to the various islands and seeing how different the islands were from living in Southwest Florida where we had relocated."

I said to Chris, "So, you knew cruising was something you could do again?" Chris said, "Oh absolutely. But life happened and we didn't cruise again for a long time."

Chris didn't cruise again for 20 years, and then in 2008 did a short "girls trip" cruise to the Bahamas on Royal Caribbean *Majesty of the Seas*. Then, in 2016 Chris retired from the school system and began cruising as a Host for *Distinctive Voyages*. Right before she was due to retire, Chris heard from a friend, an employee of Travel Leaders Network. One of her friend's responsibilities was to recruit and assign Hosts to the cruises that were part of the *Distinctive Voyages* program. Chris said, "I thought that would be right up my alley and the timing of hearing about this opportunity was perfect. So that was my entrée to *Distinctive Voyages*. Today it is a requirement for Hosts to be licensed travel agents. Four years ago, some of us who were not agents were brought into the program. I had the international travel experience, outside sales experience with a travel agency, and the education and training background, so I was accepted."

Chris at Tracy Arm Fjord, Juneau, Alaska

Chris got her first *Distinctive Voyages* assignment for a Celebrity cruise in October 2016. However, in June 2016, she was notified about a 10-day cruise on Crystal *Symphony* out of Amsterdam to Norway and Iceland that departed in July. She said, "These kinds of opportunities pop up from time-to-time because for instance, a Host might have to cancel an assignment on short notice. I immediately expressed my interest as I had heard all kinds of wonderful things about Crystal. Of course, the cabins were double occupancy, so I had to scramble to find a partner. I invited my 86 year-old mom, who used to enjoy cruising with my late dad, and we had a great time. In fact, I took her on the October 2016 Western Caribbean Celebrity cruise as well."

Since then, Chris has been on a series of bucket-list cruises for *Distinctive Voyages* throughout the world including the Mediterranean, Alaska, Panama Canal, Norway and Iceland, the British Isles, and Southern and Eastern Caribbean. So far, Chris' cruises for *Distinctive Voyages* have all been on Celebrity (*Eclipse, Equinox, Infinity, Solstice*), Crystal (*Serenity, Symphony*) and Holland America Lines (Prinsendam).

Due to the cruising lockdown Chris lost out on an August 2020 Scandinavia/St. Petersburg cruise this year on Celebrity *Reflection*. She is the assigned Host on a Celebrity *Edge* Caribbean cruise December 2021, which she told me was her first choice of the 2021 list of *Distinctive Voyages* sailings. "There are about 500 upcoming *Distinctive Voyages* cruises, and there are about 300 Hosts. Recently we got the list of 2021 *Distinctive Voyages* cruises, and then we had to respond with our top three choices of the cruises we would like to Host. And there is some other information requested, like whether you have done training offered by the cruise line for the cruises you have chosen, and how many times you've sailed on that cruise line and some other information. You submit your paperwork and the people at Travel Leaders Network go through all the requests and get back to you with your guaranteed assignment. So of the list of possible *Distinctive Voyages* cruises, my first choice was Celebrity *Edge* to Aruba, Bonaire, and Curacao, December 13-24, and I am now guaranteed as the Host! Oh, have you seen that ship?"

Chris was one of the lucky cruisers to get in a 2020 cruise before the lockdown. She did a non-*Distinctive Voyages* cruise with her family to Cozumel and Costa Maya, Mexico, Belize City, Belize, and Roatan, Honduras on Royal Caribbean *Rhapsody of the Seas*.

One of Chris favorite photos...Belize.

Chris is a fortunate cruiser to have been able to combine her passion for history and culture with her love for travel, and to have shared that passion with her family. She is looking forward to her next gaze at the water from the deck of a *Distinctive Voyages* cruise.

Chris said, "One of the best things about travel of any type is the ability to experience how people in other parts of the world live, work and play, and also how they view life—culture."

Section Five:
THE CRUISE COMMUNICATORS

The passionate cruisers featured in *The Cruise Communicators* appeal to the senses of cruise fans via the spoken word through podcasts, or through the captivating visuals that cruising is perfectly suited for on You Tube videos, or written prose of encyclopedic cruise information. The individuals featured in *The Cruise Communicators* embody the essence of the original premise of *The Joy of Cruising/Cruising Interrupted*: travelers with a passion for cruising who pursue that passion in creative ways.

Steve Kriese is creator of *DCL Podcast*, which focuses on Disney Cruise Line but also discusses matters of interest all cruisers care about when planning their cruise vacations. As an airline pilot Steve gets to see the world. As *DCL Podcast*, Steve and guests talk about seeing the world from the perspective of a Disney cruise.

Gary Bembridge founded *Tips for Travellers* as a pastime to occupy himself during his travels—two to three weeks out of a typical month—as a Marketing Vice President for a multinational firm. While Gary created *Tips for Travellers* as a part-time pursuit, he has since retired as a Vice President and now operates *Tips for Travellers*, the leading cruise specific channel on You Tube, full-time, and has maintained his record that began during his corporate career of traveling every month consecutively for over 25 years.

Erin Foster is the author of *The Unofficial Guide to the Disney Cruise Line*. Beyond cruising, Erin is a lifelong Disney fan who has answered over 11,000 questions about Disney—and they were not trivia questions. Like most of us, Erin misses cruising immensely. Yet there is something else that the cruise lockdown has caused Erin to miss even more!

DCL Podcast

As a 737 Captain for Alaska Airlines, Steven Kriese sees the world. As creator and host of *DCL Podcast*, Steve and guests talk about seeing the world from the perspective of a Disney Cruise.

Steve lives in Lake Oswego, Oregon, a suburb of Portland, with his wife Ahnawake and two children, Andrew, 13, and Alex, 9. Steve was born in California but having been raised in a military family lived in numerous places: England, Iran, Michigan, Colorado, Nebraska, South Dakota, Washington, Mississippi, New Jersey, and Oregon. Steve has spent the bulk of his adult life in the Pacific Northwest.

Steve has been with Alaska Airlines for 21 years. He learned to fly in the US Air Force where he flew C-141 cargo planes all over the world—every continent except Antarctica. Steve is retired from the Air Force Reserves, and his career of course affords him numerous opportunities to see the world. However, his affinity for travel developed long before his flying career began.

"I'm a military brat who loves to travel. So we moved all over as a kid, lived in several different countries, lived in Iran, lived in England. In the states, we lived in the Midwest but I ended up on the West Coast for college. When I was a kid, my family just love traveling and it kind of got ingrained in me. Even now, that's part of the reason of doing the job that I do as a pilot. I enjoy the flying aspect of it, but it's the traveling aspect of the job that I love. I get to travel to different cities around the United States and Mexico every week. I enjoy exploring the sites and food options in the different regions of the country—from the freedom trail in Boston, Smithsonian Museums in DC, Disney World in Orlando, running along the bay front in San Diego, to paddle boarding all around the Hawaiian Islands."

I didn't realize Alaska Airlines had such broad, diverse routes. I asked Steve to tell me more about where his job takes him. "For me the majority of my travel—living on the West Coast—I like to do what we call Transcons, which go all the way to the East Coast. So I like to go to Boston; there's a lot of history there, a lot of really good food. I like places with history and food; I go to New York City, amazing city. And of course on this side of the country I really enjoy going to the Hawaiian Islands. Such a laid back experience to be over there, go to the beach. I surf a little—not very good at it but I love to go surf. These are all on my routes. It changes month-to-month. Alaska Airlines covers pretty much the whole country, as well as Mexico, and a couple of places in Canada. We were actually the first airline to really build up Cabo. A lot of people don't know that and now everyone flies to Cabo, but Alaska was one of the first, along with some of the Mexican carriers that really helped to build up Cabo San Lucas."

Steve on Disney Wonder in front of Dawes Glacier, Alaska.

Steve's occupation certainly does enable him to do a great deal of travel. On top of that is a significant amount of travel, land-based and cruises, in his personal life. I asked him first about his land-based travel.

"My wife and I have explored New Zealand, scuba dived the Great Barrier Reef in Australia, snorkeled with the kids and the sting rays in Grand Cayman, visited Paris, experienced London, ventured through the Christmas markets in Austria and Germany. We've ridden bikes along the Danube for a week in Southern Bavaria, explored the outer banks of the Carolinas with our kids, and hiked and skied all around the mountains of the Pacific Northwest."

That's an impressive list on top of all the travel Steve has done as a pilot. I asked, "Anywhere in the world that you would like to see that you haven't seen?

"I would love to go to the South Africa area. I have been to North Africa before, I've been to Kenya. But I really want to spend some time in South Africa—see the people, experience the culture, and go on a safari. Over to Namibia as well. I think Namibia is a place that a lot of people don't know about. We actually landed in Windhoek, the capital of Namibia when I was in the Air Force. The people are some of the friendliest people I have ever met in my life, and the animals there are amazing."

Steve is relatively new to cruising. His first cruise was in 2014—a seven day cruise out of Venice, Italy aboard the Norwegian *Jade*. It helped that his first cruise was a Mediterranean cruise; certainly a wonderful way for cruising to make a first impression. The seasoned traveler was hooked right away. I asked Steve what influenced him to try a cruise.

"So, our friends had cruised several times before and they really enjoyed it. They kind of talked us into doing it. Like many others I never had a huge desire to go cruising. I didn't know what to expect, but when we sailed on our first cruise from Venice and were able to experience so many exotic ports and sites, it was amazing and I was hooked right away. We stopped in Croatia, Greece, and Turkey. I learned that nothing beats a relaxing day at sea with friends and family, and good food. As an airline pilot, I also have become fascinated with the navigation and logistics of sailing a ship from one port to the next. *Jade* was originally built to sail out of Hawaii, but after the economic downturn in the late 2000's, demand dropped there, so they sent her to the Med. It was kind of humorous sailing around the Med in this over-the-top Hawaiian themed ship. The ship had artwork and statues themed for the Hawaiian Islands; there was a large statue of King Kamehmeha in the main dining room. They have since re-themed her."

A Mediterranean cruise as the first cruise! That's on my bucket list. While a Mediterranean cruise contains a lifetime of memories for many, perhaps one memory of that first cruise Steve holds on to the most is his encounter on the water with George Clooney. Yes, that George Clooney. Steve told me, "Our ship cut off George Clooney's wedding party as they were taking motor boats out of the grand canal to their wedding reception. We departed Venice around four. We sat out on our balcony as *Jade* sailed past the Grand Canal. We saw a bunch of small boats and commotion coming in and out of the Grand Canal." Flying back home, Steve sees this story online about how some giant cruise ship had cut off George Clooney's wedding party. Clooney and his wife Amal had the wedding and they had all gotten in these small boats, trailed by paparazzi, headed to the reception. Accompanying the story was a photo of the Norwegian *Jade* juxtaposed against the small boats containing the wedding party and paparazzi—with Steve's balcony in the shot.

Less than a year later Steve introduced his sons to cruising and tried his first Disney Cruise. They cruised on Disney *Wonder* to Alaska. "My wife wanted to try a Disney cruise, and my parents wanted to go to Alaska. Our kids were five and nine at the time. We had heard good things about the Disney kids club; we knew on a Disney cruise the kids would be entertained."

Alex, Steve, Andrew, and Ahnawake on Disney Magic at their favorite restaurant,
Animators Palate.

I asked, "Were you guys passionate Disney fans?" Steve responded, "I would say, sort of. Not the way we are today. Ahnawake spent her first six or seven years in Southern California so she kind of grew up going to Disneyland. I had been to Disneyland once and a couple of times to Disney World growing up. In 2013 before we started cruising, the grandparents wanted to take our kids to Disneyland and go as one big family. We just had a great time. It was where our kids could be loud; they didn't have to be like they were in a restaurant. All the kids at Disneyland were loud! The kids could have fun, the adults could have fun and relax. That was kind of the start of considering a Disney cruise. Then once we cruised on *Wonder* we were hooked. We had so much fun with our kids, the entertainment provided on the ship, and in the ports...we were then hooked on cruising with Disney as a family. It was so easy for all of us to find things we enjoyed on the ship: my wife relaxing by the pool and the spa, me taking animation drawing classes and history of the ships, the kids playing in the clubs and with friends they made on board, and then all of us getting back together at dinner and in the evenings to spend time together."

Almost all of Steve's cruises subsequent to that first one on *Jade* have been on Disney Cruise Line. Steve has cruised on each of the ships in Disney's fleet: Disney *Magic, Wonder, Dream,* and *Fantasy.* I asked Steve if that first Disney cruise to Alaska on *Wonder* made Steve and his family loyal to the Disney brand. "I think it did. Disney had this thing called rotational dining where you meet your servers and then they go with you to the three dining rooms on the ship. Our head waiter started giving my mom a hard time but in a playful way. She's sort of a 'stick in the mud' about food but he could see he could play with her, and it was fun for us to watch. Then he started doing magic tricks with the kids. The kids were just enthralled. I have a video with my youngest son and his eyes get so big; he can't believe what he saw. And this was only the first night. And it just went from there. Another server, his name is Tiger Tom—he's now the head waiter on the *Magic*—but at the time he worked in the Cabanas which is the buffet on Disney, he came up to my son and started playing a game with him with the back of my son's hoodie. And my son who was a little tired at the time just totally turned his spirits around. We've since seen Tiger Tom a couple of times on subsequent cruises and he remembers us. It's those little touches like that. I think you could probably find that at other cruise lines too, but those are the kinds of things that hooked us to Disney."

After three consecutive Disney cruises following *Jade,* Steve returned to Norwegian Cruise Line in 2017. He and Ahnawake, with friends and no kids, did a nine-day Baltic Cruise on Norwegian *Getaway* highlighted by St. Petersburg, Russia which Steve recalls as amazing. "We visited the Amber Room and palaces of the Czars in St Petersburg. Some of the most over the top wealth I've ever seen." After *Getaway* Steve returned to Disney Cruise Lines and has gone on all Disney cruises since. I asked him if, besides Norwegian, he had considered cruise lines other than Disney.

"Yeah, I'd like to give Royal Caribbean a try. Our kids are getting older now; I listen to other podcasts and they talk about other cruise lines. I think like the Flowrider [surf simulator] and some the other fun things that they have, I think my kids would really enjoy that. My kids have seen the videos. They also have seen the go-karts they have on some of the Norwegian ships.

I think my wife and I would like to give Celebrity a try. And we'd like to do a river cruise."

Ahnawake and Steve at one of the most beautiful places they have ever been, Geiranger Norway.

After 10 cruises, Steve has seemingly experienced enough cruise highlights and memories to last a lifetime. It helps that his very first cruise was to the Mediterranean. Beside disrupting the George Clooney wedding party, I ask Steve for a few highlights. "Oh man; there's so many good memories…" I could sense his hesitation to pick one great cruise over another. (All cruises are wonderful!) I suspect he was "fast forwarding" through scenes from various cruises in his head. I said, "Pick a single day. If I could write only about one experience you got the opportunity to realize on a cruise, what should it be?"

"In 2016, when we sailed to Norway on Disney *Magic*, the northernmost port we sailed to, Geiranger. Sailing along the coast of Norway—my mother's home country—and exploring the amazing coastal towns we stopped at. Sailing to the head of Geiranger Fjord—a UNESCO Heritage site—and visiting a small farm which sat above an adjacent fjord. We met this Norwegian farmer and his wife. They raised sheep but couldn't make a living on that alone so he also brewed beer and made cheese. So Ahnawake, my parents and I had some beer and cheese with him and while we were doing that the kids went with his wife. She had a business where she made metal stamps you ink and make impressions onto fabric; she sold these stamps all over the world. The kids each got a piece of fabric stamped and my mom made them into pillows when we got home. Just that whole day; the farmers, the beauty of this fjord, the beauty of the view from this farm. You walk out their door and you look out over the mountains and down into the fjords with the ocean and everything below you. Probably the most beautiful place I've ever been."

Not surprising given what I have come to learn about Steve, his lasting cruise memories mostly involve family. On a Disney *Wonder* cruise to Alaska Steve, Ahnawake, their sons and Steve's parents did a helicopter tour and landing on the Taku Glacier near Juneau, Alaska. A cherished memory from that same cruise is having dinner at Palo, Disney Cruise Line's adult exclusive restaurant with Steve's parents while *Wonder* sailed down the Gastineau Channel leaving Juneau. Another memory was on Steve's return to the Mediterranean on a Disney *Magic* cruise from Rome to Barcelona in 2018. "Exploring Pompei with my kids after they had studied about its demise in school. The history and magnitude of what happened there is indescribable."

DCL Podcast was launched in September 2016. *DCL Podcast* is described on its homepage as *a podcast which focuses on the history of, and travel with the Disney Cruise Line. While Disney Cruise Line is our home port, we also talk about new changes and opportunities which all travelers face when planning their next cruise vacation.*

DCL Podcast is now up to over 170 episodes. The vast majority of the shows are related to aspects of cruising with Disney Cruise Line (DCL), or land-based vacations at the various Disney-affiliated resorts and venues. *DCL Podcast* also covers topics of more general interest to DCL cruisers. For instance, DCL fans provided their impression of cruises they took on a different cruise line. I asked Steve to talk about the origin and growth of *DCL Podcast*.

"I think I looked at this as my chance to create something. As you can imagine, not everyone loves cruising, and not everyone loves Disney; but with the rise of podcasts, you can find ones that cover just about every topic imaginable. At the time we sailed to Alaska there were lots of Disney Podcasts, travel podcasts, but none that covered Disney Cruise Line exclusively. I saw a niche there. Here is something I was passionate about— cruising on Disney Cruise Lines; I'm not a writer like you, Paul, but I can talk. In my job I sit in the cockpit for hours at a time and I talk to another person. I was at a point as well, where I really wanted to do some different things on my layovers, so I began planning the *DCL Podcast*. Initially, I thought *DCL Podcast* would focus more on history of the places you can visit, and people's experiences there. I had no idea if anyone would want to listen, but I figured I'd give it a shot and see where it would go. Plus, it gave me an opportunity to talk about our experiences as we kept sailing with Disney Cruise Line and other lines."

DCL Podcast often hosts guests to talk about their Disney cruises, and Ahnawake has joined Steve on podcasts as well. Several months after starting up *DCL Podcast* gained a continuing co-host, Christy Pudyk. Christy, a travel agent and creator of *Pack Your Pixie Dust*—a family travel blog with a focus on Disney—was a guest on the fifth episode of *DCL Podcast* and shortly thereafter joined *DCL Podcast*.

"Almost right away Christy contacted me and wanted to add to the show. We had a good connection; we both loved Disney, vacationing in general, cruising, and in particular Disney Cruise Line. It's a lot easier, and to be honest, more fun to produce the show with someone else than it is by yourself. So I was pretty excited when she said she'd join me in producing the show. That was three years ago, and over 100 shows together later, we've had an amazing time connecting with other people who are passionate about Disney Cruise Line, and travel in general. Chris is our newest co-host. He's a funny guy, a millennial from the Los Angeles area. It has grown into the three of us now and we have a pretty good following. We've found people really enjoy coming on and reliving their amazing vacations. In some cases, they have spent years preparing and planning for these trips, so they've put a lot of heart and soul into them, and they're excited tell others about it. On the flip side, our listeners all enjoy hearing and learning from others' experiences, so maybe they can enhance their next cruise. Plus, in those long days between cruises, it's always fun to live vicariously through others' experiences. So that's what our podcast has really become—an outlet for our community of listeners to talk about, learn from, and dream about their next vacations."

DCL Podcast is also on Facebook, Twitter, and Instagram. They just started to establish a presence on You Tube. "I just got some new software where we can all go live at the same time. It's more informational right now. Hopefully in the future we can take some videos on the ships. We call our live show *Coffee at the Cove*. The Cove Café is what they call the coffee bar on all the Disney ships. It's kind of cool because you can interact with the audience in real time."

I asked Steve how the pandemic has affected *DCL Podcast.* "Not a lot. Even though there are no cruises to discuss, we have a lot to talk about. Our audience seems to appreciate it. They are stuck in their homes, and they let us know they just enjoy hearing us talk. We get a lot feedback like, 'Hey, we're just glad you guys keep putting something out each week. It provides a stress relief and keeps the world a little bit normal.'"

In addition to introducing the live show, *Coffee at the Cove*, I wondered if *DCL Podcast* is doing anything differently during this cruise lockdown. "So we had set aside three weeks for a cruise this year to Greece which got canceled due to the lockdown. I still had that block of vacation so we went over to Wyoming, and visited Yellowstone National Park and Grand Teton National Park, practicing social distancing of course. So we are changing the scope to talk about those kinds of alternative vacations—what people are doing now that they are not cruising that they didn't plan on doing, because that is what's available to them. The frequency of the show hasn't changed. We found that we still have a lot to talk about."

Steve with his family and parents on their helicopter tour
to the Talkeetna Glacier near Juneau.

Looking beyond the cruise lockdown, Steve has some ambitious cruise plans. Steve and Ahnawake would love to do a river cruise and visit the Christmas Markets in Austria and Germany, and to sail a small ship along the coast of Italy and Croatia. The two of them also want to cruise with friends to Asia, and around the coast of South America. For the family, take Andrew and Alex to the Baltic so they can experience the sights and cultures of Northern Europe.

When Steve is not busy with *DCL Podcast* he enjoys running and has competed in several marathons, including at Walt Disney World Marathon Weekends, most recently this year—a few weeks before the pandemic. Steve also enjoys playing soccer, skiing, paddle-boarding, hiking, and studying history.

"It's been a wonderful ride; we've met so many amazing people, people I probably never would have known, yet who have similar interests and passion. We've connected and supported each other through social media and on board the ships. At the end of the day, as much as I love exploring the world, it's really about sharing those experiences with the ones you love, and others. That is the true joy of cruising for me."

Tips for Travellers

Gary Bembridge, creator of *Tips For Travellers* was born and raised in Zimbabwe and has lived in the United Kingdom for 35 years. Gary's parents are from United Kingdom, his dad from England and mother from Scotland. Gary knew even as a kid he wanted to travel, and he had a strong interest in history. The idea of travel and seeing all the places he had read about always appealed to Gary. He particularly wanted to visit England and Scotland. Gary also had an intense interest in trains and planes. That foundation for travel, history, and discovery that Gary established early was life-forming for him. When he got older and went off to work, he joined a multinational firm, Johnson & Johnson, largely because of the potential for travel. That was the beginning of an amazing travel journey including traveling every month for over 25 years.

Gary started *Tips For Travellers* in 2005 as a hobby when he was traveling for work two to three weeks a month as Vice President Global Marketing for Johnson & Johnson Baby Products. Gary worked with Johnson & Johnson teams based in the United States, Asia and Europe and traveled extensively throughout Western and Eastern Europe, Asia, South America, North America and Australia. The name *Tips For Travellers* really captures what Gary provided back at the time when the blog started: tips on things to do in a day, or two days at a destination.

Gary in front of Azamara Pursuit, Kotor, Montenegro on a Venice to Athens Cruise.

"For example, in one week I might have a meeting in Singapore and then go on to Hong Kong for a meeting. So before I went on the business trip I would plan so I would be able to see things, but I always had limited time. So in advance I would research like crazy and go to places knowing exactly what I wanted to see. When podcasting came along I had this opportunity to share what I learned through my research about a location. I already had the content documented. And then a year or so later You Tube launched, so I started playing around with video. So that's really how *Tips For Travellers* started. I was going to all these very exciting places, and I had already generated great content in searching about these great places I was going to."

The self-described geek had the opportunity to meld his technological proficiency with his deep travel background and affinity for discovering about the places he visited. Gary and *Tips For Travellers* were well-positioned to capitalize on the near simultaneous explosion in the growth of podcasting and vlogging, the cruise industry, and social media.

Tips For Travellers early focus was on podcasts and You Tube videos about destinations Gary visited on business. Subsequently, Gary added a focus on cruise ships as he got more into cruising in his leisure travel. Gary notes that in those days there weren't many travel podcasts; he checked the travel podcast rankings and he was in the top five for something that was just a casual hobby. Clearly *Tips For Travellers* was starting to take off but Gary's posting frequency and regularity was erratic given his work responsibilities. Gary retired from Johnson & Johnson in 2013.

Once Gary retired he was able to focus his efforts more on *Tips For Travellers* and use his marketing skills to analyze and understand what consumers of *Tips For Travellers* wanted. He discovered that cruise content was the most popular and it was what Gary was most interested in doing. Gary also decided to focus on video as he enjoyed that, and from a business perspective he felt that such a strategy was where he could maximize revenue and the return on his time spent on *Tips For Travellers*. "I pivoted more and more to cruising, and to video. I found that when I would go on a trip, I would always do the video first, then the podcast, and then a blog post, because video was the thing I liked to do the most."

In recent years *Tips For Travellers* You Tube channel has realized impressive growth: 5,000 subscribers in 2016; 10,000 by the end 2017; 54,000 by the end of 2018; and over 110,000 by the end of 2019. Currently *Tips For Travellers* has roundly 155,000 subscribers. Views went from 135,000 a month in 2016 to average over 1.5 million a month in 2019 and almost double that in early 2020 prior to the cruise lockdown. Most of the *Tips For Travellers* viewers are 45+ and 30% over 60.

I asked Gary when *Tips For Travellers* became primarily focused on cruising. "I went on my first cruise in 2006, so I started posting cruise content beginning then, but it became very focused on cruising beginning in around 2012. I decided to retire early from work. I had always had the goal to retire at 55. Then, I got ill; I got cancer and had to have chemotherapy. So I had the opportunity to retire a little before 55. Once I completed chemo and was back well again, I decided to focus on cruising and to take many more cruises."

I asked Gary to talk about that first cruise in 2006. "It was P&O, the ship was *Aurora*. I was like a lot of people who had not cruised: cruising is not for me, it's boring, I like to go and see places, do my own thing."

I interrupted, "You sound like an improbable cruiser; why did you go?" Gary said, "As a Johnson & Johnson marketing executive I was asked to present at a marketing conference to be held on the ship. Every year a company called Richmond Events conducted business forums at various venues around the world, and they chartered P&O *Aurora* for the Richmond Marketing Forum UK. They bring a lot of marketing directors and marketing suppliers on board and they run kind of a conference. I got on the ship as a skeptic and then even as we started sailing out of Southampton, I thought 'This is amazing.' I could immediately understand the whole appeal of cruising."

So, as is the case with most people I speak to, not all, but far and away the majority of first time cruisers, Gary got hooked on his first cruise. Gary said, "Absolutely. I would say I got hooked, you know out of Southampton as we sailed down the Solent before we had even gotten to the ocean, I was enthralled. I had toured the ship a bit right after boarding, and was like 'wow, the ship's amazing; the cabins were amazing.' I was out on deck as we sailed out and thought, 'wow this is amazing.'"

Sound like Gary was quite…amazed! I can imagine what it was like for Gary standing on the deck as the port, cityscape, and seaside homes faded into the background—and so did seemingly all his worries and stresses back on land. I have heard so many similar sail-away anecdotes from so many first-time cruisers. I'll surmise that his first impression set Gary on the path to be what he is in the world of cruising today. I asked him how soon he cruised again. Real soon. He told me, "When I returned I immediately did two things: first I booked a mini-cruise for five weeks later—three nights on the same ship, *Aurora*—for me and my partner to go on so I could show him what cruising was like. And then on the assumption he would enjoy it as much as I did, I planned a longer, more substantial cruise. I said to my partner, 'If you like the cruise on *Aurora*, then we are going to book a *Queen Elizabeth 2* Transatlantic.'"

So Gary and his partner went on the short cruise on *Aurora* that summer, and then for Christmas cruised his dream trip from Southampton to New York on *Queen Elizabeth 2*. Quite a way to start a cruising career. Gary has now been on over 70 cruises on a variety of cruise lines. I ask him for his favorite cruise line and ship. Gary laughed, "The next one I am on. I'm going to answer your question more directly. I responded that way partly because it's the way I approach each cruise: every time I go on a cruise I like to try something new. I also think about what my audience is going to like. So I always like the choice that I make of every cruise even if it's not a cruise I chose necessarily for me. If I'm choosing as a cruiser, that is, for me, I personally like the small ships. I really like R-Class ships like Oceania has and Azamara has. The R-class ships were built originally for Renaissance Cruise line and then Renaissance went bust in the aftermath of 9/11. R-class holds about 700 passengers, so if I was going to pick a ship for me, I would tend toward a small ship. If I'm going with my partner, that would be on something like the *Queen Mary 2*. He really likes Cunard—the major production shows, big casino, lots of choice."

Gary has experienced a wide diversity of cruise ships and bucket list-worthy itineraries all over the world: the Mediterranean, Alaska, throughout the Caribbean, Japan and various parts of Asia, New Zealand and Australia, Hawaii, Arctic, Antarctica, Norwegian Fjords, Iceland, and River Cruises in Europe on the Danube and Rhine. I put him on the spot to name a standout. Among several, including Alaska and Antarctica cruises, he mentioned the partial segment of a World Cruise as a standout. In 2016, Gary sailed Cunard *Queen Victoria* for a seven-week, 24-destination segment of a World Cruise from Southampton to Sydney.

Gary on Holland America Line Nieuw Amsterdam in Glacier Bay on an
Alaska Inside Passage Cruise.

I mentioned to Gary that the US cruise market tends to focus more on the mega ships like the Royal Caribbean Oasis-class for example, and the new Celebrity Edge, NCL Encore, and the like versus the UK. I asked him what his experience with some of the more US-centric mega ships has been. "Yes I have experienced some. The only major cruise line I haven't been on is Carnival. I have wanted to because it's the biggest. I have been on Royal Caribbean but not the really big ones. I actually was scheduled to do that this year but of course it got canceled."

Speaking of 2020 cancellations, it wasn't entirely a lost year for Gary. Yes, he did miss out on some major cruises—Norway Northern Lights, *Queen Mary 2* Transatlantic Crossing, Croisi Europe Africa River Cruise just to name a few. Gary did get to squeeze in a couple of fantastic cruises before it was "cruising interrupted." In January, Gary went on a Mekong River Cruise with CroisiEurope on *Indochine II*. This was a luxurious, all-inclusive, culturally immersive cruise in a remote, rugged setting. "That was fantastic. I'd always wanted to do the Mekong River Cruise—it was on my bucket list. It was all that I expected it to be. I had been to Vietnam; I had never been to Cambodia. *Indochine II* was quite small; I think it held 62 people. On my cruise it was only about 50 on board. January is not the peak season; it's the dry season. A lot of people like to go in the rainy season because it is lusher. Also, the big lake, Tonlé Sap Lake, a massive lake which is at the very end, it is only full enough for ships to cross it in the rainy season. In the dry season it is too shallow to sail so you have to get off the ship and drive around it. The good thing about the dry season is it is not as busy so we only saw small fishing boats and the like. But you see no major river traffic. Conversely, when you do river cruises in Europe, the rivers are so busy, packed with other river cruising ships. So, on the Mekong River Cruise you feel like you are out in the middle of nowhere… because you are, except for the locals. It was an amazing experience."

As I listened to Gary when I interviewed him last summer, the imagery of his description of his CroisiEurope on *Indochine II* cruise down the Mekong River made it easy for me to visualize, and even to imagine myself doing something like that—not a cruise that I had ever given any thought. Weeks later as I was writing Gary's story, it occurred to me that perhaps there is an episode about this cruise on Gary's You Tube channel. I searched his channel and it turns out almost 14,000 people had seen "Mekong River Cruise: 4 Key Things You Really Need To Know!" before I did. I won't try to summarize the video here except to say it is easy to understand why Gary spoke about the Mekong River Cruise in such glowing terms. The predominant theme in the video's comments section was: "This cruise looks amazing…" (And it was just added to my own bucket list.) By the way, the Mekong River Cruise video is a great way to sample *Tips For Travellers* if you want to get a sense for the quality and depth and breadth of one of Gary's videos before you subscribe to his channel. It is easy to see why *Tips For Travellers* is the leading cruise channel on You Tube.

Gary mentioned he was fortunate to get in another cruise in 2020, right before the cruise lockdown. "Yes, in early March I went on Holland America *Zuiderdam*. They do a 10-night Caribbean and partial Panama Canal transit cruise. Actually we were on *Zuiderdam* when CLIA [Cruise Lines International Association, the principal cruise industry trade association] announced the suspension of all cruises. My first thought was that meant we were not going to be able to complete the cruise. I had gone on the trip mainly because I really wanted to traverse the Panama Canal, and we hadn't reached that part of the itinerary yet. We actually still did the Panama Canal and finished the cruise. But then the stressful part was that the US State Department announced that they would be stopping all EU and UK citizens from coming into the United States; the way it was reported in the media is that they were banning all flights. So now I'm worried I'm going to be stranded in Miami for 30 days or whatever after the cruise." In the end the flight ban was only on citizens coming into the US but not flights to Europe, and Gary got home as scheduled.

Despite these two cruises early in the year, the cruise lockdown caused Gary to miss out on an incredible slate of cruises for 2020—he originally booked 11 cruises total. Gary would have reached well over 80 cruises in total this year if not for the lockdown. He'll have to wait to 2021 to reach that milestone. One 2020 cruise that has not yet been canceled that Gary is hopeful for is a three-week November cruise to Antarctica on Ponant.

Looking beyond 2020 Gary would like to go on a full-world cruise after having done a seven-week leg of a world cruise. Depending on how all of the world opens, he tentatively plans to do the world cruise in 2022. I asked Gary what else is on his bucket list? "Besides a beach every Christmas? A Galapagos cruise is very high on my list. The other thing I have on my list is not destination-specific; two cruise lines I really want to cruise on are, Disney, and Regent Seven Seas."

Well I know the cruise lockdown has devastated Gary's booked cruises schedule. I wondered what the impact on *Tips For Travellers* has been.

"It has had a massive impact. The obvious one is you can't travel, so that limits the new content you can develop. That results in the views evaporating. In the last 12 months before the pandemic I was averaging one-and-a-half million views a month, and for December 2019 was up to 2.9 million. In March it was down like 90%! And also what started happening at that time is you had people going onto You Tube and attacking anyone posting anything related to cruising. Inevitably you get used to the odd troll on a cruise channel trolling you a bit, but it got really nasty. People being vicious about cruising and attacking you."

I told Gary I could relate to his comments about trolls. The comments section of online news articles about cruising at the height of the pandemic contributed to my struggles earlier in the year. I know I didn't have to read them; not only did I but I had to fight the urge to respond.

Are you doing anything different with your You Tube channel to adapt to the cruise lockdown? "I experimented a little bit with different things. First of all, I found that people who are interested in cruising mostly seem to want to watch content that is around updating them and telling them about what's going on. So what I started to do—and I never used to do—is general update videos. That kind of strays away from the general aim of the channels which is about *Tips For Travellers*. At least once a week I'll do an update: what's happening and what does it mean? The updates do very well. People will watch those and they like to get your perspective. What I am also doing—and what I don't want to become a channel around cruise news because that's not what I do—so I do a second video that's more general. I do two videos a week. What I find is that, knowing people are planning for maybe 2021, I am doing content that helps with those long-term plans such as what makes Celebrity different or what makes Oceania different. That kind of stuff to help people pick cruise lines and then things like videos on cabins, and very practical stuff around choosing a ship, choosing an itinerary. So I am focusing on topics that help people plan ahead. The third thing I have started to do which I haven't done because I used to travel so much and thus didn't have control on the reliability of the internet, is a weekly livestream where I answer travelers' cruise questions and I do a bit of an update then as well. I'm finding that has been quite good in terms of building community."

Gary noted that unlike his You Tube and blog traffic, his podcast audience has remained stable. He attributes that to the fact that listeners are more likely die hard cruise enthusiasts.

Gary on Silversea Silver Cloud in Antarctica.

I asked Gary what he thinks is the outlook on cruising in the relatively near future. He believes there will be increased appeal of small ships. He noted that some of these exotic itineraries we have been seeing in cruising are going to be scaled back initially, and there will be an increased emphasis on cruises close to the home country. "The people who had a really rough time at the height of the pandemic tended to be on ships far from the port of embarkation. I think a lot of itineraries we are used to that are multiple country are going to be a challenge. In the UK we can do single country cruises; the US is going to be difficult as you can't do single country cruises because of the Jones Act. [The Jones Act is a federal law that regulates maritime commerce in the United States and does not allow ships of Non-U.S registry to embark and debark guests at two different U.S ports, since travel between U.S. ports is prohibited on foreign flagged ships.] I think the re-start of cruising is going to be very patchy, slow, with niche itineraries, and you will see many fewer passengers who are new to cruising initially. I think it will eventually realign into much more of what we are used to."

Gary actually booked a cruised for this year—pending government approval—at the height of the pandemic! Scheduled for right about the time

Cruising Interrupted goes to print, it is a 5-night UK ports-only cruise exclusively for UK citizens on the just launched hybrid-powered expedition ship, Hurtigruten *Roald Amundsen*. Hurtigruten is a Norwegian cruise line that specializes in Antarctica expeditions and offers cruises around the Norwegian coast. (In September 2020 Tom Cruise chartered two Hurtigruten ships to serve as a floating hotel for cast and crew as they film the latest Mission Impossible movie in Norway at the height of the pandemic.) In June, Hurtigruten became the first ocean cruise line in the world to re-start cruising, with short Norway cruises restricted to Norwegian passengers similar to Gary's cruise that he booked for *Roald Amundsen*.

Postscript

Alas, Gary will have to wait a bit longer to resume cruising. Hurtigruten just suspended all cruises after a Covid-19 outbreak on a Norway cruise on the *Roald Amundsen*. For Gary, cruising interrupted…again.

Erin Foster, Author:
Unofficial Guide to the Disney Cruise Line

E rin Foster is the author of *The Unofficial Guide to the Disney Cruise Line.* Erin is a lifelong Disney fan, and has been writing professionally about Disney since 2008. She is a charter member of the official Walt Disney Parks Moms Panel (currently called planDisney), which began in 2008. Erin also wrote the Disney Food for Families column for the Disney Food Blog and she is now a regular contributor to the blog at TouringPlans.com, which also creates much of the content for a series of Disney-related guidebooks including: *The Unofficial Guide to Walt Disney World,* and *The Unofficial Guide to Disneyland,* and *The Unofficial Guide to the Disney Cruise Line.*

Despite being most readily associated with the *Unofficial Guide to the Disney Cruise Line,* Erin's expertise is all things Disney. "Disney World, Disney Cruise Line, Adventures By Disney—I've been to Disneyland a few times but I don't consider myself an expert on that, and some of the international parks. I've been to almost every Disney thing there is to do except Shanghai Disney and Tokyo Disney. I have Tokyo Disney booked for June of 2021, but fingers crossed that happens."

*Erin goofing around at the Animator's Palate dining room
on the Disney Dream.*

Erin lives in Westchester County, New York, just north of New York City with her husband Jeff. Erin is originally from Maine. She considers New York to be home as she has lived in the New York area for about 30 years. Erin and Jeff have three young adult daughters, Charlotte 24, and, 21-year old twins Josie and Louisa.

In *The Joy of Cruising*, I wrote about experiencing cruising vicariously through the passionate cruisers I wrote about. With Erin, not only is she a passionate cruiser, but is passionate about The Most Magical Place On Earth. Imagine how much fun that must be! I want to experience that vicariously through Erin.

Surprisingly, given all of her Disney-related passion and responsibilities, there is a lot more to Erin's interests and realm of knowledge than just Disney. Erin's main non-Disney related avocation is theater. In the good old days—before March 2020—Erin attended a New York City theater performance twice a week. No, that's not a typo. In fact, for the past several years, Erin saw virtually every play and musical on Broadway, as well as many off-Broadway, cabaret, and concert performances. While she is a passionate cruiser like most of us, she confides, "I'm even more sad about the pause in theater than I am in the pause in cruising."

Erin's love of theater meshes nicely with the Disney side of her life. Disney Cruise Lines is renowned for consistently producing stellar stage shows across its fleet. Several years ago when I introduced my grandchildren to cruising, I wanted their first cruise to be on Disney. Our cruise on *Disney Dream* was magical; the kids loved it and it launched a new passion for me—cruising with my grandchildren each year. But when I reflect on that cruise in discussions with others, what stands out among many positive recollections was the quality of the stage shows on the *Dream*. The professionalism and theatricality of the stage productions, to me, were stunning and beyond what I had seen on any cruise ship up to that point. Not that I am much of a judge; you can count the total number of Broadway shows I have ever attended using your fingers. Erin on the other hand sees the same number of Broadway shows that I have seen—in a month!

I assumed Erin's pastime might provide her a unique perspective from which to view the Disney Cruise Line shows. "Definitely the case. How do they create a different world with just the way the stage is set up; the way a shadow falls; or the way something echoes in the theater. So I'm pretty aware and observant of the technical capabilities in theater. That's obviously much more amplified on a moving ship. They have dancers do flips and stuff—on a moving ship! How do they execute that without having someone break an ankle? How do they have lights that don't crash to the floor when there is a wave? What are the technical machinations behind the scenes? I find that fascinating. And so, I'm pretty aware of that on a land-based stage, and to see how they overcome the challenges of doing that on a moving vessel is amazing."

Did you study theatre in college? I asked Erin. "I was an English major in college but my concentration was in theater criticism. And, I was very much involved in theater in high school." Erin attended Dartmouth College for her bachelor's degree and has master's degrees from the University of Texas at Austin in library and information science, and New York University in media studies. That academic background with a foundation in research, analysis, and media would turn out to be instrumental in the direction Erin's professional career would take, ultimately leading to her work regarding Disney.

Erin's transition to being a Disney expert was gradual and comprehensive. Early on in her professional career after a stint doing research for a major advertising agency, Erin spent several years as a work-at-home mom after having her first daughter. During that time, she conducted loads of research and planned great Disney World vacations for her family when her kids were young, and in the process became the go-to person in her neighborhood, and among her family and friends, for people wanting advice on planning trips to Walt Disney World. In 2007, Erin came across an opportunity to capitalize on the expertise she had developed regarding Disney World. Erin told me that Disney was one of the first large companies to delve significantly into social media, and in 2007 launched the Walt Disney World Moms Panel, which uses regular Disney fans to answer questions online from other guests. Disney did the first round of recruiting in late 2007, and the Walt Disney World Moms Panel was launched in January 2008.

Erin went to Disney World once as a child, and then several times as a young adult, and when her first daughter was a toddler, Erin wanted to introduce her to Disney. She told me, "I was in elementary school when Disney World opened. A lot of my friends' parents were taking them to the park and they would come back to school and tell me these incredible stories. I was fascinated, and remember thinking, 'How do you make a world?' I was totally sucked in by those stories, *The Wonderful World of Disney* on TV, the gorgeous commercials. I was so freaking jealous. I vowed, even as a 10-year old kid, when I grew up I would take my children to Disney World as often as possible."

"So, while I was staying home raising my daughter, I wanted to introduce her to Disney World, and we started going on Disney vacations. I had a research background and I started doing copious amounts of research on how to plan the best possible Disney vacation. The other moms in the neighborhood would tap my expertise. I was a go-to resource, and over coffee or lunch we would just talk for hours about how to plan a Disney trip. In 2007 Disney started the Disney parks Moms Panel, and I had basically been doing what the Moms Panel does on my own for several years. So I pursued it. To get the first round of panelists, Disney ran a competition. Several rounds of written questions and then phone interviews. I answered their questions, made it through the interviews, and of the more than 10,000 people who applied, I was one of the 12 who were selected."

"Over the years I have answered over 11,000 guest questions about literally every aspect of planning a Disney World vacation. Anything from 'my kids are afraid of bugs; my child has an allergy; what ride should I not go on; where should we stay; I am on a limited budget, what are some cost savings tips—really anything. Over time, I became more and more aware of things and enhanced my expertise and got quite adept at explaining how to do Disney."

Erin spent four years on the Walt Disney World Moms Panel—later called the Disney Parks Moms Panel, now called planDisney. During that time she developed connections and relationships throughout the Disney online community. A particularly pivotal relationship Erin developed was with Len Testa, founder of TouringPlans.com and co-author of *The Unofficial Guide to Walt Disney World*. Erin became a regular blogger for TouringPlans in 2011, writing over 800 blog posts, and doing fact-checking, research, and analysis. When I interviewed Erin, she was at the Magic Kingdom working on a TouringPlans project. Erin noted, "Len is also the co-author of the *Unofficial Guide to Walt Disney World*, which I believe is the largest selling travel guide in the world. In 2014, he wanted to start covering Disney Cruise Line—adding Disney cruise content to the TouringPlans website and creating the book *The Unofficial Guide to Disney Cruise Line*. He asked me if I would co-author. I was in a support role the first few years and for the past three years I've been the lead author."

The Unofficial Guide to the Disney Cruise Line by Erin Foster with Len Testa and Ritchey Halphen describes Disney's ships and itineraries, restaurants, children's activities, and *Castaway Cay*, Disney's private island.

Erin experienced The Great Wall of China with daughters Charlotte, Louisa, Josie, and husband Jeff.

Erin has sailed over 20 ocean cruises, all on Disney Cruise Line, and has done two river cruises on AmaWaterways through *Adventures by Disney*. Erin's first cruise was in 2003 on the Disney *Wonder,* a four-night Bahamas cruise stopping at Nassau and *Castaway Cay*, Disney Cruise Line's private island.

I asked Erin if anything in particular prompted her to go on a Disney cruise since she hadn't cruised before and had not yet begun working with the Walt Disney Parks Moms Panel. "We were just fans of Disney and were looking to do something different with our kids. At the time my twins were about three and my older daughter was six. Disney seemed like the logical place to start cruising." I asked if she had any apprehension leading up to her first cruise, like fear of seasickness, concern that she wouldn't like it, worry that it might be boring. Erin replied, "Honestly, I didn't love it. I wish that I had more apprehension about seasickness leading up to the cruise. I was very sick on my first cruise, like clutching the bed seasick. One of the reasons we chose a Disney cruise is because it had a great reputation for little kids. One of my daughters happened to be in a phase of separation anxiety. So, she would be clutching to my leg while I was seasick. She didn't want to go to the kids club and I hadn't considered that and brought any toys or other things for us to do, and I was not feeling well anyway. So, the first cruise was kind of a disaster. That's one of the reasons I didn't cruise again for eight years."

Who would have predicted—if you were a fly on the wall in that Disney cruise ship cabin observing this deathly seasick mom, dragging her toddler clamped around her leg—that years later that mom would be the author of *The Unofficial Guide to the Disney Cruise Line*. "Exactly. When I look back on it it's really actually pretty amusing. I didn't go on my second cruise until 2011. Had a much better time then and have been cruising regularly since."

I was curious about what prompted Erin to try cruising again given the unfortunate circumstances of the first one. "My husband really wanted to take the girls to Europe. They were still pretty young then, and he was trying to find a way to convince me to take the girls to Europe even though they were still fairly young. So, he figured out a Mediterranean cruise might be a way to do that. You can see different parts of Europe but not have to do the whole unpacking and moving hotels thing, and trains between different cities, and renting a car in a foreign country. He also dangled the promise of a trip to Disneyland Paris. So he basically bribed me to go on a second cruise. I did a lot of research about making the cruise go better. I spoke to my doctor and got the patch, which I ended up not needing after a bit. My kids were older and not in the separation anxiety phase. It was a great cruise, 11-days, we saw all these great ports in Europe, and we got to go to Disneyland Paris afterward. After that cruise I was hooked."

Erin has sailed each of Disney Cruise Line's four ships—Disney *Magic*, Disney *Wonder*, Disney *Dream*, Disney *Fantasy*—numerous times and done nearly every Disney Cruise Line itinerary in the Caribbean, Bahamas, Bermuda, Canada, Alaska, the Mediterranean, Baltics, and Northern Europe. There have been numerous highlights but St. Petersburg, Russia and visiting the Mendenhall Glacier in Alaska stand out. I asked Erin to compare and contrast the Disney Cruise Line's ships. "My personal favorite is the *Magic*. Mostly because it goes to destinations that I like—it goes to Europe, it goes to Canada, it goes to Bermuda. They're all beautiful but I like the two smaller ones, the *Magic* and the *Wonder*. Len, my co-author likes the *Fantasy* and *Dream* the best because they're bigger and there are more different things to do."

Having cruised so much but all on the Disney Cruise Line, I was curious about whether or not Erin would ever consider trying another cruise line. She told me she would; in fact, she would have experienced one this year if not for the cruise lockdown. "Yes, I actually had a plan to do that this summer. One of my friend's daughters had just gotten a job on Royal Caribbean as a dancer and I was about ready to book a Royal Caribbean cruise so I could see her dance. Obviously I do want to experience other lines, so I can compare and contrast. The other co-authors of *Unofficial Guide* have been on other lines so they have written the part of the book about how Disney Cruise Line compares to other cruise lines. So we do have that research, but I wanted to get that insight too. My Royal Caribbean cruise, and unfortunately, my friend's job are on hold."

Despite being an expert on Disney Cruise Line—well, Erin is an expert on all things Disney—her favorite aspect of Disney travel is actually *Adventures by Disney*. "These are luxury guided tours of sites around the world. We've been on 10 including Peru, Europe, and my favorite was China. It was two weeks in this huge country. Imagine someone coming to do two weeks in the US. Where would they go? China would have been a difficult trip to do on our own, but with the *Adventures by Disney* guides it was perfect. Through *Adventures by Disney* we did sort of a greatest hits of China—The Great Wall, a panda sanctuary, Shanghai, Hong Kong." A popular way of experiencing

Adventures by Disney is through a package with a Disney cruise. That's how Erin got to experience one of her most memorable vacations. "We went to St. Petersburg, Russia and we got a private tour in the Hermitage Museum."

Erin with husband Jeff, and twins Josie and Louisa in front of the Church of the Spilled Blood in St. Petersburg.

Erin missed out on three Disney cruises due to the lockdown and looks forward to rebooking once it is clear we will start cruising again. She is also looking forward to sailing the new Disney *Wish,* the first of three under-construction Disney Cruise Line ships. *Wish* was scheduled to launch in 2021 but due to the pandemic all three ships have been delayed, and the inaugural cruise for *Wish* is now slated for January 2022. Erin does have Tokyo Disney booked for June 2021. Hopefully, we will all be traveling by then. Beyond 2021, Erin's travel bucket list is to visit Australia and New Zealand.

The Unofficial Guide to the Disney Cruise Line has been published on an annual basis to ensure it reflects the most recent information given the continual updates to Disney itineraries, menus, shows, attractions, policies, etc. Erin and TouringPlans have skipped what would have been the 2021 edition given the pandemic. As a consequence of the cruise lockdown, *The Unofficial Guide* will require substantial updating, which can't be done until Erin is back on the cruise ships. So, when we see *The Unofficial Guide to the Disney Cruise Line 2022 Edition* is available to order, we know that cruising is back!

Section Six:
BLOGGERS:
CRUISE COMMUNITY CHAMPIONS

Cruise bloggers epitomize *The Joy of Cruising*; they are so passionate about cruising that they want to tell the world about it! In an interview with one of the bloggers in this section, she told me, "When I would hear people say, 'Oh I wouldn't like a cruise…' I just know they are not right. They would like it!…I want everyone to know how much fun a cruise can be." I recall smiling about the earnestness I heard in her voice as she told me that.

Cruise bloggers champion the cause of cruising to the legions of cruise fans in the world. And at the same time, they are champions to many of these fans: providing free, valuable information, reviews, videos, photos, and cruise tips to cruisers planning a voyage, and prospective cruisers contemplating, fantasizing about their first cruise. Cruise bloggers also provide an invaluable service to the cruise lines, as well as the industry at large, including ancillary services. Virtually every cruise blog—in addition to cruise line information— reviews and/or promotes businesses and ventures such as excursions, destination attractions, restaurants and shopping, port hotels and restaurants, even port parking facilities.

In a newspaper review of *The Joy of Cruising*, the reviewer referred to the devoted followers of the cruise bloggers that the book featured as "cruise news junkies." It was said in an endearing way, and now more than ever during this cruise lockdown, readers are hungry for cruise news, as they anticipate the day in the near future when they can cruise again.

Cruise bloggers meet the needs of cruisers, while benefitting the cruising industry. They uniquely serve the entire cruise community—driven principally by passion. Bloggers are *Cruise Community Champions.*

Life Well Cruised

Before *The Joy of Cruising*, Ilana Schattauer of *Life Well Cruised* captured my attention through her blog and social media posts with her thought-provoking and always fun posts. I found them very relatable as they often involved family cruising, a big part of my cruising life. Furthermore, I noticed Ilana was from Montreal. I have fond memories of Montreal from visits there with my daughter and grandkids when my son-in-law played in the Canadian Football League. *The Joy of Cruising* lacked a Canadian perspective, and I was intrigued about the "cruising community" in Canada. So, I wanted Ilana to speak for the entire country!

When putting together *The Joy of Cruising*, I lamented that the book lacked a cruising perspective from our neighbors up north to go along with cruisers featured from all over the US, as well as UK, Australia, and New Zealand. Turns out a passionate cruiser from Canada frequented the same Facebook cruise groups and other social media forums as I. Publicly, Ilana commented on many of the same posts that I did. Privately, Ilana and I tried but failed to connect for *The Joy of Cruising* due to an email ending up in spam! In the two years hence, Ilana has cruised several more times, composed dozens more blog posts, and grew her social media following of fervent cruise fans by tens of thousands. So now it is great to have her perspective for *Cruising Interrupted!*

Ilana on Crown Princess coming into St. Thomas in early 2020;
the calm before the storm about to rock the cruising world.

Ilana Schattauer was born and raised in Montreal, Quebec, Canada and con-tinues to live there. Ilana created *Life Well Cruised*, a cruise and travel blog that she started in 2018 to help both new and avid cruisers with cruise tips, cruise reviews and port guides, and cruising inspiration. Separate from *Life Well Cruised*, Ilana works as an Early Childhood Educator with children six months to pre-school. In addition to this, Ilana has worked as a part-time cruise consultant for a local travel agency for more than a decade. Although she brings her knowledge and experience gained to her blog, her work at the agency is not affiliated with *Life Well Cruised*.

Travel was always a significant part of Ilana's existence.

"I grew up in a family where traveling was highly valued; most childhood travels were road trips to visit with my grandparents in Florida every winter. When I graduated high school, my parents encouraged me to participate in the 'European Grad Tour,' a 21-day backpacking trip across five countries with about 50 other students. I then visited Jamaica with some friends in college, and always envisioned I'd travel more in the future."

Ilana married shortly after college, and after a land-based honeymoon in the Dominican Republic, traveling was set to the side as the young couple focused on building and maintaining a household and raising a family. However, just as her family did when she was growing up, Ilana and her young family loved getting away together as a family, and they embarked on road trips to Lake George, Mont Tremblant and Florida for the holidays, where her parents spend the winter.

These days, Ilana and family are confirmed cruisers. Ilana has been on a couple dozen cruises. I asked Ilana about other travel, and she emphatically told me she has no non-cruise plans at all! "Although, my one long-term non-cruise wish list travel is to visit Israel with my husband."

Ilana's first cruise was in 2004 on Royal Caribbean *Navigator of the Seas* with her husband, Frank, as a celebration of their 10th anniversary. As often is the case with that first exposure to cruising, Ilana was swept off her feet by the experience— especially with a ship like *Navigator*, perhaps the world's premier ship in 2004.

"It was an amazing cruise on the *Navigator of the Seas*, which at that time was a truly incredible cruise ship: three pools, several hot tubs, mini-golf, a rock-climbing wall, and an ice skating rink!"

Ilana's great introduction to cruising wasn't without drama though. Most of us know the majority of first-time cruisers become addicted after that first cruise, or at least develop a strong urge to cruise again. Once in awhile something gets in the way on that first cruise that delays that feeling of passion for cruising—seasickness, misunderstandings of policies such as tipping, issues causing you to have to skip a port, etc. How about extreme weather? 2004 has come to be known as "The Year of the Hurricane," and Ilana's cruise was scheduled for the height of hurricane season. Ominously, shortly before departure for their first cruise, they were advised their Western Caribbean cruise might be diverted into an Eastern Caribbean cruise.

Hurricane Frances' 105-mile per hour winds slammed into Florida Saturday, September 4, 2004. Ilana and Frank's embarkation day originally scheduled for the 4th was postponed a couple of days. Royal Caribbean offered customers the opportunity to cancel.

"Nope!" Ilana exclaimed emphatically.

The threat of a hurricane was no match for Ilana and her husband's euphoric anticipation of their first cruise. Departure was set for Monday, and the seven-day anniversary cruise became a five-day cruise. No matter!

"This cruise was more than we thought it would be. We loved the dining, the shows, meeting people onboard, and the feeling of being at sea. By sail-away we felt at home, like this is where we were meant to be."

Wow, the process of Ilana and Frank getting hooked on that first cruise had already set in before experiencing any shows, non-stop food, and tropical destinations.

"The way we felt on that first cruise was that when we sailed away from the shore, it was almost like a physical sensation of leaving those stresses behind on land. Feeling like almost a sense of being lighter and worry-free. Physically sailing away from the shore, we knew already that we were probably going to do this again." And of course, the rest was history. After that first cruise Ilana was hooked!

Notwithstanding the unsettling circumstances, that first cruise left such a positive impression on Ilana and her husband that they wanted to turn their sons on to cruising as soon as possible. So, less than a year later they did a family cruise, also on Royal Caribbean, this time on *Voyager of the Seas* on a nine-day cruise to the Caribbean. No surprise, Ilana's sons, Julian, at the time nine years-old and Ethan, four, immediately took to cruising—they really loved the kids club, Adventure Ocean, and all the food and ice cream available—and a new family pastime was established. After another cruise in quick succession, this one also on Royal Caribbean—a multi-generational cruise with the kid's grandparents on *Mariner of the Seas*—Ilana, long past hooked, lamented:

"We didn't have large amounts left over to cruise as much as we would have wanted; how could I do this more?"

Ilana got her break shortly thereafter; one that enabled her to gain a foot-hold in the cruise travel world and really was the forerunner to *Life Well Cruised*.

"In 2006, a cruise travel agency was opening an office in my neighbor-hood and looking for part-time sales and office support. I thought I would work part-time, learn and help others with their cruise vacation plans, and earn some extra money and travel perks to cruise more often. It was a reputable agency and one that I had personal experience with—it was the agency we had booked our first two cruises with. I really respected the company and the family that owns it. It just seemed meant to be. So I applied to work part-time, get some training, and have some fun, be around cruising."

In 2018, Ilana used some of the insight she had gained through working at the agency, and launched *Life Well Cruised*. She was spurred to move forward on her plans mainly due to researching a return to her dream destination—a Mediterranean cruise.

"I was on the Internet and I kept coming across other people's blogs discussing their Mediterranean cruise. After reading a few of them I thought 'I think I could do that.' Just the idea of being creative, writing—I didn't really know what it would entail. It was a lot more work than I expected but in a good way. I am just super happy and grateful with the growth—to have just started *Life Well Cruised* in March 2018 and now *Lifewellcruised.com* serves over 100,000 monthly readers and has over 250,000 monthly page views. For a website of just one writer, for me, it's a good amount. I'm happy with it and just hope to continue to grow it. I would like to incorporate some guest posts. I'm well represented on social media. I focus a lot on Facebook; I find it so engaging and it's a great place to grow a community."

Life Well Cruised added a YouTube channel to its offering mid-2019. "Some people like to consume their content by reading blogs or listening to podcasts, and others like to consume content by watching it." Ilana said. With the lockdown Ilana is unable to create cruise vlogs and cruise tip videos, but has been creating informative videos regarding cruise industry updates, and positive news stories. Ilana says, "Despite the situation, viewership is up and our audience is growing."

Ilana and *Life Well Cruised* is very active in the cruise community. Ilana has done guest blogs for several top cruise bloggers as well as being a guest on some cruise podcasts. She also has been featured by Superstar Blogging, an online travel blogging community. Ilana has been recognized as one of the top 25 cruise bloggers.

In addition to Royal Caribbean, Ilana has cruised with Princess, Celebrity, Norwegian, and Carnival. Her favorite destination is Bermuda; she has cruised there seven times! Ilana is also particularly fond of the Dutch Caribbean, especially Curacao. Of several memorable cruise experiences, I was excited to hear about Ilana's biggest memory: her Mediterranean cruise, given my own Mediterranean cruise booked for November.

"Our Mediterranean cruise five years ago was a huge highlight for us! There's something about the sights, culture, food and wine that makes it so memorable, and I really want to return. The cruise was to celebrate our 20th anniversary, and has always been my dream since we started cruising. We cruised on Royal Caribbean *Serenade of the Seas*. We chose which Med cruise to go on based on the itinerary. It left out of Barcelona with stops in Cannes, France, Ephesus which is in Turkey, Santorini and Athens, Greece, and Italy—Florence, Rome, Salerno. We were in the car talking about it and Ethan, who was about 14, was listening to Frank and me, and said 'those are all the places I learn about in history.' We knew he would enjoy the cruise so even though it was initially a cruise for Frank and me, Ethan accompanied us."

Frank, Ilana, and Ethan at embarkation for their 2017
New Year's Eve cruise to Aruba, Bonair, and Curacao.

Ilana is one of those passionate cruisers fortunate enough to experience the ocean in 2020 before the pandemic locked all cruising down. In January when the virus was a distant threat not even in the cruising community's consciousness, Ilana and family cruised to the Southern Caribbean. Their 10-day, six island cruise on Princess Cruise Line *Crown Princess*—their fourth time on *Crown Princess* having first sailed her in 2007—had an itinerary that included taking them to visit several islands new to them that have been on their wish-list for many years: St. Lucia, Barbados, Antigua and St. Kitts. It was a wonderful trip but due to a combination of mechanical problems and uncooperative weather, they were only able to stop at half of the destinations.

"St. Thomas was as beautiful as ever. We had an amazing day at Megan's Bay Beach with new cruise friends. The highlight of our trip was St. Lucia. St. Lucia was breathtakingly beautiful from every vantage point. Plus, it was a lot of fun! We went to the mud baths and Touraille waterfalls followed by The Beacon, which was the most amazing view you could imagine."

"We had a great cruise; however, due to circumstances with the ship's generator and seas which were unusually rough, we weren't able to make it to all cruise ports. Of six scheduled ports, we only stopped at three. Princess did offer a gesture to all passengers of 35% of the cruise fare as a future cruise credit which was very appreciated. Of course, we are cruise planning and hope to visit the Southern Caribbean islands again!"

I asked Ilana about her travel bucket list. "You've done a Mediterranean cruise and you had an Alaskan cruise booked for this summer that was cancelled by the cruise lockdown. That's two from my bucket list. What's on yours?" I asked. Without hesitation she told me the Mediterranean again.

"High on the list is getting back to the Med and visiting Venice, Croatia, Kotor and the Greek Isles. Even though I've been to Italy, I've never been to Venice and that is a dream!"

Not surprisingly given what I hear from more and more big ocean liner cruisers, Ilana is looking to try a downsized cruise experience.

"I'd love to cruise with a small ship, perhaps Azamara, in the Mediterranean region, to be able to dock and experience the smaller ports, and stay and visit longer each day. I'd also like to take a river cruise along the Danube. I would love to take a Canada/New England Cruise as well."

Ilana's ultimate bucket list travel? "One day, a world cruise would be an awesome experience! In terms of non-cruise travel, I'm just not that drawn to travel where cruising is not part of the trip. There are some places. The one non-cruise trip we would like to take, hopefully in the next five years is to visit Israel. Other than that, there are a few destinations that I may want to travel to that I would hope to be able to combine with a cruise. For example, perhaps Paris, but I would want to combine it with a river cruise in France."

I wondered how *Life Well Cruised* was faring during the cruise lockdown. From my perspective, as mentioned in the introduction to *The Bloggers*, Ilana was instrumental in buoying my spirits during that period of the lockdown when I despaired about not only that there would be no follow-up to *The Joy of Cruising*, but there was even some concern about whether cruising itself would survive. "For you personally Ilana, as well from the standpoint of *Life Well Cruised*, how has the pandemic affected you?"

"Like for everybody it's definitely had an effect. A lot of the way I earn a living from *Life Well Cruised* is by people reading the articles. *Life Well Cruised* is a passion of mine, but it is also monetized, so it's also a business, and definitely when people are researching less, obviously that impacts me monetarily. Disappointing because *Life Well Cruised* was really growing—and I still expect it to grow—but this virus definitely has put a damper on cruising and people coming to the Internet for information about cruising."

Good morning from Celebrity Summit.

I had assumed that cruisers would flock to bloggers and vloggers and communicators like *Life Well Cruised* in order to fill the void, their unfulfilled need to go on a cruise, and forums like *Life Well Cruised* were the next best thing—obviously I was wrong.

"I think that could be true on social media." Ilana said. "In my case, I really enjoy all of the conversations I have with people online. I do find there is really a sense of community among people who wish they could be cruising and want to talk about cruising. But it's the research that's not there. That affects ad revenue and other income—there is a certain amount of income bloggers make as a result of selling cruise-related merchandise. So when people are not preparing for a cruise, not packing, then there is a negative impact. Similarly, with YouTube, I have heard from other vloggers that the content people would normally look at, which gets a lot of views, is down so that affects advertising income. It's not surprising. I'm not even complaining. The least of anyone's concern is how much a cruise blogger is making, but it is a side business so there definitely has been an impact."

I told Ilana, "Well you certainly seem to be holding up well spirit-wise, emotionally, during this time. I get a lot of comfort, solace from your site and your posts and your community on social media. It doesn't show that you have been negatively impacted, so I am appreciative that you are able to maintain enthusiasm and lift the spirits of your followers."

"Well you know what it is—thank you by the way—I know I am not the only one whose business is affected; in my case it's a side business. I'm disappointed that we lost some momentum that *Life Well Cruised* and the YouTube channel had. With Covid happening that really slowed that down temporarily, but I can't really get upset about it—businesses have ups and downs. That being said, I do really love the community of cruisers online. People still do chat and engage about cruising and travel and I don't think that's going away.

I asked Ilana if there is anything *Life Well Cruised* is doing differently to adapt to the cruise lockdown. "Are you doing more informative type things?" I asked.

"Yes I am. I don't consider myself a cruise news blog, and doing this part-time I don't write daily, so I just wouldn't have the time to be a news blog. Though I'm not a cruise news site, at a certain point you have to consider what the community needs. People were asking these questions so a lot of the *Life Well*

Cruised posts are trying to answer some of those. I do try to provide updates with a little bit of my own perspective because it's a blog, not a news channel.

I asked Ilana about the future, both concerning her view on the prospects for cruising, as well as for *Life Well Cruised*.

"I am hopeful that the situation with the virus doesn't continue so much longer that there is a protracted delay for cruising. The reality is that for any business, if they are not able to get back to operating in some way, that financially has to be very difficult. I do hope there is a way they can get back to cruising even with some temporary limitations or modifications—the same way Las Vegas is getting back to welcoming guests, and theme parks and resorts are getting back to welcoming guests. Outside of that, I actually think that once this is over—and I think it might take a year—I think we are going to be looking at a better product. Cruises are amazing but there were some things on cruise ships—I don't want to say they were bad, but with everything that has happened it does give the industry a chance to make things better. So far for instance, we have heard from Norwegian Cruise Line and they have talked about changing their air filtration system; I have heard with other cruise lines there are things being talked about in a similar regard. I think there will be an increased sensitivity to hygiene. There will be full-serve buffets instead of passengers serving themselves and perhaps coming in contact with the food. Will they ever get back to a self-serve buffet? Maybe they will. There are different ways to do that; you can have small platters that are already prepared. We do see that sometimes at some of the smaller eating establishments on cruise ships now. Right now we have to be hyper-vigilant, but maybe we will have a balance and be able to relax a little on some of the restrictions, but we'll always keep a focus on hygiene."

"I just hope I will continue to grow the *Life Well Cruised* brand. It's not really about me living a *Life Well Cruised*; people love to talk about their travels and their cruises and what it means to them. To me, it's a platform for other people; to be able to feel like they are living their best life while cruising—whether they cruise many times a year, once a year or once every couple years, cruising with kids, cruising to exotic destinations. I like to be able to have that venue for people."

Oh, by the way, that lost email that caused us to miss the manuscript deadline for *The Joy of Cruising* surfaced two years later in the course of our interviews! Ilana and I got a laugh out of that, and I am glad she has joined me for the journey that is *Cruising Interrupted!*

Cruise Mummy

Cruise Mummy is Jenni Fielding, who lives in Bolton, England with her husband Matt and their two children, five-year old Leonie, and Adam, three. Jenni works in the cruise industry in marketing. She is a manager for World Travel Holdings UK, a leading UK cruise company, managing search engine optimization for their subsidiaries: Cruise 118 (mainstream cruises), Six Star Cruises (ultra-luxury cruises), and, River Voyages (river cruises).

Jenni and family in Cartagena, Spain with P&O Britannia in the background.

Other than cruising Jenni enjoys going to the gym and walking with and enjoying days out with her children, and walks with her extended family including their two dogs.

In May 2019 Jenni introduced the blog *Cruise Mummy*. The name was a take-off on her Instagram account name which was, MummyMummyMummy, so named after a refrain Jenni hears incessantly from Leonie and Adam (trust me, during our interview Jenni gave me a sample of what 'mummy, mummy, mummy' sounds like coming from her kids). Maybe for the audiobook.....

Jenni was well-prepared for the technical aspects of maintaining and growing her blog. She was a social media manager for many years and initially handled social media for her current employer until switching to focusing on Search Engine Optimization (SEO). SEO involves maximizing the visitors to a company's website due to high placement on the list of search engine results.

"I didn't want to lose that skill because social media changes over time. I had invested so much in learning how to do it well. Just to keep a hand in, have a reason to stay abreast of social media and keep up-to-date with it. And it is something that I enjoy doing."

I asked about her goals with *Cruise Mummy*: Is it to educate; make money? Is it just a hobby, passion? Or all of the above.

"Jenni said, "My main goal is to educate people and share my love of cruising with other people; get more people involved with it because I know how good it can be. I also do some small freelance work which is mostly SEO and copywriting. Part of my freelancing is I write articles for other people's travel blogs. I absolutely love doing that and it doesn't feel like work and it's great to get paid for doing that. But at the same time I am thinking, 'I've got a travel blog and ghostwriting for someone else is a bit silly; I should be writing it for my own blog.' At the same time though, that's cash right away, which I need, while writing for your own is more of delayed gratification. I have got a plan in place over the next year—and I'll definitely get there with the way *Cruise Mummy* is growing—and I'll be able to do what I am doing now but exclusively for myself instead of other people."

I asked Jenni to talk about how the *Cruise Mummy* blog came about.

"I fell in love with cruising and ended up in the cruise industry. I love to talk to people about cruising. When I would hear people say, 'Oh I wouldn't like a cruise; oh, I can't afford it; oh, I don't think the kids would like it.' And I just know they are not right. They would like it, and they can afford it—it's not as expensive as they think—and the kids would have a great time! I don't want anyone to miss out. I want everyone to know how much fun a cruise can be. Rather than speak to people one-to-one, and saying oh no you would like a cruise, I decided I'll start a blog and use social media and I'll spread the word about cruising that way. And I have had people send me messages and they'll say, 'I never thought of a cruise and I've come across you online and now I am going to book one.' Or people say, 'Thank you, I've taken my first cruise and I absolutely loved it...you have been an inspiration!' That's what I want to do; I don't want people to miss out on thinking they wouldn't like something that is so much fun."

I said, "That's wonderful. It sounds like you take it as a challenge to correct some misconceptions about cruising."

"Yes, that's it. I have never known anyone who said, 'Oh, I went on a cruise and I didn't like it.' If they did, it's because they went on the wrong ship for them. After all, they didn't have the help to pick the right one for them. So that's again something I can help people with."

Besides the positive feedback Jenni has received from readers of the blog, *Cruise Mummy* has been quoted in *USA Today*, and *Reader's Digest*. Also, *Cruise Mummy* has done a number of guest posts on other cruise blogs.

Jenni was influenced to travel at a young age. She grew up having been exposed to travel frequently with her family. "We used to do quite a lot of traveling. My parents were into traveling. So we would often go abroad to countries like Spain, Greece, and Turkey and just have normal holidays like that. And we had a caravan as well, you know like what you tow behind the car, like a motorhome. So we'd often be going around UK; we'd drive to France in it. I think when I was around three, we drove to Yugoslavia. So yes, we were always traveling. I always loved to be away. It was nice to have trips to look forward to."

Jenni's introduction to travel as an adult began right after completing her studies in psychology in London. Straight after university at University College London, Jenni spent a month in Fiji, backpacking around the islands. She then lived mainly in Sydney, Australia for a couple of years, and spent some in Thailand. Jenni says this absolutely influenced her decision to pursue travel as a profession.

Jenni's entrée to the travel profession was in 2008 when she joined an online travel accommodation directory as an SEO specialist. In 2015 Jenni got the opportunity to move into the cruising aspect of the travel industry when she became SEO manager for World Travel Holdings (UK) Ltd.

The timing of the opportunity at World Travel Holdings was perfect given Jenni's newfound passion for cruising. In 2013, Jenni experienced her first cruise. Jenni and Matt did a seven-night Caribbean cruise on Royal Caribbean *Allure of the Seas* for their honeymoon. Matt had cruised once before with his family when he was a teen on P&O *Oriana*, a small, older ship a fraction of the size of *Allure*. This was quite an introduction to cruising for Jenni: *Allure* was the largest ship in the world at the time, introduced as a successor to that crown as the slightly larger sister ship—two inches longer—to the game-changing *Oasis of the Seas* introduced a year earlier.

I asked Jenni what was behind their choosing the largest ship in the world for her first cruise.

"We got married in the same year we got engaged, and left for the honeymoon immediately after the wedding, so we didn't really do much planning for the cruise. We booked the cruise really quickly in the midst of planning the wedding and so we didn't give much thought to it. I don't even know where the idea to cruise came from. I thought, 'Should we do a cruise? Yes that sounds good, let's just book one then.' So, we booked it and didn't think about it anymore. After the wedding we get to Miami, and I had never even seen a cruise ship before. And we saw the ship and were like, wow!"

Jenni's first exposure to cruising left quite an impression on her.

"My honeymoon was the best cruise I've had. I'd never even seen a cruise ship before when we got on the biggest cruise ship in the world—which we didn't even know when we boarded!"

Jenni hadn't researched the ship at all.

"We didn't have time because of the wedding. When we boarded, we didn't have a clue what to expect from the ship or about cruising. We just got lost constantly for the first couple of days. Our neighbor in the cabin next door, this older lady, noticed our confusion. She said, 'this is your first cruise?' I said yes. She said, 'I've been on 57 cruises. You ruined it, you ruined it.' I said, what do you mean we ruined it? She said, 'You got on the best cruise ship first!'"

"We loved our week on *Allure,* and then after the cruise we hired a car for another week and drove down to the Florida Keys all the way down to Key West and then back to Miami."

After their honeymoon on *Allure,* Jenni and Matt were hooked. As many of us know, your first cruise is likely to do that; but when you are on a Royal Caribbean Oasis-class ship with its botanical marvel Central Park aft, and fore, there's the Boardwalk, which replicates a beachfront carnival vibe complete with a carousel, you are likely to get amazed, and that was the case for Jenni.

I asked her what in particular about her first cruise was so special for her.

"Everything about it. We just loved how relaxing it is. You could be sitting on your lounger and the waiter comes by with a tray of cocktails: 'Medication for your vacation!' Little things like that were throughout the cruise. The staff can't do enough for you. They're all just so friendly and willing to help. It's just the best service ever. We never experienced anything like that staying in a hotel."

Cruise Mummy in front of Brittania in Monaco.

Jenni and Matt loved their introduction to cruising so much that within weeks of getting home they booked another Caribbean cruise for six months later when Jenni was pregnant with their first child.

"We wanted another cruise while it was just the two of us, as we knew that for the next 20 years, we would have to take the kids! We went to the Caribbean again. Also, we wanted to experience New York City, so we spent a few days in New York after the cruise. We had never been to New York and I don't think that is something you can do with young kids, a lot of walking. We cruised on the Norwegian *Breakaway.*"

NCL Breakaway was launched April 2013.

"Even on that second cruise I didn't do much research. I really liked *Allure;* let's try a different ship. So I googled 'best ship in the world,' and a list of cruise ships came up and it said number one Norwegian *Breakaway,* so okay let's book that one," Jenni laughed. "I really didn't do much research. I compare that to these days when I research a cruise. So many hours goes into thinking about it, researching, planning a cruise. But back then it was like, okay, let's do this one quick before we have a baby!"

Six months after the cruise on NCL *Breakaway*, Leonie was born. While on maternity leave, and having a serious case of cruising envy, Jenni made her move to become a part of the industry she had so quickly become enamored with.

"I sent an email to the managing director of a local cruise travel agency, begging for a job because I loved cruising so much. An hour after sending it I was in his office being offered a job."

In addition to Royal Caribbean and NCL, Jennie has sailed P&O Cruises, and on MSC Cruises *Preziosa* with its stone piazza and Swarovski crystal staircases. Besides the cruise lines that Jenni and her family have cruised, she has taken tours of tours on numerous cruise ships on day visits with World Travel Holdings. That sounded like it might be fun. I asked Jenni to talk about it.

"It's really what everyone in the business gets to do. It's educational and will help you do your job, particularly salespeople. It's a good way to see ships I would never get to book myself, the more luxury ones like Silversea, Azamara, those kinds of cruise lines. It's nice to go and have a look around and see how the other half lives. It's usually in a port not too far away from where we are in the UK. Liverpool is the nearest port to me, which is about an hour away. So, when a cruise ports at Liverpool, when all the passengers get off around 10 you get on when the ship is quiet. They give you a good tour of the ship and tell you about it. There's a nice selection of food and drink. You might watch a video and then normally you head to the main dining room so you can experience the full three courses. Then you have a bit more time to go and film the ship and take photos, and then we get off. It's always a fun day. I love touring a ship like that."

I thought it sounded like fun!

When I spoke with Jenni early in 2020, the *Cruise Mummy* blog was poised to generate great content and Jenni and family were slated for an exciting year of cruising. Jenni's ambitious schedule of booked cruises was started with an overnight stay on the exciting new Virgin Voyages *Scarlet Lady* while docked in Liverpool. Other cruises Jenni had booked for 2020 were MSC *Splendida* in March, Cruise & Maritime Voyages *Magellan* in June, Royal Caribbean *Anthem of the Seas* in August, P&O Cruises *Iona* in November. After a much needed break, Jenni has P&O *Ventura* in March 2021.

I said to Jenni, "Wow, that's a lot of cruises for this year."

She laughed. "Because I work in cruising, I have cruise websites in front of me all day, so there's always a temptation to book. At one point I had eight cruises booked; my mum said, 'Come on now Jenni, this is getting silly.' I reminded her that she had five cruises booked! She had only cruised once but I'd influenced her to book five more. I give a large chunk of my wages back to my employer. As my salary goes into my bank account, the cruise payments come out! Luckily, my husband loves cruises as much as I do so he's okay with it!"

Of course, Jenni shared her big cruising plans for 2020 with me before we had any inkling about the pandemic. Little did she know the disappointment that lay ahead. In that same discussion back at the beginning of 2020 she told me:

"I've been pretty unlucky. In the late 2019 I've had two cruises canceled! The first was a Bahamas cruise on Royal Caribbean *Navigator of the Seas* in September. I booked it for travel right in the middle of hurricane season, with departure on the day statistically most likely to get a hurricane! Hurricane Dorian arrived and my cruise was canceled. Then on Friday the 13th in December I was booked for P&O *Ventura* but the ship broke down so that was canceled too!"

Unfortunately, Covid-19 extended Jenni's cancellation streak to six cruises in a row! But that disappointment certainly hasn't dampened Jenni's enthusiasm. She is hopeful for *Iona* in November of this year and is looking forward to *Ventura* in March 2021, and *Anthem*, now scheduled for May 2021.

In terms of her cruising bucket list, Jenni states, "I definitely want to do a transatlantic cruise. It's very much about the ship for me; I get more excited about the ships than the destinations when I cruise. Destinations are often very nice but they don't really inspire me to choose a cruise; I'm pretty much going to choose it for the ship. And I love sea days; I'd skip ports to stay on the ship."

Cruise Mummy with Mariner of the Seas in Nassau.

When I asked Jenni about her non-cruising travel plans. She emphatically said:

"None! If it's not a cruise, I'm not coming! Cruises take up all my annual leave, so aside from weekend breaks in cottages with friends, I don't go anywhere else." Jenni did note that she has a bucket-list aspiration to take her kids to Disney World in Florida when they're older, but is quick to point out, "We will combine it with a cruise."

My Virtual Vacations

My Virtual Vacations was created six years ago by Alyson Nachman. Its aim initially was to serve as an information source for Alyson's many friends and family who often contacted her to tap her expertise about what to expect on cruises: booking advice, best stateroom location, favorite destinations and the like. Alyson had done a fair amount of traveling including several cruises with husband, Joel, and two adolescent sons, and had become somewhat of a source of travel advice. After taking a few cruises and falling in love with the idea of cruising, Alyson was excited to share her newfound passion in every conversation she could.

"My friends and family started calling me and asking me questions about booking cruises. As I dug through my mementos to share with them, I realized what a collector I was: photos of ships, destinations, and food; every activity guide, menu, excursion brochure. That's when I decided to put together all my information as a reference source for people to visit. *My Virtual Vacations, www.myvirtualvacations.net*, was born! Through my experiences, I share tips for cruising with kids, specific details of what you can expect, and my passion for cruising in a bit more of a luxury style."

Alyson with a friend in Skagway, Alaska

It helped to have a resource and partner like Joel who is a professional photographer that likes to photograph food, destinations, and accommodations. Alyson chose the name *My Virtual Vacations* because she said she likes to virtually reflect back on experiences and images of all of her travels. She originally considered focusing exclusively on cruising.

"I'm glad I didn't. Even though *My Virtual Vacations* does focus more on cruising, we have taken a number of land vacations; and, we do vacation before and after cruises. I'm a big pre-cruise and post-cruise kind of person; not that they are huge vacations but at least arrive ahead of time, and perhaps experience the beach and a little of hotel and resort life. A person might read about that part on *My Virtual Vacations* and think 'I'm not really a cruise enthusiast but this sounds like a great place to stay at the beach for several days.' So I can have that in *My Virtual Vacations* and without focusing solely on cruising it is not so limiting."

I point out to Alyson, that was kind of my thinking in calling this book *More Joy* instead of *More Joy of Cruising* as it was tentatively titled when I first approached her. A subtle change but similar to Alyson's thinking around the title of her blog—many features transcend cruising and *More Joy* is for anyone who just loves travel. Alyson responded, "Well I love *More Joy* because Joy is my middle name!"

I told Alyson I may find a way to mention that…and I just did!

Even before blogging emerged in the early 2000's, Alyson was finding ways to catalogue, organize, and share her travel memorabilia; she was into scrapbooking.

"I'm a saver; I save everything related to my trips I can get my hands on. I made scrapbooks of everything. I did photobooks; I used Snapfish [web-based photo sharing service] for a lot of my albums. I have always been into piecing everything together." So, *My Virtual Vacations* really was just a logical progression for Alyson.

Alyson lives with her family in Baltimore, Maryland. Though she grew up in Los Angeles, Alyson was drawn to the east coast by Goucher College in Towson, Maryland where she studied business management. Alyson has been in the area ever since, working out of her home office doing human resources work for a global company. Her work keeps her busy and helps pay the bills, but to satisfy her creative side and interest in travel Alyson has cultivated *My Virtual Vacations* into a hobby and passion.

Alyson enjoys a mix of cruising and land-based travel—as long as it involves the beach.

"I am a beach person! We visit Florida often and we enjoy staying on or very close to the beach in upscale hotels or resorts. With two very active boys, we've discovered that staying in resorts gives us the options and opportunities we want on vacation."

With respect to non-cruising travel, Alyson's most memorable trip was traveling to Sedona, Arizona a few summers ago; her family loved that experience.

"It was a bit more adventurous than we usually do; with their famous Pink Jeep Tour—but it was so beautiful, and I would absolutely go back to the red rocks."

In terms of prospective land-based travel, Alyson notes she has not been to an all-inclusive resort in the Caribbean and would love to do one with the family. Not surprised. (All-inclusives have a natural affinity with cruising—as mentioned in *The Joy of Cruising* it was my "gateway" to cruising) Alyson's ultimate travel wish though is to leave the boys at home and escape with her husband to Little Palm Island, the iconic Florida Keys resort sans telephones, televisions, and kids, and considered one of the most romantic retreats in the nation.

Alyson first cruise was right after college on Norwegian Cruise Line. Unlike for many, in Alyson's case that first cruise did not prompt a passion for cruising; she did not particularly care for the cruise and can't even remember the name of the ship. Despite being the demographic it was directed to, Alyson found it loud and raucous; even in her 20's Alyson had a burgeoning appreciation for luxury and refinement. Alyson does want to try NCL again as they were relatively new at the time of her forgettable cruise and she has since heard wonderful things about them.

The first cruise Alyson vividly recalls and that left her with a lasting positive impression about cruising was when she went on a cruise in her late 20's and accompanied her grandmother—it was just the two of them—on Holland America Line *Maasdam*.

"That one I really loved. I think the differences was…I really fell in love with the luxury aspect of Holland America. I really like that upscale feel when I was with my grandmother. A lot of people my age at the time would say 'this isn't my thing; I want a party ship with loud music.' I loved just the quiet, the service, the food, it clicked with me. I know it's an older crowd, but I liked that feeling."

Now Alyson was hooked on cruising. When she met her husband, she turned him on to cruising.

"We like a lot of the same things; we just clicked with respect to vacationing. So I kind of suspected he would love cruising. After getting married we went on some land-based vacations for a few years—our honeymoon and then other trips. I thought it would be difficult to cruise with babies. A fear years after getting married we had the opportunity to find out if my husband would take to cruising. My boys were now toddlers, and we brought our babysitter with us. My grandmother's 80th birthday was approaching, and a family cruise was organized on Royal Caribbean *Majesty of the Seas*."

Were you right about your husband and cruising, I wondered?

"He liked the concept of cruising. We didn't love our cabin. *Majesty* and the ships back then didn't have as many top cabins; we didn't have a balcony but rather a porthole on a lower deck. The ocean splashed on the porthole all night as it was rather rough seas. But his passion for cruising was inflamed right away."

That experience influenced their decision to stay in balcony cabins or suites. Besides Holland American, Alyson's dozen or so cruises also include Royal Caribbean, and Celebrity cruise lines.

"I've taken most of my cruises on Celebrity Cruises. They just fit my style. On one hand, I like things to do, but on the other, I don't want an overwhelming amount of choices or crowds. I enjoy good food and upscale service. I really enjoy Celebrity's suite restaurant, Luminae, which is just as amazing cuisine as you can find on land. And the exclusive lounges make it glamorous, plus an intimate gathering place for the family. My philosophy is that I'd rather cruise less, but in a larger suite."

After an experience staying in a cruise ship suite, Alyson said it is difficult to go back to a regular cabin. Her first suite experience was on Royal Caribbean in a Grand Suite on *Enchantment of the Seas*; her family loved it.

"Once we experienced a suite, it was hard to go back. We love having a butler who does all the little things for us. It's not because I need that level of service, but we enjoy the familiarity of having the same person. And, when cruising with teenagers it is very nice to have separate rooms."

Alyson's passion for cruising was obvious to me given the way she talked about it and the enthusiasm she exhibited on her social media engagement. I wondered was her family as passionate about cruising as she? Alyson's sons, now 18 and 20, were two and four when they first cruised on Royal Caribbean *Majesty of the Seas*. Besides being their first time on the ocean, the boys first cruise was a special event: it was in celebration of their great-grandmother's 80th birthday, and Alyson was accompanied by extended family. It was a joyous occasion, and the little guys immediately took to cruising (although, unlike my cruising sidekick grandchild Laki, not to the cruise ship kids camp.)

"My kids have never enjoyed being enclosed in a cruise 'kid's camp', although my youngest enjoyed it a bit more than my oldest. My oldest would scream until it was time for us to pick him up—I'm sure the camp staff loved us! My youngest would at least participate in activities. When he was six, we were on Royal Caribbean's *Enchantment of the Seas* and he was so excited to take part in the talent show—although he really couldn't come up with any talent! My whole family went to the performance—my parents were cruising with us—and waited anxiously to see what his talent would be. In the large theater on the stage, he sat there on a stool and blinked his eyes furiously. Amid future theater majors and musicians, he just blinked his eyes—yes, that was his talent! To me, I was just excited that he was having a great time and he even took home a t-shirt for a prize. That was probably the last time he participated in the kid's camp, but it still brings back great memories for me and to this day, we still laugh at his 'talent' of blinking."

What about the mega ships I wondered? The boys, and a family like Alyson's seem the ideal candidates for the cruise industry trend of the last several years. In *The Joy of Cruising* I wrote about the "*themeparkification*" of cruise ships; the trend towards larger and more "tricked-out" cruise ships in terms of gee whiz, family-friendly attractions including roller coasters, bumper cars, merry-go-rounds, surf- and skydiving- simulators, bowling alleys, laser tag and the like.

"My kids never experienced the mega-ships full of racetracks, zip-lining, or surfing, but they know how to entertain themselves, talk to adults, have great table manners, and appreciate the excitement and passion of cruising. Early on my youngest son discovered the basketball court, and my oldest son became a fan of the cruise ship specialty restaurants, which he still loves to this day. These are the kind of insights I share with families when they are looking for that perfect cruise ship for their family vacation."

Alyson typically cruises to the Caribbean or Bahamas, but in 2019 checked one off her bucket list by cruising to Alaska on Celebrity *Solstice*. In June, Alyson, Joel and the boys departed from Seattle and visited Ketchikan, Juneau, cruised Endicott Arm, Skagway and Victoria, B.C.

"Alaska was a completely different experience. Other than the breath-taking visits to Endicott Arm and the Mendenhall Glacier, we love to try local food, so we did a delicious salmon bake in Juneau. The family absolutely loved the beauty of Alaska, but admittedly missed the beaches usually encountered on our cruises."

Sunset in Alaska.

Endicott Arm Fjord Alaska

Mendenhall Glacier, Juneau, Alaska

Alyson's next cruise is rapidly approaching. In January 2021 her family will take an 11-night cruise on *Celebrity Reflection*, their third time on *Reflection*, departing from Fort Lauderdale to the ABC Islands (Aruba, Bonaire, and Curaçao.)

"It will be our first time to the ABC islands and our first cruise longer than seven nights."

I ask Alyson what's left for the cruise bucket list now that she has experienced an Alaska cruise.

"I'd love to do a European river cruise. I've never experienced a river cruise. I'm enamored by the calm water, close-up views, and small ships with personalized service. Not to mention experiencing the lovely European wine that they always promote! I also would love to do one of those true luxury lines, Regent Seven Seas, maybe if I hit the lottery!"

Several of the passionate cruisers I have interviewed also are travel agents—mainly for the purpose of booking cruises for family and friends, although a few pursue it as a business. Given *My Virtual Vacations* was largely started by Alyson to aid family and friends I asked if she also books travel?

"Do I sell cruises or want to? No way! I've been blogging now for several years and have been approached numerous times about being a travel agent. I enjoy sharing my experiences and providing information, for free! It's what I enjoy the most to do and then to talk about. As I always say, I can talk cruising all day long. And that's why I love social media. I can talk, tweet, post, and share all day long," Alyson responded.

Alyson has a presence on most of the major platforms: FaceBook, Twitter, Pinterest, and Instagram. She does all of her own website and internet work; has formed relationships with some from within the cruise industry; and done collaborations with other travel bloggers (like *Life Well Cruised* featured earlier). In addition, Alyson has done some articles for local publications; she did a honeymoon travel guide for a local wedding guide.

Besides the fact that *My Virtual Vacations* is a part-time, evenings and weekends venture, Alyson acknowledges the importance of striking that right balance between social media, family, and the other things she is interested in like cooking and being a foodie.

"What does the future hold for *My Virtual Vacations*?" I asked.

"I'm going to keep going!" Alyson told me. "I truly believe in family travel; luxury family travel; my sons are older now, they're 18 and 20 so how long can you do family cruising?" She asks wistfully. "They live at home and still love to travel. My husband will always love taking food and travel pictures, and I will always love talking about cruising so I'm sure *My Virtual Vacations* is going to continue for awhile."

Cruise Lifestyle

"2019 has been a year of cruise firsts for me," Laura mused. "My first river cruise, which was on AmaWaterways *AmaMagna* on the Danube; my first inaugural cruise, the launch of Royal Caribbean *Spectrum of the Seas* with an amazing itinerary leaving from Barcelona, through the Suez Canal, to Dubai; and, I attended my first CLIAUK Conference." [CLIAUK is the UK branch of the Cruise Lines International Association.] "And, it was my first year hosting *Cruise Hour*."

Cruise Hour is how I got to know Laura Pedlar, the creator of the *Cruise Lifestyle* blog. *Cruise Hour* is a weekly online gathering of cruise enthusiasts who discuss fun topics about cruising including cuisine, fun things to do, excursions, destinations, etc. I happened upon *Cruise Hour* on Twitter and started posting responses to the fun questions posed by Laura, often proudly accompanying my responses with cruise photos, typically of my cruising partner granddaughter. I kind of thought *Cruise Hour* was a catchy Twitter name—and didn't realize it referred to an actual *hour*! I was fairly new to social media, so I didn't "get" live events early on. Despite being named *Cruise Hour*, I thought it was just an ongoing thread about various cruise topics. It took me a while to notice that my responses tended to be many hours, even days, after the *Cruise Hour* discussion ended and the participants had long moved on to other parts of social media, or were asleep—Laura was hosting the discussion group from Cornwall, England, a six-hour time difference from me in Florida! I told Laura that story and she laughed, assuring me that others would respond even later than I used to. (I think she was trying to make me feel not so "duh.")

I asked Laura to talk about the development of *Cruise Lifestyle,* and *Cruise Hour.* "I picked the name *Cruise Lifestyle* because at that point I wanted to cover lots of different elements of cruising: the drinks, the food, what people wear, the destinations, all of those things. As time has gone on and I've cruised more and more, I have come to realize I am most interested in destinations… and the food. My posts now at *cruiselifestyle.co.uk* are about things to do at a particular destination. I also post a lot about food. I take notes about places we eat around the port and add that to my posts. Things like, 'There's one place you need to try when you are at such and such.' I also talk about food on the ship. I enjoy cruise ship specialty dining; that's one of the things on which I am quite happy to spend my money." *Cruise Lifestyle* is well represented on social media: Twitter, Instagram, and a little bit on You Tube. Laura said, "I do need to do more videos; I enjoy watching other people's cruise videos. My partner Craig likes to do videos and he has all the Go Pro gear and so he does all that."

Laura on Crown Princess, 2019

I asked Laura how *Cruise Lifestyle* is faring in the current environment with the cruise lockdown. "I am trying not to base everything that I write on the current situation. I am a fairly optimistic person and I'd like to think this is very temporary. So, the majority of what I am putting out is information that will be useful to cruisers once they can cruise again. I've looked at where I've been, and there is a list of ships I have been on that I have not written up yet because I only do this part-time. So I have been focusing more on content that will be useful to people when they re-start cruising. I am looking at longer-term rather than immediate. There are only so many videos or blog posts you can do about when cruising is starting again."

I said, "Say something about *Cruise Hour;* that's the way I came to be aware of you and *Cruise Lifestyle.*" Laura replied, "So, a few years ago I came across a similar cruise chat show on Twitter; it was once a week, about cruising, and I enjoyed it. And then it disappeared. I assumed it would come back thinking, 'maybe they just took a break.' It didn't. After a year or so, I thought why not start something myself because I enjoyed it. I like talking about cruising when I am not on a cruise; and it's nice to meet other people who have the same interests as you. *Cruise Hour* has been going now for over a year. It has been good. It's nice that I have met a lot of people, mainly from UK and US. It's really interesting the things people have done; you ask a question and they come back with all these unique answers and different experiences and it's interesting to see people's pictures. Cruisers come to it from all different angles, which makes it very interesting: new cruisers, people who have only done short cruises in the Caribbean, people who go on expedition ships."

I asked Laura if she has any particular plans for *Cruise Hour*. "More and more it's tricky coming up with ideas. And it's particularly tricky at the moment. The obvious topic would be about how sad we all are that there are no cruises at the minute and what's going to happen next. But there are only so many times you can talk about that, so I've kind of steered clear of that. For our one-year anniversary in July, we did a live video chat via Zoom. It was nice to put faces with names. We had people from all over join in. It was really nice; it flowed very well. The hour went quickly and we agreed we'd quite like to do more live video chats in the future. I also get the feeling that some of the audience wants to meet up at some point on a group cruise. That could be a possibility; we chat every week—a core group—and we feel like we know each other. Some are very apologetic when they miss a chat. Of course, there are others who dip in and out occasionally, and then people who just stumble across it. Longer-term, I would like to pursue collaborations between *Cruise Hour* or *Cruise Lifestyle* with some cruise lines."

When we are not dealing with a pandemic, Laura of course would like to be on a cruise ship somewhere. When not cruising, besides spending her time on *Cruise Lifestyle* and *Cruise Hour,* Laura teaches Zumba once a week. "When I was growing up all I wanted to be was a dancer and would love to have been a dancer on a cruise ship, but my height put a stop to that. I'm 4 ft 11 and I was told that cruise ship dancers had to be at least 5ft 6 to wear all the feathers. Zumba is how I keep dancing and a way to stay active."

Laura was born, raised and still lives in Cornwall with her significant other and cruise partner, Craig. She left Cornwall to attend the University of Worcester in 2002 where she earned a master's degree and focused on social marketing but she chose to return and settle at home because she loves being near family and Cornwall's beautiful coastlines.

Laura created *Cruise Lifestyle* in 2016 after completing her degree. "I had more time on my hands suddenly, and I missed writing. I wanted to share my experiences with other cruisers. I noticed that there was some information I couldn't find when I was researching my cruises, so I decided that blogging the details was important to helping others in the future. I like to focus on the destinations and food as well as cruise news."

Laura cruised to Hawaii on the Princess Cruises *Grand Princess* in 2015. "I found an amazing itinerary with a cruise to Hawaii, with the option to bookend the trip with stays in Las Vegas and San Francisco." This cruise was significant for Laura in a number of ways—foremost among them was that it lead directly to the birth of *Cruiselifestyle.co.uk.* Laura said, "I did all this research for the cruise and looked at all of the different excursions. And while I was doing that I came across all these cruise blogs and I was thinking 'I shouldn't really keep all of this information to myself.'"

The *Grand Princess* cruise was also Laura's first cruise as an adult. She cruised a couple of times as a child with her family, and enjoyed it immensely, but didn't cruise again until she was 31 years old. And, it was a celebration of her Craig's birthday. "I introduced my partner Craig to his first cruise; he really loved it. And for me, I started cruising again! Cruising to Hawaii on the *Grand Princess* made me realize I wanted to change the way I went on holiday. Before that, we were quite happy to either do a city break, or to go and have a beach holiday in somewhere like the Canary Islands—just somewhere to relax and not do very much. This cruise showed me there's lots of places I want to go and things I want to do, and a good way to do lots of things in one go, if you've got one holiday, is cruising."

Grand Princess turned out to be a grand way for Laura to reintroduce herself to cruising. "I learned Hula dancing and performed in the Princess Theatre. I finally had the chance to realize my dream of dancing on stage on a cruise ship! We visited Pearl Harbor, and the highlight was in Hilo—a helicopter ride over a volcano where we chose to have the doors removed so we could feel the heat from the volcano." I just updated my bucket list—well, not the part about removing the helicopter doors!

Laura continued, "We met some lovely friends on our Hawaiian cruise with whom we stay in touch. We had a lot of sea days, so we ended up sitting and chatting with people quite a lot. We made a lot of friends, all from the US, and what we did was decide to book a cruise together. We organized to meet up on a *Regal Princess* 2017 Caribbean cruise with stops in Grand Cayman, St Maarten, Jamaica, St Thomas, and Cozumel, after first getting together a couple of days in advance of the cruise and renting an Airbnb together."

Grand Princess cruise to Hawaii, Laura and Craig after helicopter ride over a volcano in Hilo. They chose to have the doors removed to feel the heat from the volcano.

Laura's first cruise was with her family in 1990 on P&O's *Canberra* when she was just six years old: a Mediterranean cruise highlighted by stops at Monaco on the French Riviera, and Portofino, Italy. I asked Laura if she remembered much from that cruise. "I remember bits of it well. I remember I spent a lot of time in the kids' club; I'm an only child, so I am used to making friends. I was quite happy. I enjoyed the swimming pool and eating watermelon from the buffet—that was the first time I had eaten watermelon! Touring the *Canberra's* bridge; drinking a mocktail called a Pussyfoot. I entered the fancy dress competition. I enjoyed visiting a number of Mediterranean ports on that cruise. We went to Gibraltar and saw the monkeys and went to a palace in Lisbon."

Laura and her family went back on the *Canberra* a few years later when she was nine. While she had fond memories of those first two cruises, it would be many years before Laura cruised again. "I didn't cruise again until five years ago. It wasn't because I didn't enjoy cruising; mum and dad and I just took a variety of different holidays. However, I remember enjoying cruising and having a good time. So, I came back to cruising. As I became an adult I was open to the idea of doing a cruise holiday." Laura traveled with her family once or twice a year including visits to Disneyland and Disneyland Paris. I asked if those experiences helped form her desire to travel as she got older. "Absolutely. It was definitely something my family saved up for. We would always go on holiday once a year, and if we were lucky twice a year. We were not a materialistic family, but our luxury was to go on a holiday. It was something, those memories, that are still important to my mum and dad. It's something I have been fortunate to be able to do."

Laura aged six with her mum, first cruise, P&O Canberra.

Since her return to cruising as an adult just five years ago Laura has experienced a number of iconic moments, ships, and itineraries. Laura has cruised with P&O, Royal Caribbean, AmaWaterways, and Princess, her favorite. In addition, as a cruise blogger and member of the press, Laura has had the opportunity to do tours of Princess, Celebrity, Cunard and Silversea cruise ships. She has cruised throughout the Caribbean, Hawaii, the Mediterranean, Canary Islands, Danube River, and Suez Canal to Dubai. In addition to the aforementioned special cruise to Hawaii on *Grand Princess,* Laura cites several memorable cruises among her cruise highlights. In 2018, prior to embarkation for a Mediterranean cruise on Princess Cruises *Sapphire Princess,* Laura and Craig explored Rome including the Colosseum and Roman Forum, and took a tour in a Fiat 500. During the *Sapphire Princess* cruise Laura had such iconic experiences as visiting de La Boqueria market in Barcelona, climbing the Leaning Tower of Pisa, and walking the F1 track in Monaco. In 2019, Laura sailed the Royal Caribbean *Spectrum of the Seas* inaugural cruise from Barcelona to Dubai. She visited the Panathenaic Stadium and Acropolis in Athens, toured Pompei on an excursion led by an archeologist, transited the Suez Canal, and experienced a sunrise hot air balloon ride over the desert in Dubai.

Laura was fortunate to be able to get in a cruise in 2020 before the lockdown. She sailed a two-week Southern Caribbean cruise on P&O *Britannia* with stops at Barbados, St. Lucia, Antigua, Dominica, Saint Vincent and Bonaire. "We were so lucky, as we went in January—we got back on the 19th. I originally had it in my mind I wanted to go on a cruise in the Far East, Japan or Thailand or somewhere in that direction. And that would have meant that we would go in the March through May timeframe. But we had convinced friends to go on their first cruise with us, and they were like, 'when we think of cruising we think of the Caribbean.' So, we went in January. Obviously, March, April, May never would have happened, so we were so lucky." Or even worse, they could have gone in March and then gotten stranded. I mentioned to Laura how I am writing about some cruisers who were stranded on the ocean due to Covid just a few weeks after her return from the *Britannia* cruise. Imagine if that happened on someone's first cruise!

As a relatively new cruise blogger who is still a millennial, Laura has a lot of cruising in front of her. Her future cruise hopes and plans reflect that. River cruising is in her near future. She enjoyed her first experience on a river cruise and wants to continue where she left off. "Our *AmaMagna* cruise ended in Budapest. I'd like to carry on from that point down to the Black Sea, and go to Romania, and those Eastern European countries." And Laura has already chosen her birthday present for her 40th coming up in a few years: sailing the Mekong River through Vietnam and Cambodia.

Laura would also like to do an expedition cruise to Antarctica and take a cruise to the South Pacific, particularly New Caledonia. I asked Laura what's on her ultimate cruise bucket list. "I'm not going to give the obvious answer. When we discuss a question like that in *Cruise Hour,* a lot of participants say a world cruise. Yes, that's a given; everyone would love to go on a world cruise. But there are several places I would like to see. So, Japan, and the Far East in general, possibly a combination of land and cruise. I'd like to cruise circum-navigating Iceland. Lots of people go to just Reykjavík, whereas there's lots of places all over Iceland I would like to see. South America as well. Hopefully I will get to see that in 2022. I have a cruise booked to Brazil and Argentina. It's on a new ship—Princess Cruises *Discovery Princess.*"

Laura also has a lengthy list of land-based travel she would like to do in coming years: Budapest, Salzburg, Rome, St Lucia, Barbados, Normandy, New York including Niagara Falls, and Venice. She would like to make a return visit to Amsterdam, and she wants to see a couple of destinations that are solemn and somber for very different reasons: Auschwitz and Chernobyl. Longer-term, Laura's land-based bucket list includes an African safari, the Grand Canyon, Rio de Janeiro for Carnival, Halong Bay, and The Great Wall of China.

Laura and Craig on the inaugural cruise of Royal Caribbean Spectrum of the Seas in 2019.

"I want to see so many places, experience different cultures, and eat local food. Cruising has enabled me to do that. However, I wouldn't refuse to visit a destination just because I couldn't cruise there. Even on cruises I like to try and stay before and after a cruise to explore more of a destination—a pre-cruise in Rome; a post-cruise in Dubai. Perhaps different than some other cruisers, I don't cruise to be on a ship; I cruise to see the world."

Eat Sleep Cruise

Donald and Heidi Bucolo are the creators of the popular *EatSleepCruise*, an award-winning blog. Don and Heidi are millennials who have been married for 11 years. They are both from the New England area: Heidi grew up in Massachusetts, and Donald was raised across the bay in Rhode Island. They attended college in the area—Heidi graduated with a master's degree from Boston University and Don graduated with a doctorate in psychology from the University of New Hampshire, and after graduating they settled in the area and live less than an hour from Boston.

Travel has been a big part of Heidi and Don's relationship right from the beginning. Even though they were both in the New England area, the first couple of years of dating they had a somewhat long long-distance courtship as Don was attending graduate school. Theirs is a modern-day love story—Heidi and Don met online, attracted by their mutual interest in travel. Seemingly they are always on the ocean but they both have full-time professions. Heidi is a physical therapist working with the geriatric population, while Don is a research director for an education service provider that works with K-12 schools. Don calls *EatSleepCruise* a labor of love.

Heidi and Don in front of Morro Castle, Havana, Cuba on a May 2017 cruise on Norwegian Sky.

Heidi and Don's first vacation as a couple was a cruise in 2007 on Royal Caribbean *Legend of the Seas*. This Western Caribbean cruise visited Grand Cayman, Belize, Costa Maya, and Cozumel. This was Heidi's first time on a cruise. Don had done a short cruise with his family as a kid, and cruised in college, but it was kind of forgettable; not because it was a mediocre cruise. It was a Spring Break cruise with a bunch of his friends! As Don put it, "What happens in international waters, stays in international waters!"

I wondered why they chose a cruise for their first significant travel together, since Heidi hadn't cruised before, and Don's cruises weren't all that memorable. Heidi explained that some friends of hers were going on a cruise and invited them along. Despite some hesitation—they were still getting to know each other and the cruise was six months away—Heidi mentioned the cruise to Don. It turned out to be a fateful decision for Heidi and Don, as they got hooked on cruising and the cruise on *Legend of the Seas* was the forerunner of *EatSleepCruise*.

Heidi's first impression of cruising was very positive and she could readily see where it fit well with her approach to things in general. "I am a very detail-oriented and structured person; I like having plans. Cruising is very structured; you have dinner at the same time every night, with the same guests, same waitstaff; there's always nightly entertainment, you have a routine. I like that. Also, I tend to be a bit of an over-packer; the fact that I could unpack once for the week and then visit multiple destinations without having to pack and unpack several times was a sure winner for me. Honestly when we started planning our next vacation, we didn't even hesitate—we just thought of booking another cruise."

It didn't take long for Heidi and Don to cruise again, going on the Norwegian *Pearl* less than a year later. Those first two cruises in rapid succession were the catalyst to three dozen cruises in the 13 years together. Although after those first two cruises, Heidi and Don did try a land based-vacation; an all-inclusive resort for their honeymoon. Unfortunately, or perhaps fortunately given the way things turned out for them, the honeymoon solidified their choice of cruising as their preferred mode of vacation travel.

Heidi said, "Because we had taken two cruises together already, we decided for our honeymoon maybe we should try something different. Both of us are kind of research-oriented, and planners. We did extensive research online and picked an all-inclusive that had high ratings. We ended up doing the west coast of Mexico. We booked a resort in Puerto Vallarta. The resort just did not live up to our expectations."

Don said, "We got married in 2009; the recession was occurring. The resort was a ghost town, so it wasn't fully functional. Not all the restaurants were open; the activities that they normally have, they didn't run because of not enough guests or not enough staff. The grounds were beautiful and the excursions were amazing. We did some crazy zipline through valleys, and a sea lion encounter, but the resort overall was lacking—the food was not that great, the entertainment was laughingly bad." Heidi added, "Every time I used the hair dryer we would trip the circuit breaker!"

Heidi and Don have not been back to an all-inclusive resort since—or any other land-based travel except vacations to amusement parks. (Heidi never met a roller coaster she didn't want to try.) Since that less than stellar honeymoon travel experience, all of Heidi and Don's travel has been via cruises. That is the cruising community's gain. Heidi and Don decided to give back to that community in August 2014 when they created *EatSleepCruise*.

"We created *EatSleepCruise* after spending years contributing to message boards as a way of sharing everything we have learned while traveling. I said to Heidi one day, 'We're doing all this work, posting information to other people's websites, we should start our own blog.' Heidi came up with the name *EatSleepCruise*. It started as a blog, and as we've grown over time we added social media—Facebook, Instagram, and Twitter as those started getting more popular—and then Pinterest happened for us in 2017 and that really exploded things for us. More recently, our YouTube Channel has grown to over 26K subscribers and has gained traction with hundreds of thousands of views a month."

Heidi added, "We have no background in journalism, web development, photography, videography, or social media, so we have been learning as we go." *EatSleepCruise.com* is truly a team affair. Don says, "Heidi may do a little more of one thing, and I do a little more of another."

On the site, their logo tagline is, "Sea the World, One Port At A Time." The topics covered are exclusively cruise related, with encyclopedic information about, and reviews of, ships and ports of call. And, there are three sections titled respectively: *Eat*, which features cruise ship dining guides and specialty restaurant reviews, restaurant and bar menus, cruise, drink package guides, etc.; *Sleep*, cruise port hotel guides and reviews; and, *Cruise*, which features anything and everything about a broad cross-section of cruise lines and ships.

I had a mistaken assumption about the origin of the *EatSleepCruise* moniker. Having researched Heidi and Don's background and followed them on social media with their indefatigable coverage of all things cruising, it seemed to me they cruised all the time—they literally eat, sleep, and cruise—and I assumed they named their blog after their lifestyle. I thought, hard to think of a more aptly titled blog!

EatSleepCruise was selected by Porthole Cruise Magazine to its list of the Top 10 Cruise Influencers of 2019. In describing its process, Porthole Cruise Magazine discusses searching for the most authentic personalities with a passion for cruising. That certainly mirrors my impression of Heidi and Don—authenticity and passion. I asked them to reflect on that accolade, and talk about if that recognition has impacted *EatSleepCruise* in any way. "We were really honored just to be included with the other honorees, some of the people in the cruise community we follow. I think that recognition holds a lot of weight in the industry. A number of the folks we have worked with reached out to congratulate us; it helped strengthen some of the relationships we already had with brands, and it allowed us to forge some new relationships. For instance, we were asked to be part of the cruise categories expert panel for the USA Today 10 Best Readers Choice Awards."

EatSleepCruise is often asked to provide expert input and perspective in publications and podcasts, and it is cited as a top blog in various blog rating venues. They have been quoted regularly in places like Forbes, CNBC, AARP Magazine, and Porthole Cruise Magazine. Recently, *EatSleepCruise* was invited to be a virtual guest presenter at the Travel Like a Pro Conference.

Heidi and Don have cruised on a diverse mix of cruise lines and cruise ship types. They are unabashedly mega-ship enthusiasts, having sailed on most of the world's largest cruise ships. Heidi and Don have sailed on all four of the Royal Caribbean *Oasis-class ships—Oasis of the Seas, Allure of the Seas, Harmony of the Seas,* and *Symphony of the Seas* which take the top four spots on the list of the world's largest cruise ships; they have sailed on Norwegian Cruise Line's largest, the Breakaway-Plus class ships; and in January 2020 sailed on Carnival Cruise Line's largest ship, its just launched flagship, *Panorama.*

"We sailed on Norwegian's newest ship, Norwegian *Encore,* and were on the inaugural cruise and were at the christening ceremony that featured a live performance by Godmother, Kelly Clarkson. A year prior, we had attended the keel laying ceremony for the ship at the Meyer-Werft shipyard in Germany."

Heidi and Don have also sailed on several other cruise lines. In addition to Royal Caribbean, Norwegian and Carnival, they have cruised on Celebrity, and MSC. They have also sailed on more intimate vessels to unique destinations: the high-end Viking Ocean Cruises and Windstar Cruises *Wind Surf*, and in 2019 they experienced their first river cruise on Viking River Cruise's *Einar*. Besides cruising throughout the Caribbean and Bahamas, Heidi and Don have also cruised to Alaska twice, Hawaii, Cuba, Bermuda, Ireland, Iceland, and Northern Europe.

Heidi and Don at the Cliffs of Moher, Ireland during their May 2018 Ireland/Iceland cruise on Celebrity Eclipse.

Heidi and Don have cruised to some wonderful destinations. I asked to them to share some stand-out experiences. They told me two that stand out that both involved helicopter tours: A helicopter tour and glacier walk on Mendenhall Glacier in Juneau, Alaska, and a helicopter tour over Kilauea volcano and the Big Island in Hawaii. Other memories they shared include: an Old Havana Walking Tour with a local guide in Cuba; exploring Chacchoben Mayan Ruins in Costa Maya, Mexico; a Viking *Jupiter* cruise with a stop in St. Petersburg, Russia where they visited multiple palaces—the Hermitage Museum, ornate churches, and attended the Russian ballet—and the cruise ended in Berlin where Heidi and Don saw the Berlin Cathedral, the Brandenburg Gate, Checkpoint

Charlie, and visited the remnants of the Berlin Wall; experiencing the Game of Thrones tour on a visit to Northern Ireland as part of a 10-day cruise on Celebrity *Eclipse* that departed from Dublin, Ireland and, during a Royal Caribbean *Harmony of the Seas* Eastern Caribbean cruise, completed the St Maarten America's Cup Racing Yacht Challenge. And, in the course of sailing state-of-the-art ships and visiting iconic destinations, Heidi and Don spoke fondly of having experienced some of the world's most enchanting beaches.

"And, we have visited some of the world's best beaches including Horseshoe Bay Beach in Bermuda, Eagle Beach in Aruba, Waikiki Beach in Oahu, White Bay Beach in Jost Van Dyke in the British Virgin Islands, and The Baths at Virgin Gorda."

Not all of Heidi and Don's cruise memories are so…well…fond. Heidi said, "To celebrate Don graduating school, we sailed Royal Caribbean *Freedom of the Seas* on a seven-day cruise to the Eastern Caribbean. During a stop at CocoCay, he lost his wedding ring while snorkeling. We had been married for less than a year! It was never recovered, and it remains at the bottom of the ocean in the Bahamas!"

The 30-somethings have cruised extensively in a relatively short time period, and have been exposed to so many memorable experiences. How do they maintain that pace? "Our goal each year is to spend more days at sea than the previous year. Prior to 2018, we averaged at most 20 days cruising per year. Then 2018, we spent a total of 34 days at sea, and for 2019 we spent 44 days at sea. And our goal is to build on that in 2020."

When I first met with Heidi and Don early in 2020 they were well on their way to building on their total sea days. They got an early start toward their 2020 cruise tally with a cruise to the Mexican Riviera on the new Carnival *Panorama* launched just a month earlier after being christened by her god-mother, Wheel of Fortune hostess Vanna White. Despite the the diversity of cruise lines Heidi and Don have experienced, the *Panorama* was the first Carnival cruise they have enjoyed together. I asked them about their reflections on the new flagship for the world's largest cruise line. "We enjoyed it.

It was much more high energy than some of the other cruise lines. The ship was well designed and beautiful. Carnival knows their target audience and they execute very well. Food was much better than expected. They were very family oriented, lots of fun activities; there's just a level of…they know what they are doing and they just do it."

*Heidi and Don on the Mendenhall Glacier during their
2014 Alaska cruise on Celebrity Solstice.*

On March 8, 2020 Heidi and Don boarded Royal Caribbean *Freedom of the Seas* in San Juan, Puerto Rico for a seven night cruise to the Southern Caribbean: the ABC Islands, Aruba, Bonaire and Curaçao, and Saint Thomas, US Virgin Islands. It was the initial cruise after *Freedom of the Seas* had undergone a $116 million refurbishment highlighted by a new duo of waterslides, *The Perfect Storm*, popular attractions on several other Royal Caribbean ships.

The cruise lockdown began while Heidi and Don were at sea on *Freedom of the Seas*. "We left on March 8th and were supposed to come back to San Juan on the 15th, but we were re-routed to Miami and we had to spend an extra couple days on the ship. We kind of observed everything unfolding back home because of the coronavirus while we were on *Freedom of the Seas*." Wow, normally I would say spending extra days on a great new ship, not having to quarantine in a cabin, and enjoying all of the amenities and food, and getting to partake in the activities, at no extra cost, would be "a good problem to have." But these weren't normal times. While Heidi and Don were on the ocean, the World Health Organization declared Covid-19 as a global pandemic, March 11; March 13 the Cruise Line Industry Association (CLIA) announced a voluntary suspension of cruise ship operations from U.S. ports of call; and, March 14, The Centers for Disease Control and Prevention (CDC) announced the issuance of a No Sail Order and Suspension of Further Embarkation for all cruise ships that were not voluntarily suspending operation.

Heidi said, "Despite all that was going on in the world, honestly, not much changed on the *Freedom of the Seas* cruise. There were increased health and safety measures—they checked our temperature when we boarded in San Juan, they added hand sanitizing stations seemingly everywhere, food was being served to us in venues rather than self-serve, and that kind of thing—but we visited all of our ports of call, all the events on the ship carried on without issue. We were actually enjoying a 70's party on the ship when social media started blowing up with first Viking announcing a halt to cruises, and then the CLIA announcement. The word started getting around the ship about what was happening back home but no one was panicking. We were kind of dreading going back home; we were looking at social media and were hearing that there was no toilet paper back home. 'Really? All the bars were open, we had plenty of toilet paper. We'll just stay on the cruise ship!'" Don added, "By this point, we had family and friends reaching out to us who were concerned for our safety and jokingly telling us we should steal some toilet paper to take home with us!"

"Sunday morning March 15, our scheduled disembarkation in Puerto Rico, we awoke to find the ship still sailing close to full speed with no land in sight. We initially thought maybe we were just going to arrive late, but we soon realized something was wrong. Around 7 am, the Captain informed us that Puerto Rico had denied our ship entry and that we were being re-routed to Miami and would be at sea an additional 2 days. The morning was a bit frantic with everyone trying to make new travel arrangements home."

Heidi and Don in St. Thomas, March 2020, in front of Royal Caribbean Freedom of the Seas, their last cruise prior to the pandemic lockdown.

The pandemic spoiled Heidi and Don's plans for the remainder of 2020 which was to be highlighted by cruises on new ships and new attractions: MSC *Seaside* stopping at MSC Cruises' new private island *Ocean Cay Marine Reserve* which opened in December 2019; an April inaugural cruise on the Virgin Voyages *Scarlet Lady* including its new private Beach Club at Bimini, the new Carnival Cruise Line *Mardi Gras* booked for September, and an inaugural cruise on Royal Caribbean's new *Odyssey of the Seas* originally scheduled for November 2020 and delayed to April 2021. When I first met with Heidi and Don in early 2020 and they told me about their plans for the year, we planned to reconnect later in the year before publication so that I could get their reflections about these exciting cruise plans. I knew readers would want to hear about these new ships, especially the innovations introduced by Virgin Voyages—no buffets, no kids—and the first roller coaster on a cruise ship, on *Mardi Gras*. But, *Cruising Interrupted*!

"We have already been invited by Virgin Voyages to sail on one of the first cruises on *Scarlet Lady* late this year. We are also in the process of re-planning our 2021 schedule. As you know, we love new mega-ships so will most certainly re-book *Odyssey of the Seas* and *Mardi Gras*."

Not only would Heidi and Don have to defer their plan to accelerate their already prodigious cruising pace, but the self-described "big kids at heart" lost the chance to check one off one of their travel bucket list items—visiting *Disneyland* for the first time. (They have been to *Disney World* in Florida.)

Looking well beyond the cruise lockdown, Heidi and Don characterize their bucket list as, 'Sea the world, one port at a time.' Heidi and Don have cruised so much and had so many memorable experiences on the ocean and visiting iconic beaches and destinations that I assumed their bucket list travel plans would include some overland travel, but Don told me their goal is to realize their bucket list items via cruise ship. And it is an ambitious cruising bucket list indeed. Their bucket list includes visiting the Galapagos Islands; Antarctica; seeing the Northern Lights; traversing the Panama Canal; a River Cruise through Egypt; Paddlewheel Steamboat cruise down the Mississippi River; Seine River Cruise; and a Greek Isles Cruise. The only land-based travel that made it to Heidi and Don's bucket list—beside making up for that missed Disneyland trip—is an African safari.

When Heidi and Don are not on a cruise or working on *EatSleepCruise*, besides shopping, Heidi really enjoys thrill-seeking activities like zip lining and roll-ercoasters, so they do like to visit amusement parks. Unfortunately they can't do that right now. Don "who has time for a hobby," is the resident nerd and loves sci-fi and watching television.

I was curious as to how the cruise lockdown has affected *EatSleepCruise*.

Don noted, "This is the longest time we've been on land in the last few years. In the last couple of years we usually cruise almost every other month. As far as the site is concerned, traffic is way down. People just aren't searching for the content for planning cruises. So we've kind of changed the perspective of what we are doing on the site and on social media. We are going to do a balancing act; we want to promote cruising but we need to be sensitive to the current situation." That's very similar to the thinking I had when I decided to restart writing of this book. Striking a balance between celebrating the passion of cruising while being sensitive to what's happening worldwide with the pandemic. Heidi added, "And also just being optimistic for the future knowing the cruise industry will return, and kind of keeping cruisers spirits alive with memories and photos of previous trips."

"Keeping cruisers' spirits alive." That's the essence of bloggers being cruise community champions.

Section Seven:

THE PASSIONATE CRUISERS
OF THE JOY OF CRUISING...
WHAT ARE THEY UP TO NOW?

I chose to re-connect with several of the passionate cruisers who were featured in *The Joy of Cruising*. Actually thanks to social media, I have never lost connection with them. However, I wanted to engage them in a more in-depth, intimate way by sharing with you a continuation of their fascinating stories.

Joe Church has one of those evergreen cruising stories that never grows old. His cruising story is dependent on a long-running relationship that will continue as long as Royal Caribbean Cruise Line exists, and Joe feels up to it. Besides having a wonderful Royal Caribbean cruise story, having been on all of their ships and traveled to every part of the globe that Royal Caribbean covers, Joe has run a marathon length distance, 26.2 miles, on the jogging track of every ship in the Royal Caribbean fleet. The story of the origin of that tradition is poignant and was covered in *The Joy of Cruising*. Since featuring Joe, Royal Caribbean has added a ship to its fleet which Joe has already conquered, and Joe competed in the New York City Marathon for the first time in his celebrated running career.

Paul and Carole, of *Paul and Carole Love to Travel* were one of three couples included in a feature in *The Joy of Cruising* called "Cuba Cruising." Paul and Carole "escorted" the book's readers on a Havana tavern crawl, and in the process of writing their vignette, I felt I was right there with them. They seem like such a fun couple of cruise enthusiasts, and after the book was published, I vowed that if there ever was a sequel, *Paul and Carole Love to Travel* would be featured in its own right.

Bill Raffel was included in *The Joy of Cruising* in a section called "Cruisers Like You and Me…Sort Of," about ordinary cruisers who had done extraordinary things in cruising. By happenstance, I learned from Bill about a "once in a lifetime" cruise he was days away from attending. I asked Bill to let me share his reflections from the cruise with you.

Finally, Sheri Griffiths, Founder, *Cruise Tips TV,* reflects on how the cruise lockdown has impacted *Cruise Tips TV,* one of the anchors of the cruise community. Sheri discusses how *Cruise Tips TV* has adapted to the lockdown, and shares her thoughts about cruising's future.

Marathoner of the Seas:
Still Running

"In the wee hours of this morning I began running laps around the *Spectrum of the Seas*. The ship has been traveling at 20 knots into a 20+ mph headwind for an apparent wind in excess of 40 mph making for a very challenging run. But it is facing challenges that makes it worth the effort. 26.2 miles/42 km (92 laps) done. 29th Royal Caribbean Line ship completed."

On December 21, 2019, Joe Church shared the above message. Joe is a 68-year old retiree with a number of passions he pursues to the fullest: he is a runner, a birdwatcher, and a traveler. While his traveling doesn't necessarily have to be on a cruise ship, he has accomplished an amazing feat on cruise ships, unmatched by any cruiser in the world: Joe has run a marathon-distance, 26.2 miles, on every cruise ship in the fleet of the world's largest cruise line, Royal Caribbean.

Marie Clark and Joe on Spectrum after Joe completed his 29th marathon distance run on Royal Caribbean cruise ships.

When last we visited Joe in *The Joy of Cruising*, he was not far removed from from a major medical calamity—a series of four heart attacks over the course of less than a day—which would have caused many to transition to a more sedate lifestyle. Not Joe though; a couple of months later he ran/walked the full distance in the Tokyo Marathon. 160 days after being rushed to the hospital he ran over 26 miles on his 28th Royal Caribbean cruise ship, its newest at the time, and the largest ship in the world, *Symphony of the Seas*.

December 2019, Joe got his opportunity to extend his unique tradition, personal challenge, and amazing feat of running a marathon length distance on each Royal Caribbean ship. Shortly after *The Joy of Cruising* was published, *Spectrum of the Seas* was launched. *Spectrum* is a Quantum Ultra-class cruise ship: smaller than the Oasis-class comprised of the four largest ships in the world—*Oasis, Allure, Harmony, and Symphony of the Seas*—but larger than Royal's previous next largest class of ships known as the Quantum-class.

Joe flew to Thailand to do some birdwatching—he is as avid a bird-watcher as he is a runner—and to run in the Chiang Mai marathon. From there he flew to Hong Kong to join up with Marie for a few days there before they boarded *Spectrum of the Seas* on December 22. As was his tradition for ships that didn't have a track dedicated solely for running and apart from the other passengers on the sports deck, Joe planned to do his run at around 1:00 am that first night on board when other passengers were not likely to be on the track.

Of course, Joe wasn't idle during the wait from the time he did a marathon-distance run on *Symphony* and the wait for the completion of the construction of Spectrum. The man has three passions, after all! Having run a marathon on every continent, 44 countries, in every state in the US (in 2020 Joe surpassed the 25,000-mile mark in his 16-year running career); and oh by the way, he is an ardent birdwatcher—idle is not in Joe's vocabulary. Last fall, while watching the calendar and counting down the days to a glorious cruise on a brand-new ship, Joe decided to run in the New York City Marathon.

Joe running in the New York City Marathon, November 3, 2019.

"I sort of backed into that one. Since I had previously run one in New York State as part of my running in all 50 states, I hadn't planned on running the New York City Marathon. But in the marathon world there is a project called the Abbot Six World Majors. It includes the Tokyo, Boston, London, Chicago, Berlin and NYC Marathons. I had previously run Boston and Chicago before I started running in other countries. After having my heart surgery I ran Tokyo, London and Berlin all in 2018. So with five already done I decided to go ahead and run NYC so I would be a World Majors finisher."

"New York City Marathon is the largest in the world with 50,000 runners. However, in the United States among runners, the iconic marathon is the Boston Marathon because you have to qualify for that one. So, if you get to run that, that's considered to be the pinnacle of your marathon-running career. Because a lot of people aren't capable of qualifying, New York City is the big one in many runner's eyes—that's the one they want to strive for. They start you on the Verrazano Narrows Bridge on Staten Island and then you run through all five boroughs of New York, finishing in Manhattan into Central Park and that's where the finish line is. The marathon has tremendous crowd support for pretty much the whole race. As you moved from one neighborhood to another you could see each has its own individuality. So, I had the opportunity to do that. It was not my best marathon ever; but post-surgery that was my fastest marathon yet. Since my days of fast marathons are over, I now spend more time soaking up the whole atmosphere of the race."

Between marathons—on the ocean as well as those on land—Joe satisfies his wanderlust all over the world often combined with pursuing his running and birdwatching passions. Joe has visited 90 countries; he's run marathons in half of them. Joe also provides moral support to his fiancé, Marie, a marathon swimmer Joe met through doing triathlons (swimming, biking, and running over long distances.)

I was curious if—in between his marathons on Royal Caribbean—Joe did some of his traveling on another cruise line. "All of my regular cruising has been on Royal. I say regular because all of my cruise line ships have been on Royal. I have taken a trip to Antarctica on a very small boat. It was to go to see penguins and whales and the like.

"An expedition ship?" I asked. Joe continued, "Yes, I got onboard a former Russian research ship, the *Vavilov* that now does these kinds of excursions. It went from Ushuaia in southern Argentina [Ushuaia is the southernmost tip of South America, "the end of the world"] down to the Antarctic Peninsula, and ran along the Peninsula for four days for sightseeing. In the process of doing it—I was onboard with a group called Marathon Tours—we ran a marathon on the Antarctica. There were actually two vessels, the *Vavilov* and the *Ioffee*, with 100 of us on each boat. [*Vavilov* and *Ioffe* were built as advanced research vessels that have been converted to luxurious passenger vessels complete with bar, library, lounge, and international chefs.] Then we got back on the boats and traveled back up to Ushuaia. So I got to cross the Drake Passage, which is considered to be some of the roughest seas in the world, on a hundred-foot boat."

I asked Joe, "What about traditional cruising; did he plan on going on any other lines?"

"I don't have plans on doing one, but if I happened to see some particularly enticing destination and another cruise line could get me there, I'm sure I would."

So for the time being Joe will remain "loyal to Royal." Joe is done running marathon distances on Royal Caribbean cruise ships…for now. Royal Caribbean launches their newest cruise ship, *Odyssey of the Seas,* scheduled for holiday season 2020. Joe celebrated the completion of his last marathon distance on *Spectrum* with a nap. When he woke up, he went over to the ship's onboard "Next Cruise" kiosk and booked marathon number 30 on *Odyssey of the Seas* for January 2021!

Paul and Carole Love To Travel

*P*aul and Carole Love To Travel* is Carole Morgan-Slater and Paul Morgan, a couple from Gloucester, United Kingdom. They have been married for 18 years. I met Paul and Carole when I did a feature in *The Joy of Cruising* called "Cuba Cruising." The essay depicted brief vignettes about visiting Cuba via cruise ship, as experienced through the eyes of three diverse couples from different backgrounds and locales. Paul and Carole represented a UK perspective, which given national restrictions and regulations regarding Cuba tourism is somewhat unique versus what tourists from the United States encountered. I never met Paul and Carole in person, but I recall as I wrote their reflections on their Cuba visit, that it felt like I was along with them on their Havana "tavern hop." I kept up with Paul and Carole on social media after the publication of *The Joy of Cruising*. Every image I saw of them, every video I watched on the *Paul and Carole Love To Travel* YouTube channel, brought a smile to my face and reminded me how I felt as I was vicariously experiencing Cuba through them. They just exude fun. The tagline on their site even emphasizes that: *A fun couple who are sharing their travelling experiences and hoping to inspire others to go and explore the world too!* So, when I decided to write what was to be *More Joy of Cruising*, I knew that I wanted to get to know them even better.

Paul and Carole Love To Travel was created in 2015. Carole said, "I wish we started *Paul and Carole Love To Travel* many years ago because we've traveled for many years, and it's only been the last four or five years that we've documented our travels, and really only the past couple of years that we invested the time to make it something that we are very proud of."

Paul and Carole on an excursion at Petra, Jordan during their
Marella Discovery Red Sea Cruise.

In 2018, Paul and Carole added a You Tube channel. Their videos are informative and capture the fun and beauty of the cruise experience. And, much more so than their blog or the static images on social media, their You Tube videos reflect the sense of humor and happy spirit Paul and Carole exude that was so obvious to me from "meeting' them through *The Joy of Cruising* and following them since. One occasional, poignant presence on their You Tube channel is Big John, Paul's 85-year old dad. Big John appears in a few short episodes reciting poetry; he also is a regular cruising partner of Paul and Carole. After perusing the You Tube channel and chatting with Paul and Carole about Big John accompanying them on cruises, I found myself reflecting on what cruising would have been like with my own dad, especially at that age. It's something we never got to do, and frankly, I had never given it any thought until learning about Big John, and admiring that aspect of Paul and Carole's cruising life.

Carole works as a nurse and manages a radiology department. She is due to retire next year and is anxiously looking forward to cruising more. Paul is an entrepreneur. He owns P&C Cars, a pre-owned automobile dealership. Paul and Carole have enjoyed traveling together since meeting 25 years ago. At the time, they were relatively new to travel and Paul had not cruised at all. Carole had some experience traveling via cruise ship by virtue of having worked at Celebrity Cruises as a nurse for a couple of years early in her nursing career. "In the early 90's I was a nurse on Celebrity. I started on the old ship the Celebrity *Meridian* that sank…not with me on it," Carole laughed, "and Celebrity *Horizon*, which is now one of the Pullmantur Cruises ships, and they just announced *Horizon* is among the ships they are scrapping due to the economic impact of Covid."

I said, "Imagine being a nurse on cruise ships earlier this year at the height of the pandemic when ships were stranded on the ocean and with Covid cases or at least, passengers exhibiting symptoms. What was it like being a nurse on a cruise ship back when you work for Celebrity?" Carole said, "I was young, free, and single. It was a brilliant experience, and I met many new friends. We worked hard, but partied hard. I did it for two years. I saved some money—you don't get to spend loads when you are working."

I wondered if Carole's passion for cruising and travel developed when she worked on cruise ships. "After I left nursing, I always wanted to get to enjoy a cruise as a passenger, but cruising was not in my budget. In the 90's it was very much a luxury holiday, it wasn't affordable as it is now. When I met Paul we would holiday a lot: Florida, Disney World, went to the Greek Isles. So we traveled a lot but we never thought we could afford cruising." Paul interjected, "You couldn't talk me into cruising anyway!" Carole added, "The other thing is Paul didn't want to go cruising. It took me about seven years to talk him into it. He didn't understand why anybody would want to go on a cruise ship and be stuck in there and be claustrophobic. It wasn't until I persuaded him to do it that we finally did a five-night cruise out of Barcelona on Royal Caribbean *Navigator of the Seas.*"

Given their active involvement in cruising today, operating the *Paul and Carole Love To Travel* blog and its growing You Tube channel, obviously somewhere along the line, Paul changed his notion about cruising. I asked if it was on that first cruise in 2011 on *Navigator*. Paul said, "I immediately thought, why didn't we do this before? Oh, so this is why everybody loves cruising. The bug bit me right away. Before the cruise was half over, I was ready for the next one."

Navigator of the Seas was Carole's first cruise as well—as a passenger. The cruising bug bit her too on her first pleasure cruise. I had assumed that as a nurse for Celebrity she worked most of the time and didn't get to experience what it was like to enjoy a cruise. She told me, "We had two nurses and how we used to do it is we would do 24 hours on, 24 hours off. You would have some time to get off the ship. They were short times as you were on call and you couldn't get off for a long time. It was still brilliant because I was going to all these places I had never been to before. Even spending a few hours on land—it was amazing."

Formal night on Navigator of the Seas; Paul and Carole's first cruise.

Paul and Carole both got hooked on cruising right away and less than a year later cruised again—a short cruise out of Southampton, United Kingdom to Le Havre, France on Cunard *Queen Mary II*.

Much has changed since those days when Paul and Carole were new to cruising. Paul and Carole describe themselves as passionate travelers whose first love is cruising. "We do love to travel; we've got our motor home, obviously we are going to be doing a lot more of that kind of travel now that we are allowed to do that, and we like to have land-based holidays. But our first passion is cruising." Paul and Carole have been to over 45 countries—mostly reaching them via cruise ship—with 20 cruises throughout the Mediterranean, Canary Islands, Norway, and the Caribbean including Cuba. They have cruised with Royal Caribbean, including *Independence of the Seas* four times, Cunard, Celebrity, Marella, MSC, P&O, and Fred Olsen cruise lines.

In addition, *Paul and Carole Love To Travel* was fortunate enough to be invited by Cruise Lines International Association (CLIA) in conjunction with Saga Cruises in July 2019 to a two-day press cruise followed by the naming ceremony for *Spirit of Discovery*, Saga's largest ship ever and first newly built ship (Saga's fleet prior to *Spirit of Discovery* was comprised of ships obtained on the secondary market.) Saga cruises are exclusively for over-50 passengers.

"Not only was this an amazing opportunity to see first-hand what Saga has to offer—yes, we have reached the required age!—but also the chance to meet some fellow travel bloggers that we had only previously spoken to online. It was great seeing some familiar faces as we waited to board this beautiful new ship, but it was even more wonderful when we were given a suite! The *Spirit of Discovery* is a beautiful ship. Saga's aimed to build a ship that would reflect the finest boutique hotels and they have certainly achieved that! The naming ceremony featured a string quartet, a Welsh choir and the Royal Marines Marching Band. It was really fit for royalty, which was lucky as the christening of the ship was carried out by the Duchess of Cornwall Camilla Parker Bowles. I even managed to get some exclusive shots of the Duchess cutting the ceremonial cake that was a replica of the actual ship and even had steam coming out of the funnel. Once the ceremony was finished, we boarded the ship and enjoyed a fantastic evening meal and were treated to an amazing performance by Jools Holland and his Rhythm and Blues Orchestra featuring Ruby Turner and Pauline Black from the Ska band Selector. It was such an amazing experience! Who thought Saga would put on the party of all parties but they definitely did!"

That sounds like a memorable experience both with respect to *Paul and Carole Love To Travel* being invited to attend such a significant industry event, as well as the pageantry of it all, with actual royalty. And, it was a cruise, in a suite, on one of the world's magnificent new ships! I put Paul and Carole on the spot, asking them if they could highlight just one cruise memory, or ship or destination, what it would be? Carole said, "We loved Norway, didn't we Paul? Norway and the Northern Lights. We have cruised to Norway four times, and it's just such a beautiful part of the world. And the Northern Lights were just a special, special time. We went to Honningsvåg in Norway, the most northerly point for the northern lights, and we had four days where we could see the lights and it was just magical." Paul added, "We had four nights where every night was spectacular. And you could just sit out on deck all day and just watch because you are in the fjords and it's just like a small river. Stunning! We were fortunate; on Marella *Discovery* we got to know some of the staff and they invited Carole and me, and my dad and my sister onto the bridge to do a sail-away, which was pretty amazing. The Captain even let me blow the ship's horn. I was like a little kid in a sweet shop that day!" Carole said, "That sail-away was from Geiranger, which is probably one of the prettiest places we have ever been. It was spectacular coming past the Seven Sisters Waterfall, past the King and Queen of Norway's house. It was all fantastic."

I wondered how *Paul and Carole Love To Travel* dealt with the impact of the pandemic and cruise lockdown. Carole said, "Well we still want to promote cruising in a positive way, but it is really difficult when you do not have real-time experiences to do that. We have started exploring our local area a bit more. Circumstances have made us think about appreciating more of our home country, so we made a few blogs about local travel—for instance, revisiting Westonbirt Arboretum in Tetbury where we got married 18 years ago; and we did a post about exploring the beautiful villages of The Cotswolds." I asked where that is located and Paul laughed, "It's where a lot of celebrities with too much money on their hands pay a fortune to live." I said, "Oh, where you guys live!" Cotswolds is an almost 800 square mile area on the edge of Gloucester comprised of beautiful semi-rural, stone-built villages and towns highlighted by stately mansions.

Carole said, "We want to create travel content that people are interested in, recognizing we can't cruise at the moment. I think everyone has noticed a drop in numbers of website hits during the pandemic, haven't they? But it is picking up again. And during this time we've invested in working with a local company here in Gloucester and having a new website built. We're really excited about that because our old website was a bit dated; it's something I built over the past five years. I knew nothing about building a website and it just sort of evolved in a clunky kind of way. Now that we've got a little presence online, I wanted to make it sleeker and more professional."

I asked, "So in addition to *paulandcarolelovetotravel.com*, talk about your online presence." Paul said, "We have a You Tube channel. We were hoping that by around this time we would have a million views. But when the pandemic hit, things slowed down. We're about 900,000 views, which we're still very pleased with."

Carole added, "The You Tube channel has been one that we are probably enjoying the most out of all of our social media; it evolved into something that we never thought it would. It started with doing hotel room reviews and ship reviews. But what seems to be really popular, that we've been brave enough to do in the last six months or so, is to just sit in front of the camera. It took us a long time to be able to do that, but we get a lot of engagement with it.

People seem to like to see us being open and honest. We've started doing some vlog-style videos and those have gone over well."

I told Paul and Carole that I am not surprised about their quick adaption to You Tube and the fact that it is going well and enjoyable for them. "Every time I see images of you on social media enjoying cruises, it brings a smile to my face. You guys seem to have so much fun. Everybody has fun on cruises, but there is just something genuine about seeing you guys out and about. I can imagine that You Tube is perfect for you in that video is a medium that best conveys your vivacious, fun-loving personalities."

Carole said, "Yes, thank you. It does seem that is the response we are getting, which is really lovely." Paul added, "We do it because we enjoy it, but I think people who watch You Tube are smart enough to know what's real and what's fake, and I think there is a lot of fakes out there. We do it because our primary reason is we enjoy doing it and anything that comes with that is a bonus."

What other platforms are *Paul and Carole Love To Travel* on? What are your favorites, what's growing? "Twitter is very good for networking, talking to people, having that in-the-moment conversation. I really Twitter," Carole said. Paul enjoys Instagram and its portrayal of stories. Both platforms are growing, as is their Facebook presence.

Paul and Carole on the Marella Discovery Red Sea Cruise.

Paul and Carole cruised right before the pandemic in February 2020, on P&O *Oceana* visiting Rotterdam in the Netherlands and Hamburg in Germany. They thoroughly enjoyed the week-long cruise, their first significant cruise on P&O—they did a two-night cruise on P&O *Ventura* several years prior. The *Oceana* cruise stoked their excitement for a two-week cruise Paul and Carole had booked for later in 2020 on the new P&O *Iona,* UK's most significant new cruise ship launch in some time. Pending their cruise on *Iona,* Paul and Carole had planned to sample some cruises by choosing short, last minute itineraries. Carole told me, "Our plan this year was to do more last minute cruises, so we were going to just take time off work and have several options to choose from, just to see if we could grab any bargains." Though the lockdown didn't cooperate with that plan, Paul and Carole have held on to the hopes that cruising starts back up in time for the scheduled launch of *Iona,* now planned Fall 2020. *Iona,* currently being constructed specifically for the British market will be P&O Cruises new flagship and at 184,000 gross tons, with a capacity of over 5200 passengers *Iona* will be the largest ship ever built for UK, and the sixth largest ship in the world.

"We're being very optimistic. Carnival, which includes P&O, canceled all of their cruises first through October 15 and we thought we might cruise this year. Now the plan is to re-start in February. *Iona's* first cruise, which originally was supposed to be this week actually, was scheduled for October and we saw an itinerary we really like for a two-week cruise to Spain so we went ahead and booked that. Now that it has been further delayed, we kept our booking and moved it to June 2021. Our rationale is many of P&O ships leave out of UK; they're saying if it doesn't go ahead, you get 25% future cruise credit. We were quite comfortable with that "because we had our first real P&O experience just a few months ago and really loved that. Should it start up February, we have some time and may book for March instead."

In the meantime, Paul and Carole satisfy their travel fix with local travel of several days at a time in their motorhome. "We go away in our motorhome every summer anyway, so we will be doing a lot of that, especially since Paul can't use it for racing right now." After assuring me, Paul does not compete in motorhome races, Paul and Carole point out that Paul races cars and uses the motorhome to tow cars to the track!

Looking beyond the cruise lockdown, Paul and Carole have a rather lengthy list of dream cruises. "We've got five actually. We've been doing a lot of talking about this with me retiring and deciding what we want to do. We want to do a transatlantic to New York on the *Queen Mary II;* that's the iconic ship to do that on. We are planning to hopefully do that next August; we've got that penciled in depending on what happens with all of this with the cruise lockdown. So that's the first on our bucket list. Next, there are two cruises combined with rail: we've always wanted to go to Australia, New Zealand, and the South Pacific. So, I found a cruise in October of '21 that incorporates part of that: *Ovation of the Seas*—I want to do one of the Royal Caribbean Quantum- or Oasis-class ships; we've not done one of those. And that cruise would incorporate a rail holiday where we start off in Perth, do a train to Sydney on the Indian-Pacific, and then do two back-to-back cruises, one to islands of New Zealand—North Islands and South Islands—and then out to the South Pacific. This would take about four weeks all in all. Another one we would like to do is a combined train tour/cruise to Hawaii, or a Rocky Mountaineer train tour combined with a cruise to Alaska." Rocky Mountaineer is a Canadian passenger rail service, the largest privately-owned rail service in North America.

Any land-based bucket list travel? "San Francisco is a place we have always wanted to go. The other thing that we want to do—we love Greece. We've talked about spending several weeks doing sort of a land-based island hop. The Adriatic region around there is one of our favorite places, along with Greece and Croatia being two of our favorite European countries. We've had the pleasure of spending a short time in Croatia; we have done a lot in Greece.

I asked Paul and Carole, "As experts, bloggers, how do you envision cruising adapting in the future to what will be the 'new normal' when we start cruising again." Carole said, "I think obviously screening. We travel a lot with Paul's dad—he is part of our cruising family—so we have been thinking a lot about this as he is 85. He wants to cruise as soon as he can. We are concerned though, because I think the cruising experience for those over 65 is going to be very, very different." He sounds as passionate about cruising as Paul is. Carole said. "Yes, he is. He loves cruising so much. He just likes sitting on a ship; he wouldn't mind if it didn't leave the dock. As long as he is on a cruise ship he is so happy. He is going to need a fit-for-travel clearance from a doctor and I think that is going to be normal for people with health issues. Temperature checking is one thing the cruise lines seem to be adapting, but obviously you can have temperatures due to various reasons."

What does the future hold for *Paul and Carole Love To Travel?* Carole said, "We are pretty excited about the future because my career as a nurse is going to come to an end July 2021. It will give me the time to actually invest in what I want to do because it is such a passion and I just get so much joy out of creating blog posts or a video. The next chapter of our lives we want to be able to devote to *Paul and Carole Love To Travel.* Gain more experiences, see where it leads. We've met so many lovely people through the world of cruise blogging. It's been an amazing journey and we feel so privileged that we got to know so many lovely people and get the opportunities we have been afforded."

Paul and Carole, as always, having fun.

The word that comes to mind when I "interact" with Paul and Carole's social media and video is "sincerity." They really do seem to live out and embody their brand, *Paul and Carole Love To Travel.*

Royal Caribbean 50th Anniversary Cruise

W̶hat do passionate cruisers who have cruised 65 times—including bucket list destinations and transatlantic cruises—do to keep the passion aflame? Well, maybe revisit some of those bucket list destinations? Nah; Bill and Rosie Raffel have done the Panama Canal four times! Alaska? Hawaii? Both, four times. What about once in a lifetime travel activities? African safari? Scuba diving on the Great Barrier Reef in Australia? Bill and Rosie, been there, done that. If you are "Loyal to Royal" like Bill and Rosie are, you join Michael Bayley, President of Royal Caribbean International, and 5500 others on Royal Caribbean's 50th Anniversary Cruise on *Symphony of the Seas*, the world's largest cruise ship.

*Rosie and Bill right after embarkation on Symphony of the Seas for
50 Years BOLD/President's Cruise*

On our *Harmony of the Seas* cruise last August, it was a nice touch to get served a mini buttercream birthday cake in the main dining room in honor of Royal Caribbean's 50th Birthday in 2019. The gesture was part of a yearlong celebration which culminated November 2, 2019 with the President's Cruise aboard *Symphony*. Royal Caribbean's 50th was a big deal for many cruisers, especially US-based, where Royal Caribbean is the preeminent cruise brand in terms of broad appeal with its wide range of ships, from relatively intimate to mega-ships with family-friendly attractions such as onboard surf simulators, and even bumper cars, carousels, and skydiving simulators. Many cruisers outside of the US are fans of Royal Caribbean as well, given their international itineraries and a fleet that includes the four largest cruise ships in the world.

Royal Caribbean's 50th Anniversary Cruise buttercream cake.

We first met Bill and Rosie of Whitefish Bay, WI, a suburb of Milwaukee, in *The Joy of Cruising*, "Cruisers Like You and Me...Sort Of." Although I found out by happenstance, I can't say I was surprised to learn Bill and Rosie were going to be on the Royal Caribbean 50th Birthday President's Cruise. Bill is well-connected in the cruise community, especially regarding Royal.

In October 2019, I decided to write a follow-up to *The Joy of Cruising* and one of the first "fascinating cruisers" I determined that I wanted to write about was Mario Salcedo, affectionately known as "Super Mario" to Royal Caribbean staff and beloved by the "Loyal to Royal" cruise community. Super Mario is an iconic retired executive who has been sailing on a series of back-to-back-to-back seven-day cruises on Royal Caribbean ships for the last couple of decades! He has been well-chronicled in the media, most prominently in the documentary, *The Happiest Guy in the World*, by Lance Oppenheim.

Obviously, Super Mario is the embodiment of a passionate cruiser, and I was hoping to tell his story in *More Joy of Cruising*. So, on a whim I reached out to Bill to ask him if he knew how I could contact Super Mario. Bill immediately responded to my message. "No, I don't know him, but I will be on a cruise with him in a few days, along with Royal Caribbean CEO Michael Bayley, and oh yeah, Hall and Oates [legendary US soulful rock stars and the best-selling music duo of all time.]"

I couldn't believe my fortunate timing! I drafted a letter to Super Mario, and asked Bill to try and deliver it to him. Alas, I was unsuccessful in my efforts to get Super Mario to be in *More Joy*. But I am so glad I reached out to Bill when I did, as it provided me an idea for a new addition to *More Joy*: The Royal Caribbean *Symphony of the Seas*, 50 Years BOLD/President's Cruise! I asked Bill to tell me about it.

"Our anticipation for the cruise started when we booked it a year in advance. We got a balcony cabin at a great price—then came the long wait." (It helps that Bill is a licensed travel agent—his only clients are Bill and Rosie, and some family and friends.)

November 2, 2019 finally arrived. The *Symphony* was docked at the new state-of-the-art Royal Caribbean Terminal A in Miami, purposely built for its class of world's largest cruise ships. Terminal A was adorned with 50 Years BOLD and President's Cruise signage and decorations.

"We entered the escalator leading from the terminal onto the ship with a tunnel of balloons above us. From the moment Rosie and I stepped onto the ship, you could tell the cruise was going to be special. As we boarded the ship by way of the Grand Promenade, we could see a lot more decorations. We could tell Royal Caribbean was going to throw their 50th Birthday party in grand style! Moments after we boarded, Rosie and I were given a glass of champagne and then seconds later Michael Bayley, CEO of Royal Caribbean walked by and we said hello."

Hall and Oates, the best-selling music duo in history, performing on the 50 Years BOLD/President's Cruise.

Bill and Rosie are the perfect archetypes of passionate cruisers. They have an amazing 20 cruises booked, mostly on Royal Caribbean. Though they have also cruised on Norwegian, Carnival, Princess, and Celebrity, most of their upcoming cruises will be with Royal Caribbean as they are close to reaching the highest level in Royal's loyalty program, which rewards fans with cruise discounts, special restaurants, complimentary Happy Hours and other onboard perks.

Highlighting their upcoming cruises—contingent on the near-term prospects for cruising given the pandemic—is a 14-night transatlantic cruise on *Allure of the Seas* in November 2020, departing from Barcelona, cruising the Mediterranean and then heading to the Caribbean for a stop at Royal Caribbean's private island *Perfect Day at Coco Cay*, and ending in Miami.

Unfortunately, due to the pandemic, the cruise lines, or Bill and Rosie, have canceled most of their future cruises. For now, they have a couple of "close to home" cruises booked with itineraries in the Caribbean including one in January 2021 on *Oasis of the Seas* to celebrate Rosie's retirement. In October of 2021, Bill and Rosie will be doing a 10-day Iberian Peninsula cruise, followed by a 12-day Mediterranean Greek Isles cruise, followed by a 12-day transatlantic, all on the same ship, *Jewel of the Seas*, for 34 days straight.

Despite seemingly having done it all, and with several years of amazing cruises booked, the Raffel's do have a bucket list—cruises and land trips in Europe, hiking and touring in the Rocky Mountains, and they would love to get back to Hawaii. And of course, incorporating family into some of that travel is part of their plan.

"Given the amount of travel that Rosie and I do, it was only natural that our two children, Becca and Brian, would become smitten with a passion for travel. We have introduced them to various places in the world as well as the love of cruising. They have cruised with us five times and one of those times included our two young granddaughters on *Harmony of the Seas* November 2018. To do everything on our bucket list we will need to win the lottery and we'll need another 50 years. I doubt that either of those are in the cards, but we will try to do as much as we can, as long as we can; until we cannot anymore! Near the top of the bucket list is a cruise around Cape Horn, a World Cruise, and lastly, a trip to the Galapagos Islands with an extension to Machu Picchu." The odds of winning the lottery or living and traveling 50 more years are indeed very low (and are about the same in likelihood.) Nevertheless, I wouldn't bet against Bill and Rosie checking off most of their bucket list!

Having experienced so much cruising, I imagined that it would be difficult for Bill to specify a single most memorable cruise. I did ask him though, and to my surprise Bill did not hesitate.

"Our most memorable cruise occurred in November 2019 on the *Symphony of the Seas*, 50 Years BOLD/President's cruise. Yep, it was a fabulous cruise and one of the best we have been on. I am not sure how Royal Caribbean will top this, but I know they will try....count me in!"

Fireworks show as Symphony pulled away from Royal Caribbean's private island in the Bahamas, Coco Cay.

CruiseTipsTV: An Iconic Brand During the Pandemic

Most cruise fans are familiar with *CruiseTipsTV*, a leading blog and You Tube channel with 90,000 subscribers and 18 million views, and star, host and co-founder Sheri Griffiths. The other co-founders are her husband, and 11-year old son, known affectionately by her audience as, respectively, Mr. CruiseTipsTV and Junior Editor. *CruiseTipsTV* is a well-respected, quality-produced, and more than anything else, fun, authentic and family-centric cruising community leader. *CruiseTipsTV* is multi-faceted—near the top in the categories of cruise blog, cruise You Tube channel, cruise podcast—and well represented on all the social platforms including creative live programming. How about a live virtual cocktail party at happy hour? There is even a *CruiseTipsTV* online academy.

Sheri Griffiths is the face of *CruiseTipsTV*, serving as the host of those aforementioned live events, and sharing the screen on You Tube videos with Mr. CruiseTipsTV and Junior Editor on some cruise adventure somewhere in the world, like jumping off cliffs in Jamaica—as they were pictured doing in *The Joy of Cruising*. Furthermore, Sheri is a ubiquitous media presence, representing a cruise community perspective in mainstream outlets such as The New York Times, CNBC, Forbes, and Prevention, and participating with and appearing in cruise-specific outlets. Such central figures in the cruising community on the passenger side like Sheri have especially been a source of insight for the media during the cruise lockdown. Cruising is somewhat of a trendy media curiosity and the lockdown affects millions of fervent travelers worldwide and has left a multi-billion dollar industry on the brink. For instance, Sheri said in *The New York Times*, The Post-Coronavirus Cruise? Not Ready to Sail, "For people to feel safe, they need to feel that the passengers around them won't be boarding the ship sick, and they need to know the crew will be held to a high standard of wellness." She added, "I will get on a cruise when the CDC says that I don't have to self-quarantine when I get off a ship." (Frances Robles, June 26, 2020).

Sheri watching the coastline fade away during sail-away on Royal Princess, her last cruise prior to the pandemic.

Sheri is an in-demand guest on cruise podcasts and has been covered frequently by cruise print media. I first learned of Sheri in 2018 when she was named one of the "10 Travel Influencers Changing How We Vacation" by *Porthole Cruise Magazine*. Sheri, and the story of the creation and growth of *CruiseTipsTV* embodied the essence of *The Joy of Cruising*—passionate cruisers who act on that passion in creative, engaging, and fascinating ways. Accordingly, Sheri was featured in *The Joy of Cruising* in a section called The Influencers. Since publication, Sheri was again named to the 2019 edition of *Porthole Cruise Magazine's* "10 Travel Influencers Changing How We Vacation."

As a leader in the cruise community, I thought it important to reflect the perspective of *CruiseTipsTV* regarding the most significant event ever to impact cruising—the Covid-19 pandemic and cruise lockdown.

For starters, I wondered how *CruiseTipsTV* is faring in this emotional time for cruise enthusiasts. "In the beginning it was a very challenging time for us. To think that we would have our content engine removed from our life, it was just hard to believe. We thought that this wouldn't last very long and we would all be cruising by July. As things progressed, we have come to grips with the fact that it is going to last much longer. We aren't able to create the typical type of content we create, which is cruise vlogs. So what we have to do is pivot."

I wondered how Sheri and her family are doing emotionally, seeing something so important to them as cruising on hold. Since we had gotten to know them a little in *The Joy of Cruising*, and they are an integral part of *CruiseTipsTV*, how are Mr. CruiseTipsTV and Junior Editor doing with this lockdown happening? "Emotionally, we are all doing well. I think at first we were all really struggling. It even trickled down to our son. He was feeding off our energy, and we figured we needed to adapt and adjust and start focusing on different types of things and the reality. We have done that and are featuring different types of content on our channel to try to keep our audience happy and to keep them entertained during this time of not having any type of cruise content to give them. We haven't cruised since November 2019, so there was nothing in the hopper at the time the lockdown hit."

I said, "So you indicated *CruiseTipsTV* had to pivot. Talk about that."

"The pivot that we made was to start creating cruise news videos regularly on our channel, which have been extremely well-received. And we started having cruise cocktail parties where we make cruise-inspired special drinks live on camera; and we have done cruise cooking shows."

The live virtual cocktail parties and cooking demonstrations sounds like a fun, novel approach. I asked Sheri if they can monitor participation. "It has been okay. Few thousand people. The big numbers are coming from the cruise news. People want the cold hard facts. So you're going to get 30,000 views on anything cruise news related, whereas you're going to get 2000-3000 attendees on a live stream event. On livestream, you do have the connection with the audience that they want, the ability to somewhat interact, and to talk to us. On the other hand, a news segment is just a recorded piece that provides a lot of information but doesn't provide a connection with our audience."

Cruise Tips TV cooking demonstration: recreating Carnival Cruise Line's famous warm chocolate melting cake.

Sheri sipping a cruise-inspired cocktail in CruiseTipsTV live virtual cocktail party.

I wondered about the *CruiseTipsTV Academy,* a fee-based course enabling cruisers to access in-depth education about cruising. According to Sheri, *CruiseTipsTV* started the academy a couple of years ago to assist cruisers with the cruise research process—through booking, planning, packing, boarding and on through to what to expect about dining, tipping, disembarkation, etc.—without them having to sift through the hundreds of videos on the *CruiseTipsTV* You Tube channel. Has the cruise lockdown impacted the Academy? "It's still going and people are still very much enrolling. They have seen this as a good time to study up on cruising. We haven't seen much of a slowdown in enrollment. It's been wonderful that people want to continue to learn. When cruising resumes, we will be adding a module that includes information that people need to know about the new cruising normal."

Speaking of the new normal, I ask Sheri her prediction about what that new normal might look like. "I think we will see a lot of the same procedural changes and health and safety protocols we see on land. I am watching other places and other types of business slowly reopen to see how they are adapting